BEYOND
THE
GREAT FOREST

By
VIRGINIA PREWETT

EST. 1852

E. P. DUTTON & CO., INC.
NEW YORK, 1953

Some of the material in this book has appeared
in the Saturday Evening Post article, "I Home-
steaded In Brazil".

The quotation from The Bhagavad Gita
which appears in this book is from the
translation copyrighted in 1944 by Swami
Nikhilananda, and is reproduced with his
permission.

PRINTED IN THE UNITED STATES OF AMERICA
BY THE WILLIAM BYRD PRESS, INC.
RICHMOND, VIRGINIA

Library of Congress Catalog Card Number: 52-12962

To my husband
W. R. M.
without whose encouragement, sympathetic
understanding and continual patient help
this book would never have been written

AUTHOR'S NOTE

To avoid a confusing duplication in the given names of minor Brazilian characters, a number of them have been altered.

BEYOND THE GREAT FOREST

1

THE great South American continent, peopled thinly even around its coasts, guards a million square miles of mystery in its heart. This region, where rivers are called the River of Death and the River of Doubt and a valley the Vale of Sleep, is deeper in the beyond than the great rainforest of the Amazon and less known to the white man than the depths of Africa or remote Tibet. In the southeastern part of this realm of uncertainty in Inner Brazil, the savage Chavante Indians have held the Western world at bay for a century and a half, until lately stubbornly continuing to kill even the gift-bearing whites who entered their lands and condescending to this day only to uneasy border parleys.

Between the forbidden forests of the Chavantes and the South Atlantic coastal plains where most Brazilians live, extends another vast backland that is still imperfectly mapped and very thinly populated. A single dinky narrow-gauge railroad labors up into this interior highland and almost halfway across it. From Anápolis, the dusty frontier town where the railroad ends, a single winding gravel road thrusts on north through the Goiás Great Forest toward a no man's land beyond. A little more than a hundred miles north along this road and five miles east of it in the Great Forest itself, there is a patch of cleared land that is my own lost world—Fazenda Chavante.

Over half of Fazenda Chavante's five hundred acres are a virgin woodland bordering the mighty rushing River of Ghosts. When I first crossed this formidable river in a leaky canoe in early 1948, my land was all forest, footprinted only by water pig, deer, tapir, jaguar and wild boar. Today nearly half of it is a farm. There is a well on the farm and a house roofed with hand-split wooden shingles instead of the usual thatch. The big clearing that I nursed from the first tree cut has borne several crops of highland rice, beans, corn and cotton. The cotton, spun and woven on hand looms, has become clothing right there in the clearing. Manioc grows tall from roots laboriously toted in over five miles of forest track and rowed over a dangerous river. Chickens run around, descendants of a cock I had to fetch from over a hundred miles away; the hens I found close by, only about fifteen miles away. When the pineapples growing there were young shoots in a patch more than a hundred miles distant, they needled my hands as I gathered them to bring them in a tow sack to Chavante, and many of the farm's young fruit trees sprouted from seeds I myself carefully saved and dried.

The farm is there because I made it almost literally with my own hands. Into it went my life's savings in money and, in a sense, my life's net balance in dreams.

From October through March heavy rains blessing this region turn the River of Ghosts mud-yellow and stir it to rise and rustle angrily. In the dry time it runs slow and clear blue. Along the river front of the Fazenda Chavante the banks fall steeply and when you strip away the brush and vines you find clean white sand. Big trees lean over the river and a huge fallen log at one place breaks the current and catches the water into a shaded pool delicious for swimming. An island splits the wide river there and it belongs to Fazenda Chavante too.

In the clearing at the back of the place nearly a mile inland from the river, a long slope rises facing the afternoon sun. This is to the northwest, since Goiás lies just below the equator. Near the top of this hill, which has a stream at its foot and a forest on its crest, there is a perfect homesite. From there you can see across the big clearing and over the river a mile away and over the forests beyond the river to blue mountains in the far distance. You could watch things growing on the farm from a house built here. It would be air-cooled by the woodland at its back during the hot hours of the day and could be made warm and cheerful in the cool evenings by hearth fires burning down-wood from the forest.

I created this place to fulfill a dream of escape. I decided to go there in the fall of 1947 and it was my intention to stay there for good. In January, 1948, I told my friends I was leaving forever the world of political intrigue and strife that I had been reporting on for years, and took my departure. The wilds of Goiás absorbed me for the better part of 1948. When late in the year, I first returned to the big South American cities of the coast, it was as a visitor. And by that time I was so deeply committed to my dream that it took another strange journey to resolve it, an exploration of the very nature of escape.

It is true that a major disappointment set off the drastic move to Goiás, but I went happily. As I saw it, my direction was forward. I was only doing what many people long to do at some time in their lives, and would do, if they were free.

In late January, 1948, I bade farewell to the great world at a luncheon held by the American correspondents' corps of Buenos Aires at the American Club there. My plans had captured the imagination of the newsmen and we had a good turnout. Asked to speak, I said I meant to create in Central Brazil the world's first authentic refuge from the Atomic Age and from its symbol, the Bomb.

Our rumor-loving little world in Buenos Aires had naturally speculated about my reasons for plunging into the unknown. I was told afterwards that most of my colleagues had at first thought my move had been set off by my breakup with Bill Mizelle, the young American newspaper man whom they half believed had been my lover for nearly two years. But when Bill and I appeared together at the last luncheon apparently on the same good terms as ever, the serene friendliness between us allayed their suspicions—according to the brash soul who later brought up the subject with me—and they dropped the idea a broken heart was sending me into the wilderness.

In a sense, however, my heart was broken, though not over Bill, who had been for so long my mainstay. I am sure the correspondents would have been profoundly surprised to know that a turn in my relationship with the press corps itself had touched off my hegira. It was the group that was important to me, not the individuals, who changed from time to time.

The publications most constantly represented at Buenos Aires while I was there for the *Chicago Sun* were *The New York Times*, the *New York Herald Tribune*, the *New York Daily News*, *Time Magazine*, *U. S. News and World Report*, the United Press, the Associated Press, the International News Service and the Overseas News Agency. (The latter two, not represented by Americans, had little part in press corps affairs.) Ernie Hill of the *Chicago Daily News* was in and out, as were other newspaper and magazine staff writers. Most of the big papers with bureaus in Buenos Aires had syndicates distributing their reports in the United States.

There are moments in history when the actions of a small group of people take on unusual meaning. If they fight their battle smack in the center of the world's stage, like the Greeks at Thermopylae or the tired RAF pilots who won the Battle of Britain, their deeds go down emblazoned in history. But there are other gallant and meaningful stands made just off stage, and these, barring a great poet or historian to mark them, pass unnoticed. In Buenos Aires, from 1945 on through three troubled years, a handful of American newspaper correspondents, backed at first by a firm-willed American ambassador, broke a censorship of the same hostile kind that had for years gradually been isolating the United States public from real understanding of the rest of the world. The gap we made in censorship brought a flood of hope to a captive people and our continuing reports defeated a very crucial attempt to pass

off enslavement to the state as freedom. This was the significance of the Buenos Aires press corps' little sally into history
and of its emotional importance to me.

The Buenos Aires press corps' story began in June, 1945
when Ambassador Spruille Braden was sent to Argentina with
a difficult assignment. The Argentine "colonels' regime" which
had seized power there in 1943, and had since ruled without
benefit of constitution or congress, had been caught the year
before plotting revolutions in other Latin American countries
with German Nazi help. When the unholy partnership suc-
ceeded in Bolivia, alarm ran through the Hemisphere. Argentina was quarantined diplomatically after the colonels' spokesman, Juan Perón, made a saber-rattling speech, and the country's representatives were not asked to attend the Inter-American Conference on Problems of War and Peace, which con-
vened in February, 1945 at Mexico City. At this meeting,
called the Conference of Chapultepec, the other New World
republics drew up a mutual defense pact. By design, Article
VI of this pact's Declaration pledged the nations signing it to
submit it to their respective congresses for early ratification.
The Argentine colonels, asked to sign, did so, and thereby
promised the American republics to restore constitutional rule
and hold elections, which were necessary in order to have a
congress to ratify the pact.

I had had my baptism in today's Latin American realities
in July, 1940, in Mexico when I saw unarmed Mexicans time
and again brave the flying bullets of soldiers detailed to keep
them from voting an administration out of office; the people
finally set up their own ballot boxes near the polls and cast
votes in them, so great was their thirst for suffrage. I had
covered the colonels' regime from the first in a column on
Latin American affairs that I wrote for the *Washington Post*
before joining the *Chicago Sun* in December, 1944. At that
time I had just completed a book on the New World republics and their conference system and could realize the exact
meaning of the Chapultepec pact with its all-important if
half-concealed device favoring constitutional governments.

When I covered the Chapultepec conference for the *Chicago Sun*, I was well aware our representatives there felt the strong current of opinion that favored making an example out of the Argentine colonels' clique. But from my previous coverage of Latin American affairs I knew our State Department was sharply divided; this division showed up when Secretary of State Edward Stettinius, he of the pearly smile, flew to Mexico City from the historic meeting at Yalta and ordered the Argentine trouble smoothed over. The half-concealed catch-clause written into the treaty was an attempt to do indirectly what the order from Yalta would not permit to be done directly, that is, to clean up rather than to smooth over the political chancre at Buenos Aires.

I myself was not very sanguine that the Chapultepec agreement would ever be more than a scrap of paper. But as I traveled southward from Mexico City, stopping over to make reports from each country after the meeting, I was forced to recognize it had had a profound effect. Men of good will everywhere believed that the United States, in sheer self-defense, had turned against the tyrannies, and it had raised among them a spirit like that of the days when the New World broke the yoke of Spain.

Fair stood the wind for liberty. Though under attack, democracy was working in Latin America—in Uruguay, in Chile, in Colombia, in Costa Rica. Mexico was on the road to it, and elsewhere young democracies were getting started or democratic forces were pressing hard against dictatorship. Dictator Batista of Cuba had been forced to hand over his power to an elected opposition; Vargas of Brazil had had to promise constitutional rule. Most exciting of all, the Argentine colonels had found the democratic current so strong they had signed the Inter-American pledge to restore constitutional government. The wind stood fair.

Spruille Braden, under whose uncompromising eye Cuba's Batista had been impelled to hold the elections that ended his strong-arm rule, was sent to Buenos Aires to make the Chapultepec pledge stick. He was also told to make sure that the Argentines fulfilled their mutual defense promises by turning over certain top German Nazis to the Allies for trial as war criminals. I got back to Buenos Aires the day Braden held his first press conference with the American correspondents and I asked him about over-all policy. Braden told us that "the United States wants to see democracies everywhere." When I asked if we could quote this, he said yes.

Our cabled reports called Braden's remark a major policy statement. It meant the Argentine colonels could not stage-manage a fake return to constitutionality, but must genuinely give control back to the people themselves, as the men at Chapultepec intended.

The next day the press services in New York cabled back to their Argentine clients the New York papers' stories on Braden's statement, by-lines and all. The Argentine censors, for fear the United States might really mean to get tough, permitted the Argentine papers to publish these dispatches.

This was the first crack in a strict censorship. The news of the firm American policy ran through Argentina like a train of burning gunpowder. For years before the colonels took over Argentina, a Conservative oligarchy skilled at rigging elections—a trick they themselves called "patriotic fraud" —had been holding back the political progress and the social advances sponsored by the mass party, the moderate-progressive Radicals. The Argentine people now had a chance to break both the captivities, the old one of patriotic fraud and the new one of military clique rule.

Immediately after our cable on the new American policy appeared in Argentine papers, crowds of men and women began to hold orderly, peaceful demonstrations for their rights, which the regime had indeed pledged the American republics to restore. And now the colonels revealed themselves: they sent militarized mounted police to break up the public meetings. We cabled out this news and the press associations cabled the reports back. Again the Argentine censors were afraid to use their blue pencils, though they repressed the Argentine reporters' stories of the same events.

The American correspondents soon found themselves in a strange situation. We were not only the unique source of news on political events in Argentina for the world outside, but also for the Argentines themselves. Our cables telling of the renewed police repressions showed the colonels' regime was not making much of an effort to observe its Chapultepec pledge. Our simple, factual news messages, cabled back and published in Argentina, raised popular emotion ever higher. The Argentines felt they were no longer alone now and their courage rose. They swarmed about Braden, symbol of American firmness and of the Hemisphere will to respect "American principles of liberty and justice," one of the specific promises of the Act of Chapultepec.

This story had never been one I could cover in the spirit of the newspaper hack; it had been from the first a war story, that of the Hemisphere's Trojan Horse, and my coverage was my part of the war. I had learned in Mexico how courageous our Latin American neighbors can be in trying to establish civil rights. Now I saw with my own eyes that our international relations are not merely a matter of diplomats in their Sunday suits signing pacts around a shining table; instead, they are intimately concerned with aroused civilians braving the flashing sabers of militarized centaurs on a cobbled street. "*Asesinos!*" "Murderers!" the Argentines would shout at the charging police, and the word was the only weapon they had to hurl.

The American correspondents became a stumbling block for the colonels' clique. Their strong man, Juan Perón, had always believed he could build an all-controlling state much more cleverly than had Hitler and Mussolini, and without us he could have gone about his own "patriotic fraud" at leisure. Already he had decapitated the unions and put his stooges in direct control of organized labor, in preparation for erecting the familiar one-party state supported by a captive labor movement. But his opposition was snowballing tremendously, censorship was breaking down and the New World's mistrustful eye was on him, all because of the news going out.

Terror and vindictive violence had been the regime's weapons of control from the first; now we began to receive death warnings. In June, 1945, Arnaldo Cortesi of *The New York Times* heard that an Army group was plotting his murder. The *New York Herald Tribune*'s Joe Newman, threatened by telephone, took refuge in the American Embassy Residence. Ernie Hill received threats and I got calls I chose to ignore because I did not want the *Chicago Sun* to get the idea it was no spot for a woman to be in.

Ambassador Braden took up these threats with Perón at least twice during June and at one meeting, Perón launched into a vicious tirade against the American newsmen, saying he might not be able to control his "fanatics." Braden strongly warned him that American public opinion would not tolerate attacks against our lives or our cable rights. He also pressed for delivery of the wanted top Nazis, some of whom had backed Perón in his rise to power.

Braden stood firm, the correspondents kept filing, and the opposition to Perón kept rising. At length, in August, the colonels' clique was forced to restore a measure of constitutional liberty.

From the first I did eyewitness reporting, a strenuous, exciting, round-the-clock job. For weeks the situation hung in precarious balance. The police still harried the civilians' political meetings. Exiled opposition leaders were allowed to return, but the mounted police charged the crowd that met them at the boat.

Perón was not secure, however. Younger Army officers, under civilian pressure and unhappy over Perón's overweening personal ambition, would gather in small, discontented caucuses at Campo de Mayo, the garrison dominating Buenos Aires. Perón, who had informants everywhere, would at once speed to Campo de Mayo in a long black limousine, to harangue and rant and stamp around until he beat down the incipient revolt. Tipped off by my own informants, I would meanwhile live for hours or days tied to my telephone by the potential red-hot news break. The Argentine Navy also periodically threatened to pull out of the Buenos Aires harbor and turn its big guns against the military government. My sleep was ruined many nights when my sources telephoned through the small hours to report on the Navy's vacillations, and I came to wish heartily it would steam out into the Río de la Plata and sink itself.

Ambassador Braden has been accused of intervention in Argentina during this period; this is the "historical lie" started by Perón to cover up his defiance of the Chapultepec pact and spread by others with selfish motives of their own. The first leaflets that ever appeared in Buenos Aires picturing Braden as a "cowboy" bullying Perón came immediately after the American ambassador pressed the Argentine strong man to call his own bullies off the American correspondents and to deliver the war criminals. I was a witness to a meeting in which an emissary from an army-civilian group told Braden they would overturn Perón by force if the ambassador could guarantee that their ensuing *de facto* government would be recognized at once by the United States. Braden, in my presence, sent word that he obviously could make no such guarantee, as it would constitute intervention. . . . (Someone said to me while I was still writing the editorial column for the *Washington Post* and Braden was outfacing Dictator Batista in Cuba: "You favor the Braden policy, don't you?" To which I replied, "No, he favors the Prewett policy!") The fact of history is that Braden in Argentina advocated only a line of policy previously approved at the White House and agreed to by all the American republics in the Chapultepec pact. What I "advocated" there was an American correspondent's right to report the news.

Dramatic events came ever faster. In early September, Cortesi, Newman and I broke the terrible story, confirmed by medical reports, of the torture of political prisoners under the colonels. Among the ex-prisoners whom we interviewed was a handsome sturdy youth of about twenty who had been driven insane by application of the electric goad to his testicles.

The popular forces opposing Perón swelled and organized

until on September 19 in Buenos Aires, they massed in the historic "March for Liberty." Although Perón himself had threatened violence in a radio speech the night before and his state-controlled unions had paralyzed transportation in the city at his order, roughly a million people marched or stood watching and cheering along forty city blocks.

This was the most thrilling event I have ever witnessed, modern history's greatest mass expression of a people's opposition to tyranny. And it was part of a stirring in many lands, something profoundly important to my own country's very safety. The American correspondents reported that a sound truck in the parade played "God Bless America," an expression of friendship to the United States completely unprecedented in Latin America's history, if not the world's.

My cable on this march filled a column on the front page of the *Chicago Sun*, but I needed the pen of an inspired prophet or poet to do it justice. We say an unarmed people can never face down the hostile guns of a dictator and this is true, they cannot do it all alone. But these people did face down a tyranny with only the symbol of American support among them. They were a beautiful sight, hundreds of thousands of men and women marching in a triumph of the human spirit; they were shining in their courage and hope.

At once the military regime announced they would hold elections without entering a candidate of their own.

But immediately also the chill wind I had feared began to blow upon us. Spruille Braden, symbol of America's firm insistence on the fulfillment of international promises, and on government by the people, was recalled. Ostensibly he was promoted, and became Assistant Secretary of State for Latin America, but in effect he was kicked upstairs.

Braden left Argentina on September 23. On September 27, the military government jailed hundreds of civilians in all walks of life on the time-worn charge of plotting a revolt, and suspended constitutional rights again. It was that quick.

But the fight went on. The students of Argentina's six autonomous universities went on strike, barricading themselves in university buildings. (I managed to get through police lines and inside the barricades one dark night.) Beginning on October 4, the police turned their guns and tear gas on the students. In La Plata, not far from Buenos Aires, scenes of indescribable horror occurred as students inside the building battled police with improvised weapons, chair arms and benches. Outside, unarmed townspeople tried to fight their way in to help the students in the battle, drawn by the awful noises of breaking windows, smashing doors, screams of the girls, shots, the angry defiant shouts of the young men. Repulsed brutally by the police, many of the grownups burst into tears of agony and rage. When ambulances and Black Marias finally came to take away the boys and girls, the helpless watching crowd sang the national anthem with its refrain, "Liberty, liberty, liberty . . ."

Reports of other brutalities to the students ran through the country and the anger and the anguish of the people grew terrible. Public expressions were suppressed in a rule of terror, but the opposition organized pressure by letter and telephone on the younger officers of the Argentine Army. On October 9, these officers forced Juan Perón to resign his posts as vice-president and secretary of labor.

During three anxious days the anti-Perón Army men and the civilians tried to form a "caretaker" government to hold elections. If there had been in Buenos Aires an American ambassador who favored "democracies everywhere," his very presence would have proved decisive. Braden's presence in Cuba had kept the Batista forces from defying the pressure for elections. In a Brazilian crisis running parallel to the Argentine one in 1945, an American ambassador who stood for "American liberty and justice" stayed quietly at his post after an Army coup ousted Vargas, and elections were duly held on December 1, turning out the old dictator and his followers. As it was, in Argentina, peaceful crowds gathered day after day outside the building where the young officers were negotiating, in moral support of the liberation cause.

But the peaceful crowd, without any direct or indirect

support from the democratic peoples of the world, was pitiably vulnerable. The Buenos Aires militarized police, deeply involved with Perón and fearing reprisals for their brutalities, appeared in force and almost without warning machine-gunned the anti-Perón crowds. Censorship clamped down and early hospital reports of thirty dead were denied; the real total of dead and wounded will never be known. I managed to telephone a dispatch to Chicago at a cost of something like four hundred dollars.

Strict police rule was clamped down on Buenos Aires. While the young Army men were still shaken and the democrats stunned, members of a meat packers' union in nearby Avellaneda controlled by a gangsteresque labor leader named Cipriano Reyes staged a riotous pro-Perón march on Buenos Aires. The police now turned the city over to this crowd. Reyes and the Perón-appointed governor of Buenos Aires province had actually begun organizing this demonstration as an answer to the democrats' "Liberty March" before Perón was exiled. The late Eva Duarte, then Perón's mistress, acted as go-between and pay-off woman for the marchers and later the legend was created that she organized it all by herself.

The pro-Perón march on Buenos Aries convinced the older Army officers who had come up with Perón that he could build his labor façade with police backing and they swung in behind him to reinstate him. A new Perón-controlled cabinet announced elections for February, 1946, and Perón came out as candidate of the "Labor Party" which he was forming through the Secretariat of Labor.

The opposition, with everything rigged against it, fought on; you could not fail to give your heart to such a people. In the election campaign, the power to govern by decree, as well as the police and the public treasury, helped perfect the rig. As a bribe to working people, Perón ordered all employers to pay them a bonus of a month's salary. Opposition speakers were banned from the radio. Independent newspapers were squeezed financially and attacked by Perón's goon squads.

The killings went on. Two students were killed in a battle between democratic and native Nazi groups who clashed under my apartment window. The sidewalk was slippery with blood when Arnaldo Cortesi, UP's Bob Buckingham and I walked toward the fracas. The urbane Cortesi, with his long cigarette holder in hand, strolled up to the line of fire. Bob followed out of bravado and I came along because I figured the *Chicago Sun* could do anything *The New York Times* and UP could. We became very familiar with spilled civilian blood in Buenos Aires. A group of the correspondents once counted up to a hundred civilians who had been killed to our knowledge. Many times the hearses of the dead democrats were followed to the cemeteries by large crowds and often the police broke up the crowds protesting the killings other police had committed in breaking up other crowds.

The constant violence was meant to scare people out of the opposition's ranks. When the opposition presidential candidate traveled through the country, his train and his rallies were shot up. I counted a hundred bullet holes in one side of a coach in the train. On his return to Buenos Aires, a huge welcoming crowd was fired upon by the police.

This was the "free" election campaign, one so heavily weighted against the opposition as to make a true referendum impossible. The vote count was not even monitored by the opposition. The ballots vanished into the hands of the Perón forces, and as results trickled out over two months, a smooth fifty-five per cent majority was built up for Perón. With the cat counting the votes of the mice, how could it have come out otherwise?

During this time the correspondents all realized the firm American policy was melting like ice cream in the summer sun, though the American Embassy chargé d'affaires still helped protect our right to send cables. As the election returns crept in, confirming the farce, I wanted to get as far away from Argentina as I possibly could and probably would have gone except for a turn in my personal life that made it bearable.

A newspaperman named William R. Mizelle, born in the South like myself and lately released from the U. S. Navy, came to Buenos Aires to work for the United Press. I had a desk in the UP office and we met there. I was on vacation at the moment and had just restlessly deserted a house party at Uruguay's fashionable Punta del Este beach; instead of re-opening my flat, I had checked in at the plush Plaza Hotel where I was running up a considerable tab for daiquiries. I liked Bill on sight and at once started doing the town with him, more soberly, since he did not drink. Because I could not at the moment bear one more thought of unhappy things, we started out on a note of utter frivolity. The first attraction, beyond my simply liking the cut of his jib, was the new-comer's ability to make me laugh. I had not laughed in a long time, not in all my life, it seemed.

Not yet entirely spoiled by Peronism, Buenos Aires was a wonderful city for a light romance. Bill had been solemnly warned that I was a tough, a very tough newspaperwoman, but this seemed to amuse him more than anything else. We were thrown together quite naturally after my vacation was over and as we got to know each other better, I discovered many things about him that suited me besides his light manner.

First of all, Bill was sufficiently sure of himself not to resent a woman's being competent in his own field, and this enabled us to share an absorbing interest in writing. I had been pound-ing out my dispatches and rushing them off to the cable office with little thought of how I phrased things. I began to watch my use of the language again, and though my daily cables of the running story continued, I took more interest and pains with the weekly nonpolitical feature columns I sent by mail. After work and on week ends, Bill and I roved through Buenos Aires picking up color for these columns and we got to know all sides of the city. This helped to counter-balance the unpleasantness I continually had to report on in covering the political story.

For as soon as the election returns were in, the reprisals began against every element or institution of society that had opposed Perón; the constitution itself was finally to be changed. Thousands were forced out of their jobs in widespread personal reprisals. Not long after Perón's inauguration *La Prensa* wrote: "There is no sphere of industry or commerce, no profession or trade or vocation or art that is not under the thumb of the state. Curiously, slavery is thus being revived in the name of the people's welfare."

Perón was destroying the independent papers one after another and creating his own press, which smeared me as a "spy of Wall Street." Cortesi and Newman were gone and for a while I was the only staff correspondent for an American newspaper in Buenos Aires. I did my own leg work and felt deeply the importance of verifying fact and avoiding confusion, for the Perón propaganda machine ceaselessly tried to conceal and twist truth in an attempt to win international respectability for the regime on the grounds that it was the freely elected choice of a labor majority.

I had done my eyewitness reporting on the election fracases in constant risk of flying bullets or charging horses, and I continued to report the growing state slavery at risk of an intentional shot in the dark. I never knew when or how Bill might be attacked. ("It would be like them to send four goons to jump you in the dark as you go home from my flat some night," I said to Bill. "If they do I'll send them back their pants the next morning," observed my war veteran, but I was not reassured.) The Perón brain trust naturally hated me because I had recorded their true history with names, dates, incidents. I had been a witness to the fact that Argentina's privileged classes, the "oligarchy," whom Perón's saturation propaganda always claimed were his sole opposition, were only a minor part of it. I knew that several times, the "oligarchs" were asked for but did not give money to buy arms for a civilian uprising. Now I witnessed and recorded the last-ditch resistance of the large Argentine middle class, schoolteachers, clerks, newspapermen, lawyers and doctors, and of the independent labor leaders who had been forced out of the captive labor unions. The captive labor rank and file tried many times to go into independent labor unions, as an on-the-spot investigation by the American Federation of Labor later proved. But legal bans and police raids blocked them. When *peronista* labor leaders themselves attempted to seize independence, they were ruthlessly ousted. I had all through Buenos Aires, even close to Perón, sources who trusted me completely and I was able to get at, and publish, the incontrovertible detail of all this. I was a thorn in the side of the official propagandists, who continued their pressure against me.

Bill Mizelle and I had fallen into the easy habit of constant companionship and as time went on, I became devoted to him. Most of all I liked his healthy independence toward life. He had had family tragedies, as most people have. The war had taken five full years out of his newspaper career. He had volunteered before the war started for reserve officer's training and had been commissioned in time to see his first battle action at Pearl Harbor in the Japanese attack December 7. He saw continuous active sea duty in the hot spots of the naval war until a Navy eye chart caught up with him the last year of it. Then, beached, he had done a most dangerous job in test-firing the rockets mounted on our rocket bombardment ships.

Bill took up his newspaper work and came to Buenos Aires just before the Argentine government began its big squeeze on the United Press. When the UP began to reduce its force nearly a year later, Bill, as last man on, was among the first men off. I understood the UP's plight, but I resented the whole deal, remembering where he had spent the years that made him last man on. Not so Bill; instead, he turned to and began free-lancing magazine articles. Before long he had sold to *Collier's* and had cover stories in other top-ranking national publications.

I liked a man who wasted no time in resentments and would not allow setbacks to set him back. From the first I depended on him for pleasantness in my life and as the difficulties of my work multiplied, I grew to depend on him for more—for moral backing, encouragement, personal protection against the constant threat of thug attacks, and finally, even for solace when I was nervously half-ill.

In the summer of 1946, new stresses began to surround my assignment. Round Two began.

George Messersmith, a career diplomat, was sent to Buenos Aires as ambassador. He believed he could wheedle Perón out of his moment in history by sundry pats on the back, and save face for the now floundering American policy. Mr. Messersmith entertained President Juan Perón and his new wife, Eva, at the American Embassy Residence. It was the first time an Argentine president had entered the Embassy since the colonels' clique took over, and I wrote that it marked an American policy change toward cordiality. Mr. Messersmith did not like this.

He called me in and told me it would be more appropriate for me to record the bare facts. I said interpretation of events was my specific assignment and I believed events in Argentina or any other foreign country unintelligible without them. Later on, we differed on other details of the foreign correspondent's function; at length we descended to spatting over the telephone and I asked him if his attitude implied coercion.

Other newsmen who had lately come to Buenos Aires also had talks at the Embassy over the philosophy of news reporting.

The pressure around the American press corps rose. Our sources told us the Argentine Foreign Office had informed Mr. Messersmith his mission "could not be successful" if the American foreign correspondents were not muzzled.

The United States wanted Argentina to hand over one hundred Nazis. Mr. Messersmith was promised forty-two, but only thirteen were delivered. (We never got any important ones.) In December, he was called to Washington for consultations. I sent a dispatch saying his appeasement policy had failed and that Buenos Aires sources believed he would return only briefly to Argentina after a hospital checkup in the United States.

On January 14, Mr. Messersmith called at the White House to talk with President Truman, and a crowd of White House reporters buttonholed him in the lobby. One of them asked the ambassador if it were true he might not remain long at his post. The question inspired him to say:

"This is completely off the record: There is a very active but very malicious little lady out there [in Buenos Aires] who would be better off in a sanatorium than writing news stories about me." He repeated his unkind remark directly to Tom Reynolds, the *Chicago Sun*'s White House correspondent, who rallied to my defense.

Thus he was quoted by the *Chicago Sun*, which put the attack on the record, printing it with an editorial to this effect:

"We have known for a long time that Ambassador Messersmith wanted to get Virginia Prewett, our correspondent in Buenos Aires, out of his hair. Miss Prewett has insisted, in her dispatches to this paper, on telling the truth about Perón's rotten fascist regime. Mr. Messersmith, anxious to appease Perón, wants to soft-pedal the truth.

"The ambassador has now resorted to one of the most despicable tricks of the trade. Standing in the White House lobby, he launched a vicious tirade against Miss Prewett before 20 newspaper reporters who sought to interview him on Argentine affairs. He called Miss Prewett's work 'malicious' and said she ought to be in a sanatorium rather than writing stories about his activities. Whereupon the ambassador, having slandered Miss Prewett publicly, undertook to make his remarks 'off the record,' which is a diplomat's way of refusing to assume public accountability for his remarks.

"The Sun won't stand for that kind of malevolent irresponsibility. If Mr. Messersmith wants to blow his top about Miss Prewett's reporting in a way calculated to injure her reputation as a newspaperwoman, he can do it publicly and take the consequences. That is why we stripped him of his 'off the record' immunity by publishing his remarks.

"Miss Prewett's professional competence needs no defense before others of her craft. . . . Her assignment for the Sun

will be to go on telling the truth about Argentina—ambassador
or no ambassador."

The Perón government, being authoritarian, could not
imagine that a reporter for a privately-owned newspaper
could survive a difference with a government official, and
they were pleased over what they considered my downfall.
But I carried on as usual; it was the ambassador who left. Mr.
Messersmith returned for a while to his post, for a face-saving
period of several months, then he left Buenos Aires and soon
after, the diplomatic service.

The *peronistas*, jubilant over the wedge driven between
the Embassy and the correspondents, became extremely bold.
Frank Kluckhohn of *The New York Times* was threatened,
his family annoyed, and he finally left. I always let Bill Mizelle,
my constant companion, know where I was in case an "accident" should happen. A number of Argentines and at least
one foreign writer had been taken out and badly beaten by
men in plain clothes who said they were from the federal
police. Bill and I shared a liking for guns and I kept two .25
caliber automatics and a .38 revolver in my flat. Sometimes
I said, with a big hollow laugh, that I wished they would
come for me—I'd shoot it out and make the story of a lifetime.

I did my best not to let all the tension and fuss eat in on
me, but it did. I had no special consciousness of fear, but I
could not adjust to the illogic of what was happening, that a
great nation could pour out money and blood to defeat a
system and then stupidly condemn a neighboring people to
the same evil system. Nor could I answer the Argentine democrats when they asked me to explain it.

In this period there existed a strong tendency among Americans visiting Buenos Aires to take Perón at his own evaluation,
as our official policy did. These visitors would often come
to see me and, in the American way, would "needle" me to
get the information they wanted. I always reacted with elo-
quence if not indignation, but it exhausted me. Information
became hard to get and visitors allowed themselves to be

leceived by appearances. At a time when I was writing a
eries revealing Peronism's persecution of the Jewish com-
nunity in Buenos Aires, a Jewish American, a former Con-
gressman, came to the city. He visited the Embassy, which
nad no contact men the Argentine resistance trusted and
knew only what the Argentine government told them; then
he visitor walked around a bit and called on me. "What's all
your shouting about?" he said, in effect. "Everything's peace-
'ul here." At the expense of great pains in a roundabout ap-
roach—for the Buenos Aires Jews were terrified—I arranged
a secret meeting for the American so that he could hear from
his own people the story of money levies, of the bombing of
ynagogues and other typical Nazi persecution. The visitor
wrote and thanked me afterwards.

The continued stresses were inevitably reflected in my life
with Bill. Increasingly I drew on him until after nearly two
years, I came to feel it was very unfair to him. I had had one
unhappy marriage. Bill was in no position to marry even if
he had wanted to, and I knew we would have to separate
some time. We had come to laugh less and less and I snapped
nervously more and more. I got so I could hardly be polite
o anybody.

Though I cared sincerely for Bill, my emotions were deeply
involved in my job. It was not only the realization that the
whole business meant so much to the New World's democratic peoples and the security of my country. I could not
orget the individuals, the dead university boys, the slippery
blood, the brutality and cynicism that had won power for the
now "respectable" regime, which used the same anti-American
propaganda as the Russians. I could not forget the unctuous
harangues Perón would give from the balcony of the Presidential Palace before he sent his goon squads to attack the
La Prensa building. I could not forget the little school teachers
who had lost their humble jobs for opposing Perón, and had
been blackballed from teaching; nor the men who had kept
on resisting long after all hope was gone, and had been arrested and tortured for it. I knew then as I know now that the

backbone of the Argentine nation who had opposed Perón so stubbornly were never converted, but were merely silenced. These people had taken their risks in the belief my country wanted "to see democracies everywhere," and it had not proved true. I myself felt betrayed and in part guilty for their betrayal, for I was one of the American people on whom they had counted in vain.

A few months after the Messersmith incident in the White House, real disaster struck the press corps. A minor employee of the AP failed to blue-pencil sufficiently a wired-in story about Eva Perón, whose spicy history was then much in the news, and official ire fell heavily on Ray Ordarica, AP chief in Buenos Aires. In an all-out smear campaign, the Perón press accused Ray of organizing fantastic plots against the regime. The operations of the agency were harassed in a number of ways. Soon Ordarica went to the United States. His replacement told me he was not removed from his post because of the pressure. However that may be, the effect was the same as if his removal had been forced by the peronistas. They believed they had won a great victory.

Not long afterwards, most of the American correspondents at Buenos Aires went to Rio de Janeiro for the Hemisphere meeting called the Conference of Petrópolis. While we were away, the Perón regime, growing ever bolder, shut down ten more Argentine newspapers and I foresaw new trouble after we should return. The peronista delegation to this conference rode high, though they had made a farce of complying with the Act of Chapultepec. Their high, wide and handsome behavior at Petrópolis sealed the tomb on the Act of Chapultepec and the Inter-American conference system as instruments of New World defense against Trojan Horse totalitarianism. The wind no longer favored democracy and in due time, new dictatorships were to burgeon in Latin America and old ones were to be revived. Long before Hitler and Mussolini and Stalin, Latin America was familiar with tyrannies built up on the pretext of aiding the masses. After the Petrópolis meeting, the eyes of power-greedy men everywhere were turned in admiration on Perón's "co-operative" state, in which a clique around The Leader, Perón, kept everything in their power, including a small token opposition which they permitted to survive for purposes of confusing world democracy.

At the time of Petrópolis, Spruille Braden was out of the State Department, but Norman Armour, who knew Perón of old, was Assistant Secretary of State for Latin American Affairs. Mr. Armour had been ambassador to Buenos Aires when the military coup occurred in 1943. I had known him there in 1941, and I took to him the troubles of the American press corps in Argentina. He was genuinely distressed and assured me the new ambassador, James Bruce, and his chief aide, Counselor of Embassy Guy Ray, would back up the newsmen once more.

The conference of Petrópolis also brought a turn in my personal life. Bill went to the conference, but the dreadful day-and-night race to cover it inevitably broke the close daily association to which we were accustomed. For the time being, each of us had to transfer a greater interest to other people. Rightly or wrongly, I felt impelled to precipitate the break I had foreseen. I was extremely anxious not to scar the man on whom I had leaned for nearly two years and I honestly believed it was best for us to part while things were still sweet, if not so shining. There was no question of another person with either of us.

Bill, at first surprised, took it well, as I had known he would, though he grew a little impatient with me at the last because I was worried about him. We did not beat our affection to death with words; little was said, nothing that could hurt, and we parted.

In great weariness of spirit after the conference, I went to Central Brazil to report on the opening of a new farming region I had heard about in the state of Goiás. What I found impressed me deeply.

First of all, the natural beauty of the upland appealed to me as none ever had. The crisp air was good after my troubled years in the heavier atmosphere of the coast and I could get long, sweeping views to distant hills with forests on them. The raw backwoods life was completely unlike anything I had ever known, closer even to nature than the rural life of my native American South. A great nation's frontier was moving forward here; by comparison, it was the brightest and most hopeful-seeming spot on the map of South America. The change was a relief to me and I bought five hundred acres of virgin forest land as an investment, with the idea I might retire to it and write novels at some time in the vague distant future.

When I returned to Buenos Aires in October, 1947, I stepped directly into my final round in the long press corps struggle to preserve the right to inform the American people.

All the other staff newspaper correspondents were new. I was the lone veteran now. Mr. James Bruce, an American businessman, had assumed his duties as the new American ambassador a short while before. His more experienced career adviser, Guy Ray, asked me to come to our regular Friday press meeting a few minutes early.

Guy received me alone—we had met in Mexico some time before—and told me the Argentine Foreign Office had suggested the American correspondents might like to have a friendly interview with President Perón. The new ambassador favored the idea, he intimated. But the Embassy would be embarrassed if any of us asked indiscreet questions, for instance, about the Argentine First Lady. The world press of late had freely implied that when young, she had been no better than she should be.

I had no desire to ask the President about his wife's past, I said. I'd never even written about it. But I would want to ask a question about freedom of the press.

Guy shook his head, slowly and a little sadly. That would be considered indiscreet, he was sure.

"Then I'll have to consult my paper," I said. It was obvious the *peronistas* thought they had the troublesome correspondents packaged and wanted the new ambassador to deliver us in a pretty-pretty interview that would have made Perón look good. I had looked on at Perón's conferences with Argentine newsmen; if we were not permitted to ask polite questions turning on real issues, I knew we should be made vehicles for his smooth propaganda and should have to lend our by-lines to it.

The press corps, which had steadfastly refused to write the history of Argentina according to Perón, would now set the final seal on his new "respectability," created by his propaganda and by the vacillations of American foreign policy. Perón was realist enough to know that without the seal of the embattled correspondents, his respectability would never be entirely accepted.

Guy explained to me a little apologetically that his assignment was to get along with the *peronistas* and to try to manage them that way. I said my assignment was strictly reporting and that I believed he'd never get anywhere by trying to appease the regime. I'd seen all similar attempts fail, I said. On this note, we went into the main press conference.

In the full conference I met Mr. Bruce for the first time. He said very little in the ensuing discussion, beyond remarking that the correspondents themselves had asked the Embassy to arrange the interview.

I could have said that nothing about Perón or his beliefs or his government had changed and that if I signed my name to a story whitewashing him it would betray the truth, my paper, my principles and my country. Instead, I said I'd have to consult the *Chicago Sun* on agreeing not to ask the question about freedom of the press. I knew the paper would never tell me to tie my hands on a legitimate question.

The press corps had apparently been ready to go along with the interview, I learned. Guy Ray was the Embassy spokesman in trying to talk me into it.

I said that freedom of the press was the big story in Argentina, the only one we had. At the time, the Argentines were supporting a Russian stand on the press in the United Nations. It was also a practical issue with all of us, I pointed out. I knew the new staff correspondents had been having difficulties over their permits to cable to their papers. Ridiculous delays had been put in their way. One newsman had even been asked for a small bribe to get his press card. I asked one of the staff newspaper correspondents if it weren't true he was at that moment forbidden to send out press cables.

"He told me not to file for a few days," was the answer. ("He" was a petty Argentine press bureau official.)

"Then you're suspended?"

"No, I'm just not filing."

"Why, if you're not suspended?"

"I didn't want to bait him."

I began to feel sick. The constant attack on the press corps, our trouble with Messersmith, Ordarica's fate—it was all adding up to timidity on the part of the newcomers.

"What would you do if a big story broke, would you 'bait' him then?" I asked.

A new voice spoke up.

"When Jules Dubois of the *Chicago Tribune* was here he couldn't get a permit at first, so he filed on an AP cable blank and his message got through."

"But that's a one-time trick," I countered. "You can't run a newspaper operation like that. We've got a right to file and we ought to keep it."

"Oh well, he got his card a few days later," said someone, as if that made it all right.

I hit as hard as I could.

"News that's a few days old isn't good enough for the *Chicago Sun*," I said.

The discussion became less calm.

Guy Ray said that when President Truman visited Mexico, his press aides indicated to the Mexicans what questions would be suitable.

"Then let the Argentines tell us what we can and can't ask," I offered.

This wouldn't do.

Arguments were tossed at me from various quarters. The

old hands of the magazines and press associations, most of whom had done excellent and daring work at one time or another and had gotten into very hot water for it, kept quiet. I suppose they knew I'd never agree. But I would have appreciated a word of support. I felt entirely alone. I missed Bill Mizelle, who had taken a stand similar to mine in a private interview with Guy Ray, but who did not attend Embassy press conferences because he was a free lance.

I was heartsick over the division among the press corps. Perón and his followers believed they were smarter than the representatives of "Wall Street capitalism," as they called us. They believed they could outmaneuver and outlast us, as they had our diplomats. And they had finally managed to start a split in the press corps itself. The bright moment was over: the last beachhead would have to go.

"The rest of you have the interview and I'll cover the story from the outside," I said.

This was not agreeable. I could almost see the boys shudder at the thought.

"Then I'll have to consult my paper," I repeated, and the meeting broke up.

My cable to the *Chicago Sun* brought a reply supporting my reasonable desire to ask a question about press freedom, or any other politely phrased, legitimate question. But even before the cable came, I launched a campaign to hold my ground without any further divisions among the press group.

I started with Ambassador Bruce. After he heard the facts I brought out in the conference, he had offered to take official action to relieve the newcomers' difficulties over their filing permits. I went to see him and showed him a number of clippings of my news stories reporting how Perón was squeezing free enterprise and American firms out of existence and was playing footie with Russia and her satellites. This was to show him exactly where I stood on matters of general American public interest. The new ambassador apparently gleaned a good deal of information from the clippings. He said frankly he didn't see why Perón shouldn't be asked a question about freedom of the press and that he would say so at our next press meeting.

The ambassador's backing assured immediate victory, but not the kind I wanted, for it gave the Embassy the balance of power in the affairs of the correspondents. I had had three years of full editorial responsibility for a weekly newspaper and one year on a city daily even before I could vote; the independent instinct of the American press was strong in my veins.

There was another reason why I did not want to depend solely on Embassy support, even from the friendliest ambassador. Since I had begun writing about Latin America in 1940, I had seen our Latin American policy abandon the bases of principle which Cordell Hull tried to establish and had watched it reverse and contradict itself. While in Buenos Aires, I had seen its vacillations gut the Inter-American system of co-operation as national policy-makers dedicated to expediency tried to settle among themselves just what policy it was expedient to adopt. I had seen the concept of expediency change and change and change again as this or that personality enjoyed momentary ascendancy in our State Department; I had seen our basic national policy vary from country to country, according to the views of the incumbent ambassador. Even if a correspondent wanted to hitch his point of view to official policy, he would have to fall into continual self-contradictions to negotiate the hairpin turns. It was not only unethical, but was also a practical impossibility and something no responsible reporter would consider.

To restore the surface solidarity of the press corps, I went to several of the men who had spoken out in our last meeting and told them I'd agree to limit my questions to requests for comment on Perón's previous public utterances. This would of course have permitted me the widest latitude for asking about freedom of the press or anything else. The wilted backbones of the newcomers had stiffened perceptibly since Bruce had promised to get the *peronista* bureaucrats to stop hazing them, and they agreed to my formula. At an early meeting with the ambassador, who said he saw no reason why we should not ask Perón about freedom of the press, we all agreed on the point.

But Perón could not afford to accept such a condition, of course, and the friendly get-together with him was not held.

The experience was traumatic, for I had never believed any of us would fall into the *peronistas'* trap. Theoretically, I knew that all the trouble the press corps had had at Buenos Aires could lead to weakness, but I had never expected it to happen. In my mind I knew that overseas reporters without strong backing could not hold out forever against all the pressures and the harassments of a hostile foreign government, yet I had expected them to do so.

I considered myself a reporter, not a politicker or monitor among my peers. I had no desire ever again to be the professional conscience of any press group on a question of freedom of the press. When the Chisun told me they were abolishing their overseas syndicate at the end of 1947, I was genuinely relieved. For foreign correspondents, the time might be out of joint, but I could no longer try to set it right single-handed.

As I remembered the very different world I had dipped into on my visit to Goiás, that country seemed to be the somewhere-else I had always longed to flee to at bad times in my life. I decided to go there without delay, to have done with all else. I could use my severance pay and small savings to build a far retreat and I would practice nonviolent nonparticipation and think things out. For a living, I would clear land in the forest and make it fruitful; and it would heal me. The thought made me happy.

I had not seen Bill Mizelle since my return from Brazil, but one day in mid-December, after my plans to leave were made, I glimpsed him, quick-moving as a swordsman among the crowds. We spoke and he told me he had gone to work for *The New York Times* bureau. A mutual friend had informed me he had not hastened to replace me. It seemed harsh for us to spend the holidays apart though in the same city—there had been no quarrel and I felt emotionally safe because I was leaving. So we celebrated Christmas and the New Year's Eve together and completed a transition from sweethearts to friends. It was possible because we had never formed the habit of cross-examining each other on our emotions and because I was determined neither to cause nor suffer pain. I could not bear to think that either one of us would ever look back with longing and I was sure that if we remained friends, neither of us would. I asked him to sit by me at the farewell press luncheon.

At this farewell luncheon with the press corps, I invited those present to visit me in my refuge far away. I said nothing of my feelings about our abandoned beachhead.

I could have told my colleagues that as they gave up their rights, their liberty would gradually become jeopardized. Representatives of the American press were in fact arrested and jailed in Argentina not many months afterwards, on trumped-up charges of fomenting a strike. I could have said that when we yielded this outpost, the position of every American correspondent was weakened the world over, and the embattled remnants of the Argentine free press were weakened and the remaining free press everywhere in the world was weakened. I could have said this:

"The American foreign correspondent, by actual count, is a vanishing breed. Of those still functioning abroad, how many have the moral backing that made it possible for a few of us to break a censorship right here in Argentina and keep it broken for so long? How is the American public to know what's going on in the world and what its representatives abroad are doing? The curtain of silence is not only being shoved down on us, we are pulling it right down around our own necks. . . ."

But I didn't say it. I was not Prince Hamlet any longer.

BEYOND THE GREAT FOREST

2

THE January sunlight poured into my little flat high in the Edificio Safico overlooking the broad white city of Buenos Aires. In a few days I was to leave for Goiás.

"Roger Ward is bringing a power saw from the States later on and I hope I may be able to make a deal with him to cut my timber when we start clearing. . . ." I was writing a letter to Susana, who had been my best friend in Argentina for over two years. This truly elegant little Argentine, about five feet one but with a jaunty set to her shoulders that made her look taller, had been born with all the disadvantages of an overprivileged Latin American woman, but with intelligence and will, she had long since freed herself from these bonds without sacrificing anything of her native femininity and good taste. Susana had lived in the United States; she believed in our way of life and at times, I think, had more faith in the United States than many Americans have themselves. A crystalline wit completed her thoroughly delightful personality and made her company always a pleasure. Susana had traveled with me on my first exploratory trip to Central Brazil and when I decided to go there to live she agreed to come soon after for a long visit.

Roger Ward was the third member of the small party recruited to invade the Goiás frontier. I first met him in 1946 when he had just come to South America selling airplanes for Boeing, and he customarily joined Susana, Bill and me for Sunday jaunts around Buenos Aires when he was in town. Our group had often discussed half in fun how we'd like to found a remote community for escapees from the woes around us and Roger, who traveled for Boeing in Brazil also, made the first contacts with people in Anápolis. After Susana and I visited Goiás in September, 1947, Roger made a trip there and bought land next to mine. Our common interest in Goiás helped us all decide to go there.

Susana had lived through years of upheaval and tension in her country. I was leaving a conflict that became intolerable when the Buenos Aires press corps ceased defending itself. The nearest Roger ever came to giving a reason for his move to Goiás was to say he wanted to work for himself for a change. He had done a big job in aviation during the war and I am sure he was tired of cities.

The friendship among Roger, Susana and me had always been kept on a pleasant level of civilized impersonality, which we meant to continue in the wilds. To pay for developing his land, Roger intended to start a small brick factory in Ceres, the tiny frontier post twenty-five miles from our land. Susana and I planned to find a place to live in Ceres too while I had land cleared and built a house on the farm. In my last weeks at Buenos Aires the planning of this house became my constant pleasure. I sketched one that could grow from year to year as the old homes did in the American South. It was to have broad picture windows and flowered terraces; it would combine graciousness with the utmost in convenience. I hoped to make a place where other friends also could find safe haven and rest.

Captain Leek A. Bowen and his wife, Joan Lowell Bowen, were the couple with whom Roger had made the contact that introduced us into Goiás. Seeking their own El Dorado, the Bowens had gone into the Brazilian wilderness in the mid-1930's. After suffering real hardship, they had established themselves at Anápolis in a comfortable home where they offered hospitality to other newcomers arriving to buy land.

The Bowens owned forest land and sold both Roger and me our tracts along the River of Ghosts. When I was reminded that Joan Lowell was the center of a dispute over the authenticity of her best-selling book, *Cradle of the Deep*, in the late 1920's, I vaguely recalled the book's dust jacket, which showed the photograph of a beautiful girl with a mane of streaming black hair, climbing the rigging of a sailing ship. When I first met Joan at the airport at Anápolis she seemed a slight, black-eyed, middle-aged woman, dust-beaten to a smooth brown. Dressed in slacks and T-shirt for travel in the backlands, however, Joan seemed to grow taller and the years fell away. As you knew her, her flashing eyes became memorable. Against the forest, I later observed, Joan's dark skin was gypsy-brown, not dust-beaten, and her immense self-confidence gave an impression of unusual vitality.

Not long after my official farewell in late January I set forth by air from Buenos Aires for São Paulo, where Captain Bowen met me. Son of a seagoing family of Port Republic, New Jersey, Captain Bowen was a master mariner in his twenties and for years commanded Munson Line luxury liners in South American waters. At one time he was New York port captain for this line, which he left to plunge with Joan into the wilds of Brazil. This slight, blue-eyed, fair American, fiftyish now but wearing his years well, always counseled caution in the face of too-exuberant enthusiasm and the vast inexperience of the newcomers. Joan's sense of adventure often kept her from feeling the difficulties that befell in Goiás, but the Captain was aware of them and was adept at picking up the pieces.

I had had a second-hand Plymouth station wagon shipped to me at São Paulo, and I meant to drive it the eight hundred miles to Goiás, but the Captain told me the roads and travelers' inns along the way were terrible and advised my going with him by plane. He sent for a driver to come down from Anápolis by train to take the loaded vehicle back. While my car was clearing through customs, I shopped for the wilderness in holiday mood. I already had denim pants, cotton shorts and riding boots, and I bought very light, long-sleeved cotton blouses at Captain Bowen's suggestion.

The Captain looked on with amused tolerance while I selected tools with which to make camp furniture for my house. The rest of my purchases were three horsehair mattresses, two big kerosene table lamps—Aladdin lamps with fragile mantles that glow with a brilliant white light—a kerosene lantern, flashlight with spare bulbs and batteries, six Collins ax heads, six L-shaped flat steel brush hooks for cleaning out the underbrush, a hammer, a pocketknife with bottle opener, a big butcher knife, a machete, a huge jar of Elizabeth Arden cleansing cream and a big bottle of skin tonic, a big box of vitamins, a can of DDT, a pair of eyebrow tweezers, six silver-plated table knives, forks and spoons, and one large and very beautiful dessert bowl, imported from Sweden, with six matching dessert plates. These last items were my gesture toward bringing gracious living into the wilds. I bought several cases of canned goods—figs, tomatoes and processed meat. My library included my own two nonfiction books and a novel written by my sister, Bowen Ingram, plus a Webster's Secondary School Dictionary, How to Build a House and F. L. Green's Odd Man Out.

As Captain Bowen shepherded me around São Paulo's shopping district, he gavè me my Boy Scout drill on how to avoid the pests of Goiás. There were few poisonous snakes in upland Goiás, I learned, and no malaria along our routes. Goiás had wood ticks, although they were not known to carry fevers. These were worst in pastures but could be found in matted greenery in the forest. The stinging gnats of the forest you could best avoid by wearing long pants with socks and a light blouse with long sleeves. Scratching the bites of the gnats often produced ulcerous sores. The pest most frightening to me was the berne, which bores into the skin of animals and lays an egg that becomes a burrowing grub. The Captain said they seldom got into people but could do so if you were careless. In its boring stage the berne usually got to people via clothes hung on infested bushes. I was told never to hang my clothes on a bush and never to wear clothes that had not been pressed with a hot iron after washing. You couldn't keep the backland washwomen from hanging your clothes on bushes to dry, but hot irons killed the insects.

The Captain told me there was a good brick house standing empty on their place at Anápolis. He suggested Susana and I could put in glass windows and use it.

"I think we'll stay nearer the farm, at Ceres, a few months while I build the house in the forest," I told him, demurring.

The Captain looked thoughtful.

"You two women may not want to go into the *mato* to live right away," he observed finally. *Mato* is a common term for the forest in Brazil.

"Why not? We can have a Brazilian family to live with us. And there'll be the men working the place. What's wrong with the *mato*?"

The Captain brought his attention back from something he was gazing at in space and his eyes blazed up as do many blue-eyed people's when they smile.

"Well, the *caboclos*, the backwoodsmen, say the *mato* will kill you or make you fat," he told me. "Maybe you and Susana will get fat."

After a few days my shopping was done. We left São Paulo's big, bustling airport and flew northwest for over four hours. For a long time the rounded green hills of São Paulo state were under us and we caught glimpses of the bright red earth that grows so much of the world's coffee, with white gleaming towns in the distance and the tracery of roads. The signs of man grew fewer as we flew inland; the country rose, the hills flattened, the forests were lush only in long vales. Goiás is a long state, larger in area than France, and Anápolis centers its southern half. Southern Goiás is near enough to the equator to be forever free of frost, yet high enough to be spared the curse of Amazonian-type jungle vegetation and temperatures. For a good while before you reach Anápolis, you fly over cattle country. The rolling gray-green landscape below looks scabby with patches of green, like moss on a gray rock. Though somewhat paler, from above it recalls the tones and patterns of a GI's jungle-camouflaged uniform.

The Aerovias DC-3 came down at sun-drenched upland airports, Uberaba and Araguarí, and as the red of the earth came up to meet us, the green of the shrubbery around the blazing white buildings was vivid and the sky all over and around us a high, deep blue. Best of all was the crisp, tangy upland air, as invigorating as a tonic. I drank it in; this was what I had longed for, a new world, blotting out every thought of my life before.

The Captain began to watch for landmarks out of a forward window and finally, as the plane flew over a sort of low rim into a shallow bowl, he called me. There ahead was a sprawled-out town, with one big white building seven or eight stories high shining in its center. This was Anápolis, railhead and jumping-off place for the deep interior.

Joan met us in the Bowen's big old Chevrolet station wagon and we lumbered over a rough graveled road several miles through country very much like the sagebrush Texas plains till we came to the deeply pitted and rutted and very narrow streets of Anápolis itself. We rattled through the short main street of the teeming little frontier city and through gently rolling country east of it. Some six miles out we turned into a gate and coasted down a long drive to the Bowens' comfortable brick house. Unlike most Brazilian homes, this house was protected from heat and glare by a grove of thick trees. It was built against a long slope that ended in a rushing stream down behind it.

My new friends made me feel very welcome. They themselves were just starting a new gasoline filling station and truck agency in Anápolis, and soon I plunged into busy activity along with them. I found there was nothing to rent in Ceres, so I accepted the Bowens' offer of the little house on their place as a reception center for Susana and me; Roger could also use it as a base till he got his start at Ceres. I ordered glass windows to supplement the wooden shutters on the house and decided to build two fireplaces and new partitions. When I asked the Captain's permission to make these changes, he said I could do anything I damn pleased and the house became known as Liberty Hall.

Feeling very much a pioneer, I began building myself a bed out of two-by-two's of a local hardwood. I bolted it together and ran wire through the side rails like an old colonial cord bed. I cleaned up an old door and made a dining table out of it. For a dining nook I repainted handmade straight-backed seats that had come out of an old bus. Some Brazilian backlanders make their own crockery of native clay, and we found a woman who agreed to bake plates and cups and saucers for me. I used a cloth woven and dyed locally for table runners, gay blues in stripes and checks, and put white string mats used for saddle pads on the floor for throw rugs. I began to assemble rustic kitchen-type chairs, camp cots to make into studio beds, and boxes out of which to make stands, shelves and other furniture. I painted my box furniture blue and green and yellow and hung my big hand-painted Paraguayan straw hat on the newly whitewashed wall along with a pair of locally made yellow chaps. When everything was done, the little house was fresh and bright, with a charm of its own. I loved the soft red of its worn brick floors and the clean look of its white walls.

All this was quite a change of occupation for me but it was not exactly a lark. I began to learn what it means to live in a frontier town. I had spent some of my childhood in a Tennessee town of two hundred population, but it was nothing like the Brazilian back country. There was no choice of anything—nuts, bolts, nails and paints of even approximately appropriate kinds were wrested from local supply houses by dint of interminable personal research. My Portuguese was not good enough to use over the limited telephone system. To send a messenger was to invite disaster, since nobody could decide for me. Difficulties did not stem from the legendary Latin American *mañana* attitude, for people

46   BEYOND THE GREAT FOREST

were obliging and tried to help. But every detail took so
much going about and hauling back and forth, I began to
feel like a person trying to swim with one arm tied to his
side.

I had been in Anápolis nearly a month when I finally saw
my land for the first time. I want to make clear the location
of the places that I'm going to tell about, because I'll name
them again and again. The Bowens' Anápolis home, called
the Chacra—Portuguese for small country place—is about
six miles northeast of Anápolis, the railhead city. We had
to drive back to Anápolis to get to the big road that runs
north a little over seventy-five miles to the Goiás Great
Forest, or *Mato Grande,* and the *Colônia Agrícola.* The
Colônia is an enormous new homesteading project launched
in this thousand or so square miles of forest in the early 1940's
by Dr. Bernardo Sayão for the Brazilian federal government
at the direction of Getúlio Vargas. Between Anápolis and
the *Colônia* headquarters town of Ceres there was one town,
an old community called Jaraguá situated about sixty miles
north of Anápolis. At Ceres the big road crosses the Rio das
Almas, boundary of the farm colony, and then runs near
the river for many miles northward. About twenty-five miles
north of Ceres, at Kilometer 171, a right-hand turnoff leads
over about five miles of rough trail to the Rio das Almas, or
River of Ghosts, so called because of the many who died in
its floods during a gold rush long ago. Across the River of
Ghosts at this point lay the Bowens' land and mine and the
tract bought by Roger.

One Saturday morning in late February, Joan and I and
Joan's part-Indian driver Santinho ("Little Saint") piled into
the Bowens' old Ford station wagon and set forth to the
north, due back on Monday. We took along another tenderfoot, Davino Cuaresma, who had recently come from Southern Brazil to open farm land bought from the Bowens by
his brother, an Aerovias pilot, Comandante Nilo Cuaresma.

My mood was one of happy anticipation; Goiás is a region
always blessed in my eyes for the beauty of its long vistas

and I looked forward even to the tiresome, jolting drive
because of the countryside we would go through. I've seen
the truly splendid varieties of the American South, of deep
Pennsylvania, of upstate New York with its tanglewoods;
have felt the impact of the rugged, wild Central Plateau of
France, and of the broad, stark plains of Castile, where you
see too far. The geographical drama of Latin America from
Mexico to Tierra del Fuego far surpasses all these, magnificent
though they are. And in far Goiás, the one hundred miles
of varied country that stretches from Anápolis to my farm
in the *Mato Grande* caught and kept my love from my first
experience of it like a symphony of great music. The day
we went north to visit my land I looked at it with new eyes,
for I had come to claim a part of it as my own and I truly
felt that it held the rest and serenity I longed for, and would
be my home forever.

The big road running north rises gradually from the shallow bowl where Anápolis lies. There the earth is pinkish-gray
under its silvery gray-green vegetation and it rolls away east-
ward to soft-rounded, immensely old hills. The old Ford
labored up to the rim, and away to the west we began to see
deep valleys, steep-sided with wooded slopes, filled with blue-
black shadows. The road cut across low ridges and valleys;
there was always ahead of us another high slope and beyond
it another valley with its rushing clear stream. The scrub
growth gave way to thin woodland as the hills rose, for we
were going up to cross the range of low mountains beyond
which lies a basin split by the Rio das Almas. Southward from
this high region of Central Goiás the waters run down to
empty eventually into the Atlantic through the Río de la
Plata past Buenos Aires. The streams rising within the basin
of the Rio das Almas proper join it and flow into the Tocantins, which in turn merges with the mighty Amazon far
away.

As we approached the ridge, the aged Ford labored up a
winding road among long slopes. Here cattle trails made
brown crisscrosses in pastures where through thin grass you

could see the stumps of trees that marked them as earlier clearings. Every now and then we would pass an old *fazenda*, the seat of a cattle baron, a small, desolate, dusty and sun-beaten tile-roofed house with growths of cane and small coffee groves nearby. There was a Sunday stillness about these quiet slopes and valleys, where the only thing that moved was a glittering stream.

The month was February, before the harvest began, and we saw very few people on the road, not one in ten miles. The old car ground gradually up the hills that grew ever higher till at last they were low mountains. We topped them and began to glimpse on the curves a vast descending region beyond, a panorama backdropped by another range of mysterious mountains in the far distance. Goiás forests are always green but now at the end of the rains the country was especially lush with renewal, and as we rounded the mountain curves, deep shadows of valley green and blue drew the eye powerfully. The descent on the north is quick and not many miles beyond, Goiás again begins to ring her changes—miles of rolling land somewhat like the Texas plains, backed by a far wall of misty hills. Near the old gold-town of Jaraguá, which was nearly a ghost-town till the big road cut through to bring it new life, an abrupt, jagged black mass of mountains suddenly looms nearby on the west, balancing the ghostly blue of the range known as the Serra dos Bois, dimly seen far away to the east.

Northwest beyond the old town the basin continues for long rolling miles till at last the line of the earth begins to rise and swell and grow into the range of medium hills bearing the Goiás Great Forest or *Mato Grande*. With each gentle ridge flowing somewhat higher than the one before, the forests on the upper slopes grow thicker and taller and the road cutting through them shows earth glowing redder and richer with each mile. Here where the stout forests begin and the earth is fertile for planting crops the new settlement was creeping forward, and scars on the forest and the earth now partially healed over by growing grain marked the frontier's advance. The tender green of the tall unirrigated rice concealed most of the blackened knee-high stumps and prone trunks of great trees tortured by fire, but you could still glimpse these charred skeletons of the forest along the roadside at the edges of the fields.

In small clearings kilned by the sun were the first homes of the arriving farmers, ugly huts made out of unpeeled sapling poles driven lightly into the ground and roofed over with rice straw or palm fronds. There was no transition from clearing to forest. The newly opened land with its thin covering of planted green ran abruptly against the towering, black-shadowed walls of motionless, silent trees. There were very few people about—only occasionally we saw small naked children, warm brown against the red earth, playing in front of a hut, or a barefoot farm worker clad in white homespun shirt and faded homemade cotton trousers, trudging along the road.

At last we came over a big hill and saw below us the Rio das Almas, beyond which lay the *Colônia* headquarters, Ceres. But on the hither side of the river a wildcat town had sprung up, called Barranca, or "Riverbank," and it was at this settlement, barely more than a wide place in the road, that I had my first experience with the backland spirit of helpfulness. I had lost a light jacket and tried to buy some kind of a sweater in the settlement's one small emporium that carried ready-made clothes. They had nothing at all except men's rough shoes and trousers, but the storekeeper insisted on lending me something of his own. When with a pleased smile he brought out a newly laundered linen coat, not much too big for me, I realized he'd be offended if I turned it down. I borrowed it and it served me well.

We crossed the bridge, a pontoon span swaying on floats made of gasoline drums, and briefly visited the barnlike wooden structure that was the *Colônia* headquarters. Davino wanted to take up a homestead on the *Colônia* side of the river across from the property his brother had bought, and he had to file his request for land here.

Leaving Ceres, we rattled down the winding, narrow, graveled road, amid steep hills that closed in around us. On our right, we could see now and again the winding Rio das Almas, Ghost River, yellow and swift and swollen with five months of rain. The forest on these rounded hills grew even heavier as we went north, although it was tough and thick everywhere. We passed a square little tile-roofed house, a school established by Dr. Sayão, chief of the *Colônia Agrícola*, at great cost in time and trouble. We passed the thatched sapling huts of the homesteaders in occasional clearings hugging the road. In one clearing a mule patiently walked around and around pulling a beam that turned homemade wooden rollers and crushed out the pungent juice of sugar cane, ready for boiling down into sugar. In another, men were operating a backland "sawmill." They had hoisted a big ax-squared log on high supports; one man pulled a long saw from above, another from underneath to gnaw rough boards off the log.

About halfway to the turnoff at Kilometer 171 the forested hills gentle down again to long sweeps of plateau that dive into occasional sharp valleys, then rise and sweep on. We passed Córrego Sêco—Dry Creek—the only way station between Ceres and the farms. From somewhere the owner, José Maier, had got lumber to build his small station. The weather-beaten plank house with bearded, lanky backlanders lounging on its small porch and pigs grunting nearby might have been a scene in the Ozarks or the Smoky Mountains of Tennessee. All that was lacking was a hitching rail and horses. We passed many homesteaders walking along the road after we left Ceres, but not one horse-drawn vehicle and only one or two riders, leather-chapped cowboys herding cattle.

Beyond Córrego Sêco the high flats roll sweetly and the forest rises taller and ever taller. This land was part of a big splotch of ultra-rich soil that lay also on the other side of the Rio das Almas where we Americans had our holdings. It may be slightly less fertile than the fabulous red soil of São Paulo, but it is a type that lasts longer and is fertile enough for any purpose whatsoever. It is equal to the best land in Goiás or anywhere else in the world, in some experts' opinion.

In midafternoon we reached the homesteader's hut that marked the trail the Bowens had opened to their first small clearing the year before. The sun had been hot on the highway and it was a relief to get into the forest. The old Ford could barely creep along the rough track. About a quarter of a mile in from the big road we bumped over the first bridge, a rustic culvert made of sapling poles. The Ford stalled trying to get up the steep little grade on the other side. Her brakes were none too good and while Santinho, Joan's driver, tried to revive the engine, Joan and Davino and I attempted to hold the station wagon on the grade. All at once, she bucked out of our hold, rolled backwards and crashed into a tree at the edge of the stream by the little bridge.

I was appalled by this disaster, but Joan and Santinho were sure no serious damage was done. We pawed through our supplies and got out our knapsacks and a food basket. My pack held a clean cotton shirt, a bottle of anti-insect liquid, spare boot socks, a small towel, my little gold-plated .25 automatic, an extra clip of cartridges, small bottles of distilled water and fluid for my contact lenses, soap, aspirin, vitamin tablets, sleeping tablets, fountain pen, pencil, small notebook and camera. I had on my elegant Argentine riding boots and carried my leather coat that had cost a hundred and seventy-five dollars when I had it tailored in Buenos Aires. I wore heavy denim pants and a thin white shirt. My snappy little straw hat had come from Paraguay and my green and red wool scarf from Saks Fifth Avenue. I was to sever my last tie with the latter institution by losing the scarf on the march in to the river.

The long ride through the country I so admired had put me in a high mood for taking possession of my land, and the unexpected accident caught me off balance emotionally. So long as I was in the car, I was a machine-age visitor to the great forest but now, before I was ready for it, I had to meet it on primitive and, to me, unequal terms, that is to say, on foot. I looked around me somewhat uncertainly as we started to trudge in to the river. It was like going into a green-walled alley with porous sides, an alley with a green awning over it. My big surprise was the thickness of the underbrush; there was such a tangle of it I could not see how a cat could get through it, much less a jaguar. From the ground there rose a mat of vines, little shrubs, young trees, weeds, blending into low bushes which in turn dovetailed into higher bushes. These were closely topped by young trees with their own abundant leaves. The big trees thrust through it all to continue the living wall of towering greenery far above us. Only rarely could you see any distance into this anarchy of foliage. Except where the road ran through clearings for a few hundred yards the sunlight reached us only in flickers.

I tried not to show it, but I was not in physical condition for the hike. The coat and pack I carried were heavy and soon I was sweating and staggering through the sunny clearings under my load. But in the forest-shaded stretches of road the air bit sharp and cool. I alternately sweltered and shivered and then I grew hollow and desperately hungry and when we sat on a log to eat cold turkey sandwiches, the stinging gnats made their appearance. I had neglected to dig the insect repellant from the bottom of my pack in time and soon my hands were covered with itching lumps. We had to trudge on and the road seemed without an end. My boots were stiff and my pack and leather coat gradually grew heavier till they seemed to weigh a ton.

At long last we reached the riverbank and a shout from Joan brought her chief tenant Getúlio and his half-grown son to fetch us across in a narrow, leaky canoe. Though it was late afternoon, the light was still good when we pulled out into the river. As I huddled on a narrow thwart in the shaky canoe, Joan pointed about a quarter of a mile upstream to the island and river front that were mine.

There it was, more lovely than I had imagined. The shelter-ing island, the flowing river, the huge trees bending over . . .

I knew Joan was anxiously awaiting some recognition of this historic moment and I did the best I could.

"It's beautiful," I said.

Inside I felt curiously numb. I thought at the time that this was caused by the weariness of the tramp in from the wreck. (Joan afterwards half seriously insisted my voice "broke," as it should have to round out the drama.) It was the first time, but not the last, that I was to feel closed out, pushed away, by the beautiful forest.

The *caboclos* nosed the canoe into the steep bank and we scrambled up its perilous little incline. Two soft-voiced dark men, other tenants, smiling gap-toothed smiles, took our burdens now and we filed through a thicket and up a long rise sowed in corn and beans. The clearing was a rolling, burned-over tract of more than fifty acres with two or three tenant houses along the valley. I was reeling with weariness by this time and found it trying to have to climb over the big charred logs that continually obstructed our way. Again and again I banged my knees cruelly against these prone remains of the forest giants sacrificed in the rite of clearing.

Getúlio's hut, made of rough-split young tree trunks and roofed with hand-split wooden shingles, was long and dark and cool. A fire glowed in a clay stove built on low stilts. There was one long board bench inside the hut, and also to sit on, low boxes which had held pairs of five-liter gasoline tins. Platforms of saplings to sleep on in a partitioned-off space at the back of the hut were the only other furniture. I stretched out exhausted on the board bench, my head on my pack. Dona Piquitita, Getúlio's wife, made food for us. Her soupy brown beans, boiled-down rice and pot-fried chicken tasted good. She infused coffee in a can that once had held motor oil. We helped ourselves on enameled plates and gratefully drank the heavily sweetened black brew out of tiny cups of enamelware.

Around sunset time, I went with Joan to bathe in the Rio das Almas. The yellow water was deliciously cool, life-restoring; like the good air, it seemed to penetrate and carry away all weariness of soul and body. The current was so strong we dared not swim here, but could only bathe while hanging on to a tree root with one hand. One false movement and our bones might next find quiet waters where the Amazon River flowed out to sea over a thousand miles away.

After the dark fell we went back to the hut and I recaptured my place on the board feeling better. Joan and the *caboclos* sat around on gasoline boxes and swapped news in the firelight. Soon we heard the Ford's horn blowing over the river and Getúlio went to fetch Santinho, who had found a team of oxen to pull the car back onto the road and had got her running once more. Joan and Davino and I went to sleep in a small thatched hut built farther up in the clearing. By the light of flickering backland wick lamps, we strung up our hammocks and climbed in fully dressed except for our shoes.

I was trying to get comfortable in the limp hammock when we heard not far away a sound like a woman screaming.

"*Onça,*" said Joan. Jaguar.

The jaguar is in Brazil the king of the forest. Often confused with the panther or leopard, which is native only to Asia and Africa, this big cat is aggressive and ferocious and is said to track men for miles to kill them. For the backlanders, the *onça* is the symbol of the hostility of the forests. They will not even have jaguar skins in their houses; they say they bring "*azar,*" bad luck.

The jaguar screamed again, not too close.

"It's probably a female calling her cub," said Joan. "There's a stream behind us here and I suppose they're on their way down to drink."

The next morning the light of the high tropic dawn awakened me. I swung out of my hammock, put on my boots. All around the hut grew tall blue-green mountain rice of the kind that grows like wheat, without constant flooding with water. The long heads of rice were heavy with crystal dew. I walked out into the rice and stripped the dew off with my hands; it was sweet to the taste and cool, soon my hand was wet with the pure distillation. The light morning mist slowly rose to linger in the upper air, watering down the intense blue of the sky. This was not only a new scene, it was a different age, back at the beginning of things, with raw tree stumps in the growing grain and earthen-floored houses roofed with thatch. Soon I saw a little black head bobbing through the dew-fresh rice. It was Getúlio's younger son, Durvalino, bringing us a can of black sweet coffee for an eye opener.

Setting out early to explore my river front, we traced our way back through the towering corn past the canoe landing. Beyond it, upriver, we found a faint trace of a trail. Pausing once in a while to hack through fallen creepers, we worked our way slowly through the dense underbrush of the forest. We could hear the river, but could not see it and I was never sure when I first set foot on my land. The fact is that the down-river line had not yet been located.

Our goal was a little branch that ran along the upper boundary, which had been marked. We reached this clear brook and knelt to drink from it and bathe our faces. The forest was very still, we only heard little nearby rustling that must have been lizards. The only sign of life that we saw were the tracks beside the stream, left by deer and jaguar and wild boar.

We pushed our way back and I returned to Getúlio's. By noon the heat was heavy on me and I drowsed half-sick on the board. Joan went to see a tenant family in another part of the clearing. I tried to talk to Piquitita a little, but my backland Portuguese vocabulary was not yet very large. I did learn from her that it takes about three years to get a pasture when you put down forest. I wondered about my turf, the green turf so necessary for my white house. I had seen nothing of my land; my walk on it had been down a tunnel of foliage. Things were not turning out exactly as I had expected.

The Ford's body was ruined, but it took us back to Anápolis without further mishap. After a good night's sleep at the

Chacra, I forgot everything but the newness, the beauty and the strangeness of the forest. I wrote a long letter to Bill Mizelle telling him about it. At the end of the letter, I said we figured it would take about forty new families of *caboclos* to open the land that Roger, Nilo, Susana and I wanted to develop. And I mentioned in passing an important change in my master plan.

"I will build a small place at Ceres," I wrote. "We will build a lodge or *rancho* at the farm for the first year or two. We will go down there from Ceres on week ends to see things go. . . ."

This record shows that from my first real acquaintance with the forest I began to become aware of the difficulties which would postpone the white house where I meant to live ever serene. Till we had some food for a mule or horse, there was no way to make the bricks for the house—the clay had to be mixed in a mule-powered "peeper" or small mill. I found out on the first visit that there was no food available for a mule for miles around, nor could I ship hay or fodder from Anápolis. Transporting bricks even from Ceres would have been extremely costly and I was not even sure we could get them across the river. These obstacles alone were enough to make me put off building in the forest for a year at least.

3

THE somewhere-else that I had longed for in bad times throughout my life was in my mind first of all a place of sunlight, sunlight and cool shade. When I was in the fourth-grade room in school, a chalk-dusty prison in the big brick school building that was the pride of the little Tennessee town where I was born, when spring afternoons were hot and the sunlight blazed down on the dusty baseball diamond just out-side our window, I used to shake off the sleepy spell of the drone around me and gaze away over the shimmering yellow-ish earth to the cool woods beyond, and be drained limp with longing for those woods. I knew the tall trees were a roof for caverns of quiet. I longed to go there, yet I never played hooky, not for even one afternoon, to go and walk in their shelter.

Clear sunlight and far forests were the first enchantment that Goiás offered me and after I scouted the country on my original visit, I spent some of the happiest hours of my life dreaming about them, like a child about to break out of school's imprisonment. This was the time between my decision to go there and my arrival. Once there each step of the new life was strange and when I looked at the country I felt I must know it as well as see it. The Spanish have a concept expressed by the word *compenetrarse;* it means to become "I in thee and thou in me," the ideal of completed understanding. My first visit to my new domain, in which my forest unexpectedly closed me out, set me to groping for this.

For money reasons, I of course had to get my feet firm-planted on a workable reality. In long evenings at the Chacra, Joan and the Captain coached me. Joan's dramatic instinct led her to emphasize the drive to the west, the mighty battle to wrest riches from a new land, and she dwelt on the many chances to profit and progress. The Captain, different in nature, was far more cautious and more conscious of difficulties. Other people often gave me information that conflicted with both their points of view. Nobody seemed to keep records on farming and even their weights and measures were chaotic.

As I bogged down in conflicting advice, I realized my movements were also limited in Goiás and here, with an immensity of wilderness around me, I began to feel encircled. The Bowens went in to Anápolis to business early every morning and stayed till dusk, and if I went with them I had to stay in town all day, since there was danger on the roads. The Chacra was on a migration route into Goiás from Bahia, a thousand miles away. Bands of black *bahianos* wander ceaselessly around Brazil, working a year here and a year there, then walking back home again. On these migrations they live off the land and often turn bandit in lonely places. I was told by Judge Alceu, senior judge in Anápolis, never to travel without a pistol and never to drive alone in my car outside of Anápolis even in the daytime. At the Chacra a pack of big trail dogs were a major protection and there were also people living on the place. But even so, we never went out after dark nor did visitors come at night.

For a while, I tried to avoid the confinement of the town by staying at home in the daytime to put finishing touches on my little house.

Liberty Hall was pleasant, sun-drenched, clean and simple. In front, the ground sloped away and in the bottom of the valley not far below a secret stream hidden by deep banks and heavy tropical foliage whispered to itself. Beyond, a low, steep hill rose up, part pasture, part thicket and woodland. The green of Goiás wild growth blazed under the violent blue of the sky. A line of trees marched across the high skyline of the hill in stylized procession. The sunlight fell with incredible clarity everywhere, making everything more vivid instead of killing the colors. Though the farm had animals and people on it, you rarely heard a sound. A few yards away from the stream even its whispering was lost and quiet congealed again. Time stopped, everything stood still, brilliantly still, as if waiting.

There was a quality in this scene that made it hard for me to work. I used to pause often and stare and listen. When Joan and the Captain were there, it was different. When I was alone, I saw it all too clearly, as through a stereopticon device. The unbelievably patterned march of the trees across the skyline of the hill was a trap for my attention. I used to wonder what lay over the hill and beyond that and beyond. I walked a little way up the valley once or twice, but there was no invitation to continue. The Spanish say expressively, "the wings of my heart fell," as we would say "I had a sinking feeling." When I went a little way up the valley, expecting the wings of my heart to lift, they stayed stubbornly folded. I had dreamed of repose, but this heavy quietude was like the emphatic stillness before a storm, except that the sunlight was part of it. It was like an invisible wall, shutting me out.

Once and once only in these days did I touch the force I sensed just beyond me in that beautiful land and feel it friendly to me. It happened at night, when Joan and the old Indian cook Vitalina and I went looking for a young bitch that had strayed. We walked past Liberty Hall in opaque darkness and went on up the valley till we came to a place where we could cross the stream as it ran through a small meadow. One of the season's late rains had fallen in a heavy downpour in the afternoon, thinly flooding the little flat so that we had to take off our shoes and wade.

My feet sank through the cool, slowly running water, at

first on grass; then I stepped on silt left by the afternoon's flooding and my feet sank through the soft, liquid mud to hard ground. This hard bottom surprised me by returning warmth to the soles of my feet and the feel of the warm earth under the cool water was strangely comforting. For the first time I felt contact with something kindly within the rich growths, the whispering streams, secret valleys and waiting hills. It was as if for a moment my touch had reached to the bare skin of the earth my mother and her warmth had suffused me. The unforgettable momentary pulse of feeling and the thought that came with it were new to me.

The cure for my bafflement about this new land with its ancient forces vaguely felt was of course to get into action. I was told that the forests were cleared under arrangements that combined grubstaking and sharecropping. You advanced a family of land workers the supplies they needed for a year and in repayment, the man cleared about twenty-five acres of your forest and planted it in crops, out of which he paid you for the supplies, plus twenty-five per cent of the total yield. On land previously cleared, owner and cropper shared fifty-fifty, often without grubstaking.

I knew from the dawn of memory how many ways a sharecropper could cheat the owner, since my parents had been fairly large landowners operating on a tenant-farm system in the American South. At the same time, under the Goiás system, the owner could make the sharecropper a virtual slave. I disliked the idea and decided to work out some money deal with my tenants that would obviate grubstaking.

The big problems in our forest were transportation and supplies. Susana wanted to buy land near Roger's and mine and I figured there would be at least forty tenant families in the vicinity who would have to be fed. All this led to the interlocking projects—Project Truck, Project Pigs and Project Store—which began my education in Goiás.

For several years, trucking rates had been high in the Brazilian backlands and the figures indicated that if they continued so I might even finance the first year's operation at the farm out of a truck's earnings in the coming harvest. I found a secondhand International K-5 in good condition for around twenty-four hundred dollars. I paid half of this out of my dollar funds and borrowed the other half from a local bank.

I hoped to advance cash rather than supplies to our workers, but there was no store for many miles at which they could trade. The Aerovias pilot's brother Davino and I decided to set up a small supply post to serve the whole community of farms. Till Davino could clear his lot near the river, we thought it best to locate the store on the big road, and rented part of the hut at the turnoff for the time being. I was to buy supplies in Anápolis and send them north. Davino would run the store.

In any problem of supply in the backlands at the time, the question of *toucinho*, or pork fatback, loomed large. Hogs were scarce and high prices were draining them to the coast cities. The backlanders can exist on rice and beans, but they combine them with heavy portions of hog fat, which they prefer to fry out of fresh or salted pork themselves. Joan and I decided to go into the pig supply business, buying forty pigs or so to fatten for sale at the store. With farm, store, truck and pigs I now was in a fair way to become a combine in the business life of Goiás. Or so it would have appeared from the plans.

In the creaking old Plymouth I bumped painfully around Anápolis' rutted streets assembling stock. My list included staples such as sugar, salt, macaroni, brown beans, matches, thread, *mandioca* flour, needles, the hard twist tobacco that the *caboclos* shave up and make into corn-shuck cigarettes, crude handmade men's high shoes and the wooden clogs used by the few farm women who ever have money to spare for footware. I bought axheads, grubbing hoes, brush hooks, headache tablets and a few preferred patent medicines, fishhooks, small tin basins, enameled plates, a few enameled coffee cups.

One fine sunny Saturday morning we loaded the store supplies into my newly-purchased truck, together with two thousand tiles Davino had bought for his building and several small shipments we were hauling north for pay. With Santinho driving the truck and Davino in the cab, more than a dozen *caboclos* climbed up on the load and away they went. I watched them go with satisfaction. It was real action and as I rattled home that afternoon with the Bowens to the Chacra I began to feel that I was at last biting into reality.

This was quite true and reality did not hesitate to bite back. In the still-dark hours of the next morning I was awakened by a most unusual sound, tires swishing down the long sloping avenue that led from the road to the Bowens' door. The big trail dogs always knew whether anybody who came on the place was friend or foe. They must have smelled Davino, whom they knew, for they barked very little. In the small hours in deep Goiás the soul has very few defenses, and my heart sank as I identified Davino's voice calling Joan's name softly.

He had come to tell us the truck was wrecked.

It could have been much, much worse, for nobody was hurt. Another trucker with a flat tire had stopped square in the middle of the road, down in a little dip. Santinho had steamed over the little rise and was almost on top of him before he saw him. My driver could have taken a bank or a deep ravine, but wisely chose to hit the truck head-on, since either other maneuver would very likely have killed some of the people riding on top. As it was, the heavy tiles rammed the cab forward and barely missed crushing both Santinho and Davino. The truck was completely wrecked and though insured, was not to be repaired for over six months.

This one stroke not only took away my immediate prospect of financing the farm work out of the truck's earnings; it also crippled the supplying of the store and tied up my credit and my spare cash.

We started the store, however, with stock salvaged from the wreck. And now the pigs arrived at the Chacra. The man who sold them to us brought them after dark and when I saw them the next morning they looked to me like the type of long-snouted razorback that you can never fatten. At least they knew how to eat corn, which some Goiás pigs have to be taught. But they soon began to sicken and though we vaccinated them, many died.   ·

We had spoken for three other fat pigs ready to kill and the Captain and I decided to go and fetch them, to be sure we got no more doubtful animals. We took the back seats out of the Plymouth and creaked across town to bring them from the other side of Anápolis. The little city was never more beautiful; its low white houses, shining against a sunset of spectacular green and red and gold and violet, were like a stage set of long ago and far away, sharply focused, hyperreal. Easing out of the rutted streets, we crept through deep, red-walled lanes lined with gracefully bending frondy plants and decorative wild shrubs. Wood smoke from lazy kitchen fires drifted upward; gleams of cheerful blaze could be seen through open doorways as women in quiet domesticity stirred the evening rice. There was utter peace in the air.

A small whirlpool of frazzled emotions soon surrounded the Plymouth, however. First, the men struggled to get the stupid, quivering hogs on board; then our battery died. With the help of the men who sold us the hogs, we spent nearly an hour shoving and swearing and sweating to start the car, but were grimly stalled till rare good luck brought a truck along this untraveled back lane and it pushed us to start our engine. Yellow fever years before had left the Captain none too strong and we were both exhausted as we drove silently out to the Chacra through the rolling country I always found so lovely. The quiet slopes and timeless hills were bland and smug, as if mocking us.

Though all this was failure to find the harmony with nature and man that I had looked forward to in Goiás, at least it served to put the turmoil and strife of my life in Buenos Aires completely out of my mind. But soon a feud as full of violent threat as any I had known in Argentina began to absorb our tight little world and it affected me as none of the other violence had.

The Bowens together with a group of Americans in São Paulo had financed a small and badly-needed sawmill in the Colônia, and installed a young·American as manager. Because of the inevitable difficulties and some mistakes, first of all in buying a mill unsuited for cutting the type of hardwood that grows in Goiás, the mill had trouble getting into operation. The Bowens withdrew and the other owners fell out with each other. A big replacement saw blade for the mill had come through the Bowens and the São Paulo group had notified them not to deliver it to the manager, who was by now being sued by his Brazilian workmen. He badly wanted the blade, and the Bowens would not release it. There was much carrying of tales back and forth, with hints he would try to take the blade away from them.

The Captain had to go to São Paulo on business, and one evening when Joan and I were quietly reading after supper the old foxhound named Onça padded into the living room. This was unheard of, and our attention was sharpened by the way she came over to nuzzle Joan, all the while looking over her shoulder at the front door. We had heard some of the dogs barking up in the pineapple patch a short while before but had paid no attention to them. The old hound was insistent, however; Joan went over to the door and sure enough, we had left it unlocked and a tiny crack open. Joan fastened it and Onça padded off to the kitchen satisfied. We followed and learned from Vitalina that she had surprised two men lurking around the house a short while before. Vitalina had let out three of the dogs, who had chased them through the pineapple patch and over the hill. The cook said she thought they might be a pair of local jagunços, backland paid killers, sent to try to get the saw.

I knew a neighbor's house had been raided and the man killed by jagunços not long before. I got my little gun and told Joan I wanted to go out and look around for the prowlers, who of course could have shot the dogs and moved in on us if they had really wanted to. She laughed at me, but I insisted. I was neither frightened nor angry, but determined on positive action. A shot or two peppered from the rear would probably have discouraged any idea of attacking the house. Joan was firmly against my idea, however, and I yielded.

That night I had a nightmare and dreamed I shot and killed a man. The blood spread red over his white shirt; I don't know who he was or why I shot. But it was a terrible sensation and I awoke with a burning feeling in the pit of my stomach. I lay in the dark a long time thinking about it. Had there been marauders around the house, or had Vitalina's imagination supplied details she thought Joan wanted to hear? I pondered my curious but very real desire to go out and shoot at the supposed enemies. I had been used to guns since childhood, but had as an adult grown to hate the thought of killing even a rabbit or a bird. I thought seriously about gun-carrying in Goiás and decided that if I ever had to shoot a human being in self-protection, I would regret it very much, but I would shoot to kill.

The next day was Saturday and we packed ourselves off to the forest. On the road there occurred a sequel that shook even Joan. Some of the backland truckers hate passenger cars and on a narrow part of the road over the divide, a trucker kept swerving back and forth across the road in front of us, to keep us behind him and in his dust, for he knew he would otherwise have to eat our dust all the way up the grade. The road overhung a sheer drop and as Santinho tried to get by, the trucker would swing over on our side again and again. Finally, he almost crowded us into the ravine. He did it once more and this time, before I knew it, I had snatched out my gun in a burst of anger. Joan grabbed my arm and Santinho, shocked at the pantomime, slowed the car to let the truck climb away from us.

"He was deliberately trying to murder us!" I said defensively. I was weak with reaction from my anger. The others did not argue with me, but they indulged in no talk about feuding on this ride.

I had business with Davino, so I decided to sling my hammock at the store for the night, while Joan and Santinho continued on to the river and her farm beyond.

Our store, the only supply post in many miles, was a partitioned-off space about seven feet wide by twelve feet long in the dirt-floored sapling hut of Anastásio, the farmer who had the corner lot at the turnoff. The store space was about evenly divided by a rude plank counter, behind which Davino had arranged his small stock on gasoline boxes and narrow plank shelves. Behind the store was a narrow passage leading into Anastásio's part of the hut and there Davino hung his hammock at night. The hundred miles of jostling had tired me and soon after we ate our supper of watery brown beans and boiled rice, I asked Davino to put up a hammock for me in the passage. Through cracks in the pole partition, I could see and hear quite clearly what went on in the store and here had my first introduction to the part of Brazil that was eventually to become so important to me, the landworkers' world.

Most of our customers had to walk for miles and it was after dark when they began to arrive. With murmured greetings, they appeared in the open doorway, their bare feet silent on the baked earth. Clad in loose, light, worn cotton shirts and trousers, with weather-beaten felts on their heads, these men had a deceptive air of frailness about them. I say deceptive because they can hack down mighty forests on a diet of rice and beans.

These people are very courteous, punctiliously addressing each other as "Senhor," which they slur to "S'hor."

"S'hor Davino, do you have any *toucinho?*" The request for hog fat was nearly always the first one made. Then began a long dickering.

"No, Luiz, but we're going to kill tomorrow. I've promised other people nearly all of it, though."

"S'hor Davino, we haven't had any *toucinho* at our house

for four days. My family is going to get sick!" Luiz is wheedling, laughing softly, as if not expecting to be believed. "I've had to stop my work because we don't have any *toucinho!*"

"I'll try to save you a kilo, Luiz."

"How will you sell it?"

"At twenty-five cruzeiros a kilo."

"S'hor Davino, that's *muito caro!* Very high."

"I'm not making any profit, Luiz. I'm selling everything at a loss. I have to be here all day, I don't know when I'm going to get to clear my land," says Davino gently.

Another deeper voice from among the little group of men: "Dona Virginia ought to bring up some *pinga* from Anápolis. We wouldn't care about *toucinho* then."

This is followed by a general laugh. *Pinga* is raw white rum, the Brazilian poor man's drink.

"You know Dr. Sayão won't let anybody sell *pinga* in the *Colônia*," says Davino. The store, unlike my farm on the other side of the Rio das Almas, was on *Colônia* land.

Weak light from a flickering kerosene lamp gleamed on their dark faces. I liked the look of the people because they were so lean, a pleasant relief from the white, plump Argentines of the great port city, Buenos Aires. Every face aroused in me a regret that I could not record it in paint or clay. The dark men of the soil range from a deep sun-brown through mahogany to blue-black. Their features tend to run much finer than those of Africans in the United States. The few white men among them have long heads, narrow through the temples, deep eyes, usually long noses, and prominent chins. The darker the man, the more his head tends to roundness and his nose and chin to be short and round. Brazilian Indians of the tribes I've seen have round heads and squarish faces, with a yellow tinge underlying their brown color. You don't see much trace of this in the farm workers, although Indian blood is thinly there. Some of the blackest of these people have thin, straight noses and chiseled lips.

The soft wrangling went on. Credit and barter inevitably

entered, and offer and counteroffer finally became highly complicated.

"But S'hor Davino, two fifty a kilo for sweetening! I can't do my work without coffee and I have to have sweetening for my coffee. In Ceres, they're selling *rapadura* for two cruzeiros."

Rapadura is brown unrefined brick sugar, moist, molasses-sweet. Two cruzeiros was about ten cents at the rate of exchange then but a man's work earned only about twelve cruzeiros a day plus a day's food, which was reckoned to cost eight cruzeiros.

"Give me two kilos and I'll pay you next week."

"Dona Virginia couldn't even find any *rapadura* in Ceres, Waldevino. Besides, you already owe me two sacks of rice."

"But S'hor Davino, you count that rice at fifty cruzeiros a sack and when it's cut and threshed, it'll be worth eighty, if not a hundred."

"I'd be willing to take your hundred cruzeiros now and not wait for the two sacks of rice," said Davino.

"S'hor Davino, let me have a kilo at two twenty-five and I'll pay cash when my brother starts cutting his rice. I've promised to help him."

"Your brother hasn't got any money to pay you with. He owes me money."

"Jacomosi gave him two *contos* in advance yesterday for his rice."

"*Ah, sim? Pucha!*" An exclamation of surprise from the group. The interjection, pronounced "poosha!" meant that it was very early for Jacomosi, a trucker and rice buyer, to be advancing money against the harvest.

"Let me have the *rapadura*, S'hor Davino, till next week. My wife is sick and I can't go to Ceres."

"I'll credit you for a kilo at two fifty, Waldevino. What's the matter with your wife?"

"She's got *maleita*." This is the term the *caboclos* use for malaria, or for any kind of fever, even for bad colds. "She's been shaking for two days. I want to get one of those injections you gave Dona Ana. My wife will come tomorrow. But I can't pay five cruzeiros for it."

"I'm only charging four for the shots. But will you have the money?"

"S'hor Davino, when are you going to dig that well? I could give you some work on that."

"I've got enough days' work already promised to dig the well. But I don't like not to sell you the medicine." Davino is regretful.

A new voice, from a slight youth, brown and impassive in the pearly light.

"S'hor Davino, I've got three days on that well. Gervásio owes me two hundred cruzeiros and says he'll pay half of it next week. I'll pay you for half a sack of the rice I owe you, then I'll just owe you two sacks and I can let Waldevino have one of my days on the well."

Davino thinks a minute.

"But half a sack of rice is twenty-five cruzeiros and I'm not going to pay more than twelve a day for work on the well."

"But the food, the food . . . that's worth eight. Twelve and eight are twenty," insists the youth. "They'll be paying twenty-five a day by the time you start that well."

This went on interminably, each transaction complicated into an ever-widening tapestry into which were woven the price of rice, present and future, a day of work to be delivered, the illness of a woman or child, miles to be walked, and the cost, always uncertain, of everything.

Few had cash but those who had were very exigent. The hard-luck story, stock in trade for extracting credit, was replaced by mild indignation as a bargaining tool.

"But S'hor Davino, I can't use these middle-size axes. I've got to have a heavy one!" says Sebastião. "And this is *nacional* (made in Brazil). You expect me to pay twenty-five cruzeiros for this?"

"Collins axes cost thirty cruzeiros in Anápolis and they haven't even got any in Ceres," says Davino. "These new *nacionais* are nearly as good."

"You can't get anything up here in this *mato*," puts in Waldevino, inclined to swagger now that he has his purchases safely in his cotton sack.

"What made you leave Minas Gerais, Waldevino? You kill a man?" This from the deep-voiced, lamp-black Manoel.

"*Ai!* Kill a man? I was starved in Minas Gerais! This *mato* is rich. *Pucha*, what good land!"

Davino patiently handed out small sales, carefully recording his complicated transactions in his grubby book as men came and went. The store closed late and the last customers padded away into the night.

The night was cold and Davino and I both shivered as he busied about moving my hammock into the now-empty store front. The little oil lamps guttered and smoked.

"How is it going, Davino?" I asked. "I don't see how in the world you keep up with it all."

"*Ai*, Dona Virginia, these people are hard to deal with, "*ó!*" This curious Brazilian terminal exclamation, "*ó!*" (pronounced "augh!") expresses chagrin.

"Have you had to sell much on credit?"

"I have to, Dona Virginia. They haven't got much money and won't spend what they have. But you let them get too far in debt, they never come around again. I haven't got but a few cruzeiros in the box now."

This meant putting in more capital if the store was to continue. We had hoped to do business for cash on a narrow profit margin, but the idea was beginning to appear unworkable.

"Have you found any people to clear our land?" I asked.

"These people don't want to clear land for money. They want to clear it to plant crops of their own. You're not going to be able to work it any other way. If they clear land for you and don't plant it, they haven't any work for the rest of the year."

"All right, I'll pay for the clearing and keep them on as tenants."

"I don't know how I'm going to manage to clear my own land," mourned Davino. "I can't lock up this store, there's no way to do it. If I leave it, there won't be anything here when I get back."

"Can't we hire some people to build a store on your lot?"

"Dona Virginia, there'll be no work hands free for maybe two months. All the extra people have come to help their kinfolks in the harvest and get land in the *Colônia* for next year. . . ."

The life of the pioneer is not simple.

It was cold in the night and I turned and twisted in my hammock, stiff and uncomfortable. The moon rose and shed a light white as new-minted silver over the world. It was completely quiet, although the tall forest was near. Deep in the night I heard for the first time a fearsome sound—the crash of a mighty forest tree. There was no wind, and the terrible rending crash in the stillness hinted at an angry presence moving in the forest itself. I was to hear this sound again when other lightly rooted dying giants fell at last of their own weight, and it never failed to make me feel small and vulnerable.

It was dark when Joan, Santinho and I started home the next day, and our mishaps continued. About five miles out of Ceres the Plymouth caught fire. Santinho tore off his own shirt and attempted to smother the flames that flared from a short circuit in the wiring. Joan and I gave him our raincoats but it did no good. In a moment, one of us thought to scoop up from the roadside handfuls of earth dampened by an afternoon shower. The mud put out the fire and Santinho taped up the raw burned wire with adhesive from my first-aid kit. We got better repairs at Ceres and reached Anápolis very late. We stayed in town at a friend's house for once.

The next night we heard that mysterious cars had been seen creeping past the Chacra in our absence, but Joan and I dropped the subject of the feud; perhaps she saw I was entering too realistically into the spirit of the drama. In succeeding days my habit of waking in the early hours of the morning continued and the complications of my new life churned round and round in my mind. It was velvet-dark in my room when I awoke for my night thoughts. Around the top of the room partition glowed a puzzling thin line of phosphorescence, like a tiny fringe of indirect lighting. I felt the force of the strange land, so lovely, with so much that I could not yet grasp, so much that was as unaccountable as this tiny line of light.

I wondered at myself, why I had felt compelled to go out after the supposed marauders, why I had hotheadedly grabbed for my automatic on the road. This was certainly not self-completion or nonviolent nonparticipation. Where was the tranquillity I had come seeking? I had reacted with indignation against the violence all around me in Argentina; here the impulse to violence was entering into me, to drag me back toward savagery.

My financial calculations gave me no comfort. Everything cost far more than I had thought it would and the various accidents, especially the truck wreck, were crippling. But I was used to financial insecurity; my unease arose from something else as well. When Susana and Roger came, I thought, we'd really get going and everything would change for the better. I pinned my hopes on that.

4

THE gracious South American custom of seeing friends off
or welcoming them at the airport makes meeting a plane at
one of the continent's many beautiful flying fields like going
to the post office for the evening mail in an American village:
a social event where grapevine news about people's private
lives flies thick and fast among chattering groups of friends
and relatives. These gossipy interludes make South America
one great sounding board. I read once that in the Dark Ages,
Paris scandal was known in Rome by some mysterious means
before a traveler could cover the distance. In South America
today, indiscretions of vacationers in Santiago de Chile are
joked about by their friends in Rio de Janeiro just as soon
as the fastest plane can traverse the wide continent.

These sunlit airport gatherings, gay and carefree and full
of surprise meetings with friends from all over the map, always
held charm for me. The day in late April when we went to
meet my friend Susana, I was happy, exhilarated by the light
intoxicating highland air and the clear friendly sunshine and
the bright expectation of a good thing about to happen. I had
had a cryptic cable from Susana saying she was bringing a
friend with her. This was nothing unusual in those countries
of my love, Argentina and Brazil, where people may bring a
friend a thousand miles to visit, borrow an airplane, abscond
with a fortune or plot a revolution, all with casual grace. But

when I saw whom Susana had brought, I must confess I was surprised.

Perla, the unexpected guest, was an Argentine who by sheer ability and will had fought her way to success as a lawyer in her early thirties. As a woman, and moreover one without wealth or prominent family connections to help her, she had had to overcome more obstacles than the average Latin American professional man. I was surprised to see her because she was so essentially a city woman.

"Virginia, I had to bring her for a visit," Susana explained to me hurriedly. "I found her in Montevideo, sick and depressed. I couldn't leave her."

"It'll work out, Susana," I answered, hoping it would.

As Susana and Perla settled down with me at Liberty Hall, Susana preserved her cheerfulness and good spirit in the strange, even harsh surroundings. Perla, though unused to the luxury that Susana had been born into, from the first obviously recoiled from the dirt and disorder of the backlands. I felt her instinctive revulsion and tried to cushion the crudity of our living conditions. We finished furnishing the house with beds, bedclothes and chairs. I got mosquito netting from town, tacked it into the windows and hung it in the kitchen doorway to keep out flies. In a little outhouse we rigged up a crude shower bath with a perforated bucket rope-hoisted over a rafter, the bucket made out of a big square kerosene can we had brought to the house.

The kitchen fire was a hellion, smoky and balky to light no matter how many times we might fling kerosene into it at risk of singed eyebrows or worse. In the creaky old Plymouth I searched for days around the side streets of Anápolis until I found a man who had a two-burner oil stove to sell us. It proved to be a junior hellion, intricate to clean and giving no warmth against the morning and evening chill.

Without much success, we tried to divide up the cooking and cleaning. We hired the blue-eyed, towheaded twelve-year-old daughter of a farmer across the way to wash dishes and sweep. But she had to be taught and retaught the most elementary cleanliness and finally started filching our silk underwear and trinkets, which led to a running battle to get them back.

In dealing with our seemingly trivial, yet actually fundamental daily difficulties, the little house ceased to seem a sweet, cool retreat to me; rather it became the Alamo of my resistance to petty complexities. Nothing like this had figured even remotely in my original plan. According to schedule, I should have been at work hacking down a forest on the Rio das Almas, more than a hundred miles away.

Susana had from the first wanted to buy land in Goiás and soon purchased a tract of about a thousand acres lying a good many miles north of my Rio das Almas property in a locality where prices were lower. She decided not to clear her land yet, but we went along from day to day on the assumption that our original idea would be carried out and that Perla's stay was temporary. With my expenses running much higher than I had expected, I became seriously worried about getting the farm work started. At last I made the start, however, and the farm began to absorb my attention.

In the late spring after what seemed like a very long time to me—I had lost all real sense of the passage of time—four men who heard at Davino's store about my need for workers came down to Anápolis to sign on. So now on a spring day I stood behind a rough wooden counter in the cavernous, shadowy shed behind the Bowens' gasoline post and surveyed the men who proposed to build my haven for me. They lined up in a row, dressed alike in stained and dirty cotton work clothes, holding battered felt hats in their hands. The man on my right was big for a Brazilian, chocolate-brown, twenty-five or so, with an easy smile and surprisingly good white teeth. I spoke to him first, probably because he was smiling.

"What is the *senhor's* name?" I asked, using the formal and polite third-person form of address, rather than the more familiar "*você*."

"José, *senhora*, José da Lima Amaral, *ás ordems*." (. . . at your service.)

"Do you know how to grow rice?"

"*Ai, senhora,* I was born and bred in the *mato,* there isn't a man in Goiás who can cut down the big trees better than I can. I've been working in construction in Goiânia, but there's no cash in that town and I want to get back to the woods."

"I see." This was to be my self-designated Paul Bunyan. "And you?"

The second and third men in line were in their late forties or early fifties, their shoulders stooped by a lifetime of hard work and poor food. They were both mahogany-black, with deeply furrowed faces, tiny deep-set eyes, broad noses and sparse fuzzy beards. One of them answered me in a painfully drawn-out drawl.

"I'm . . . Emílio . . . Feitosa . . . da . . . Silva . . . and . . . this . . . is . . . my . . . brother . . . Ezequiel," he said. They were very much alike, their faces resembling those of weary chimpanzees more than anything else. Emílio was somewhat larger and younger, less battered than Ezequiel.

"Do you know how to farm?" I asked them. "Have you been living in Goiânia, too?"

"*Si-i-im, senh-o-ra* . . ." They told me that they originally came from Minas Gerais, where they had farmed, and that they'd been looking for a chance to go back to the *mato* for three years.

"Three years!"

"*Si-i-im, senh-o-ra.*" The Feitosas had a habit of answering in unison, as if responding in a litany.

I turned to the last one.

"*E o senhor?*" ("And you?")

This man had been looking past my shoulder like a soldier at attention on parade. Of medium height, hard-muscled, blue-black, he was ramrod straight and his thin chiseled nose, tight-lipped mouth and indrawn cheeks conveyed at first glance an impression of pridefulness. He was one of the long-headed Afro-Brazilians, with a broad, high forehead, and his face in repose was strong and tight-held. He appeared to be in his middle thirties, though I later learned he was over forty.

"Florenzo da Souza Carlos, called Manoel," he said. I flinched as I noted that, like so many poor Brazilians—and most Brazilians are very poor—he had lost some of his front teeth.

"Are you a farmer too?"

"If José thinks he can cut down trees, you ought to see what I can do," he said tersely. The men thought of clearing, rather than of cultivating the soil.

"But have you ever planted rice? Or coffee?"

"Ha! *Em tôdo o Brasil!*" ("All over Brazil.")

I looked at the men and they gazed solemnly back. How could I check on what they were telling me? Did they get drunk on *pinga*, the raw white rum of Brazil? Had they ever been in bad trouble, in jail? In the flux of the growing frontier, it would have taken me weeks, if not forever, to get references on them.

I have mentioned these men's color, but neither then nor later did I ever say to myself, "This is a negro," and I am sure they never thought, "This is a white person." Brazil has not solved the race problem entirely and most of her people, black and white, are a good deal worse off materially than most of our negroes. But in Brazil, you don't think of people in terms of color. I thought, "This is a *roçeiro*, a farmer-backwoodsman," and I'm sure they thought, "This is the owner, the American lady." A *roçeiro*, who lives the rough life and does the rough work, may be any shade from white through *café au lait* to black. The brown backwoodsman of mixed white and Indian blood, with little if any negro, is called a *caboclo* and the black Afro-Brazilians are usually termed *pretos*, but on the landworkers' level they intermarry freely. In my experience, the darker the *roçeiro's* skin, the better the man.

"What kind of a contract do you want?" I asked them.

After a moment of waiting, José spoke up.

"Well, *dona*, we understood that you were offering to grubstake and give us seventy-five per cent and that's the deal we want to make." This meant that I would advance supplies through the rains and charge them accordingly, collecting the debt and one-fourth the yield at harvest time. "We heard you want to plant coffee next year."

"I hope to," I said. "If we do well, we'll make another contract then. I'll supply you with a reasonable amount of medicine free, but I can't have any drinking on the place. Is that understood?"

The men nodded assent.

"*Si-i-im, senh-o-ra.*" The intoning Feitosas reminded me irresistibly of an old adventure film I had seen in which a mad scientist trying to turn apes into men drilled his changelings in just such responses at the crack of a whip.

My newly-acquired tenants said they each wanted to cultivate about two *alqueires* of land (about twenty-five acres) the first year. They asked for a small cash advance, about six dollars each, and for their families to be taken to the farm later on from Goiânia. One truck trip would do it, at a cost of about a hundred dollars, they estimated. It was customary for the owner to supply axes and brush hooks for the clearing and to collect for them at the harvest.

When I brought out the axes I had so hopefully purchased in São Paulo, they met with lightly veiled scorn from Manoel and José, who asked me to get them heavier ones.

"And I want one of those mechanical rice planters," added Manoel.

"So do I," said José.

I had visions of a mule-drawn rig such as we used for planting wheat in Tennessee.

"How can you use them among the stumps?" I said, well remembering how I bruised my shins on stumps and logs in the Bowens' clearing.

"Oh, they're hand planters. They only cost about ninety cruzeiros." This was about three dollars. The Feitosas said they'd plant in the usual way, making a shallow hole in the soft earth with a hoe or with their toes.

"Very well, I'll get each of you a book and you can write everything down in it. I'll keep my own book for each one of you and that way we can keep things straight."

There was a long moment of silence, in which no one stirred. Puzzled, I looked down the line.

"Isn't that all right?" I asked. Keenly aware of the bad name that abuses have attached to the practice of grubstaking, I was anxious for our records to be clear and unequivocal.

Manoel, with a bitter twist to his thin lips, spoke up. The thought grew on me that he looked the way the Moor of Venice must have looked.

"You ought to know, *dona*, these *roçeiros* here in this Brazil don't know how to sign their names."

It was a moment of embarrassment for me, one I was to experience again and again when I had to find out if people in the backlands could read and write.

"Well, we'll manage somehow," I said hurriedly. "Thank you very much—and let me know when you want your families brought. *Até logo*." ("Until later.")

"Until then, *senhora*."

If I were vulnerable to them in my ignorance, how vulnerable also were they to me, I thought. We shook hands and they left to catch a truck for the north. The new venture, a frail cockleshell caulked at the seams only by our mutual promises, was launched on its sea of uncertainty.

Not long afterwards, my tenants returned in a body to say they were ready to fetch their families. They had two recruits: Francisco Araujo de Magalhães, nicknamed Chico, a slight, soft-voiced young man of almost pure African descent in spite of his sonorous Portuguese name, and his partner Claudinho, whose last name I have mercifully forgotten. Claudinho was a gangling white man. He spoke with a whine and I despised him on sight, but we needed more workers and the others said he'd do. Chico, to my relief, could read and write and I made him our recorder. It was not enough that I knew they wouldn't be cheated—they had to know the accounts were fair, and Chico could guarantee this.

Santinho brought the families from Goiânia in a truck and piled their scant possessions at the gasoline post while I arranged for them to lodge overnight at a cheap *pensão* nearby.

The men were all married; the Feitosas had nice-looking half-grown youngsters and the others baby children. I noticed that brown Chico's timid little wife was white and that white Claudinho's was a dark girl.

The one trucker available the next day would only take us as far as Ceres. I watched while my tenants loaded their pitifully meager possessions for the move.

Manoel, Claudinho and José had flat bedsprings, without bedsteads. All the families had shapeless bags of ticking filled with straw for mattresses. José, Pedro and Manoel had fashioned chairs by nailing wooden legs onto gasoline boxes with the top and one side cut out of each. Manoel had carved the "arms" of his chairs into a curve and they were worn to a smooth, dark slickness by much use. The families had no stoves, but only long flat slabs of iron, each with three round holes for cooking vessels; they were stove tops for which mud-and-stick stoves would be built.

Each individual carried a few personal possessions in a limp flour sack, extra changes of their thin cotton clothes, I supposed. They had the rest of their belongings in open gasoline boxes: the tinny, soft-metal knives, forks and spoons used by the dirt-poor who make up the majority of Brazil's population, old-fashioned box-type coffee grinders, white enameled coffeepots, the shallow enameled soup plates they use for soup and solids alike, tiny enameled coffee cups and various full-bellied iron pots for cooking.

I advanced each of them a few more dollars for basic supplies—rice, beans, dried meat, brown brick sugar, coffee beans, fatback, manioc flour and salt. We also took along a crate of oranges from the Bowens' trees; fruit of any kind was always a great treat in the *mato*. The men did not ask for money to buy very large amounts of supplies, though it would have obviously been cheaper and easier for us to buy all we could haul rather than hire another truck later. But I had been warned and rewarned not to let them get "too far ahead" in their debts to me.

Since the Plymouth station wagon was in the shop with

another broken spring (streets of Anápolis!), I traveled with my dusky tribe in the truck. About dark we drove down the raw gash of red earth that was the main street of Barranca, twin city to Ceres. Then we crossed the unquiet, ever-whispering River of Ghosts into Ceres and continued to the Chateau, the little house owned by our friend Mr. Cecil Cross about half a mile beyond Ceres. Here we unloaded and my tenants quietly and efficiently set up an overnight camp in the front yard. The house was locked and I had not brought a key, so I unrolled my sleeping bag on the little back porch of the empty cottage. I followed a path through a canebrake to the edge of the river and bathed my face and hands in its cool waters.

My tenants meanwhile gathered big stones for a fireplace and, starting sticks to burning among the stones, put on rice and coffee to boil. They also pot-fried some fresh meat they had bought in Anápolis. These backland people are born with a natural hospitality that can make a hut more gracious and pleasant than many a palace. When I came back to the little group around the fire after resting a short while in my sleeping bag, they made me feel a welcomed guest, gently competing to serve me one of their tiny cups of pitch-black coffee sweetened with raw sugar.

Manoel had set two of his box chairs in front of our fire and with a lordly air he invited me to occupy one of them, taking the other himself. Soon we ate our simple supper and the long hours we had spent on the road made the food taste good. For our dessert I opened several cans of figs that I had bought, a treat that the children pitched into with quiet avidity. After supper, the women retired into the shadows with the younger children and the men drew up low gasoline boxes on either side of Manoel and me in our chairs. They began to fashion cigarettes, patiently smoothing out oblongs of dried corn shuck with knife blades against their palms, then whittling shreds of their hard twist tobacco into the softened shuck as filler for their slender roll-your-owns.

José started telling me that they had walked back along my

boundaries, where a narrow trail had been cut by the surveyors, and had decided to locate the clearing nearly a mile back from the river because a good stream ran through a gentle valley there. *Caboclos* prefer the soil near slight depressions and streams; they call it "moist."

"What about the soil up there, is it good?" I inquired.

"Getúlio said it was about the best anywhere around here." In Goiás, you judge forest land according to the size and type of the trees that grow on it and the grasses under the trees.

José gestured widely, our self-styled great axman whose childishly bubbling energies made him seem at times like a bumbling half-grown puppy.

"*Ai*, Dona Virginia, there are trees up there that two men can't span with their arms. *Pucha*, that's a brute of a forest! We're going to break some axes up there for you, Dona Virginia, I can tell you."

"I want you to grow a lot of rice, too." I turned to Chico, who sat looking into the fire, a straw in his mouth. "What do you think about it?"

Chico rarely spoke without appearing to ponder a little first; he had a thoughtful way about him.

"Dona Virginia, it's good. We'll grow good rice there, all right—and good coffee too, *se Deus quiser*." (God willing.)

Ezequiel and Emílio, beyond him, stirred and murmured agreement. Ezequiel, the oldest, blackest and most wizened of the group, began working his face in an effort to break his habitual reticence.

"Dona Virginia," he finally got out, "you can be sure of one thing. You may not make money, but you're sure not going to lose any money on us."

This struck me as a very strange observation.

"Look, S'hor Ezequiel," I said, "just breaking even is not enough. I want to plant coffee next year and clear more land. It costs a lot of money to get a farm started. I want us all to *make* money."

Manoel was leaning back in his chair, holding his sleeping baby son.

"*Roçeiros* never make any money," he observed dispassionately, his edge of bitterness sheathed while sharing informal duties as host. "It's the *granfos*, the big rich, who get everything. At the end of the year, people like us find themselves with a big debt for little dabs of food they ate through the rains and when that's paid up, they're lucky to have a few cruzeiros left over."

This stung me. These old evils had no place here in this new country and above all, nothing to do with me.

"There aren't any *granfos* running my business, Manoel," I said. "If my land is good and you farm it right, what's to keep you from making something? The price of rice is up and they say it'll go higher next year."

"The land should belong to the man who works it," answered Manoel, as if reciting an article of faith.

I had left behind me on the coast the Virginia Prewett who for nearly ten years had written about Latin America, past and present. Now Manoel's statement and the way he made it brought back a flash of the former life. The cry for land was old in history; my own forefathers had crossed a wild ocean and tamed a wildernesss for freedom and land; nearly a century and a half ago a Mexican priest, Miguel Hidalgo, had led one of the New World's first revolts against Spain with exactly this demand. Yet in modern times, communism has seized on this aspiration to make it a world-wide slogan on which to ride to power, and when Manoel voiced it, an alarm bell rang in my mind warning of trouble.

I thought a long time before answering. Trouble I definitely did not want, but I had a bargain with Manoel, a verbal contract.

"Manoel," I said finally, "you know they're giving away lots to homesteaders right here in this farm colony. What do you say, I'll see the chief engineer here tomorrow and we'll get you your own land to work."

I had never seen Manoel looking other than tense and grim, but now he turned the pleasantest kind of smiling face toward me.

"Why, what do you mean, Dona Virginia?" he asked. "What I want to do is clear forest on your place, like we agreed."

"I bought my land out of my savings and it was hard work getting the money together," I told him, unconvinced by this change of tone. "And I certainly don't want anybody on my place who can't be happy working as a tenant."

He did not answer directly. "The tenant should only give twenty per cent of the yield," he said. This was another familiar slogan; I had seen it chalked on walls in Anápolis, along with the hammer and sickle.

"I asked all of you in Anápolis what kind of a deal you wanted," I said. I myself had never liked the grubstaking part of land clearing in Goiás and had been trying to work out in my mind a way to get around it.

"I'm not talking about you, Dona Virginia," said Manoel, almost too smoothly. "I just say the *granfos* ought to give the worker who produces the crops more of their profits."

The group had been listening intently, their faces closed. José now gave a snort of laughter.

"This Manoel!" he exclaimed. "This Manoel . . . he's always gabbing. . . . If he can put down those big trees as good as he can talk, how much rice you'll have next year, Dona Virginia!"

Manoel remained unperturbed. "We'll see who's the best man when we get to swinging those axes up there," he said.

There came a strange moment for me: in some curious way, another part of my life, one left far behind me in my Tennessee childhood, echoed down to me. A woman, white and a foreigner, in this flickering firelight under brilliant stars in the far South American wilderness, I was as remote from what would seem to be my own world as if I had been in the depths of Africa surrounded by a band of savages. I would have been a blind fool not to realize how easily I might become a target for all the resentments piled up over centuries against white owner-masters; resentments fanned very successfully for half a generation by communism and fascistic demagogy alike. But when I was young, people with skins different in color from mine had been an important part of my child's world; I had often fled to them and their part of the house seeking sanctuary from my unjustly stern father. I looked at these dark backwoodsmen and I could not see them as an alien people. I was sure that Manoel could be dangerous, for his attitude was an open challenge. Yet I believed that I could handle the situation and prove to these six men that I would help them, that their old resentments need not apply to me.

I took another tiny cup of coffee, playing for time.

"I have an idea, Manoel," I said at last. "Let's make a capitalist out of you. You raise a good crop on my land and then next year you move to the *Colônia*. We can put your name on the register now. And we can do the same for the rest of you, if you like." I looked at Chico, our recorder. "Will you remember this, Chico?"

Chico was still gazing into the fire, detached. "*Sim, senhora,*" he said. His answering tone lacked conviction and I wondered what pictures he saw in the pulsating glow of the embers.

"You know, there's one part of our arrangement that I don't like myself," I continued. "I'd much rather *not* advance supplies to you people if I can help it. S'hor Davino and I have the store there, not too far away; I'd like to suggest that we change the deal and that I pay you for clearing the land at the going rate. With that cash, you can buy most of what you'll need, I should think. You all know that when people farm land already cleared for them, the division is half and half with the owner. I'll give you more than that, I'll give you sixty-five per cent."

All this was a new idea and it took a little time to soak in. Finally Chico spoke.

"I think that would be better for all of us," he said, thoughtfully. "They're paying a *conto* and a half an *alqueire* for cutting trees and if we each cut two *alqueires*, the three *contos* will almost take us through the rains." José, Emílio and Ezequiel made sounds of agreement.

"I'll check on the rates and we'll settle it that way, then," I said. "You all know by this time that I don't intend to run my place the way lots of people do. I want you to do the best you can up there and I'll see to it that cutthroat prices aren't charged at the store."

Since there was no objection or further comment, I thought this was a good time to break up our council and go to my sleeping bag.

The next morning before the thick mists of the deep and narrow river valley had risen much above treetop height, I was lucky enough to hail a passing truck whose driver was willing, for a good stiff fee, to take my little tribe to the river port near my land.

When we reached our turnoff about midmorning I left my sleeping bag with Davino at the store and continued on with the truck. The men quickly unloaded and the trucker left us, shaking his head over this picture of the trousered foreign woman and the jumble of *roçeiros*. I had brought some bulk supplies of sugar and coffee, and I now divided them out among the families.

It was now understood that in the future I would pay them cash to cover the cost of clearing. We agreed to let the present debts stand against the harvest. There by the river we ate a meal which the women had prepared with rapid skill. Then the men began to ferry the household goods across the river in the long, narrow canoe which danced erratically with its top-heavy loads. The early afternoon shadows were inching forward when I wound up the final detail, shook hands all around and left to walk out to the main road.

The farm was well started behind me and the complications of Anápolis were far away. I had toughened up physically and I was proud of my self-reliance in traveling with the land people; this made me feel I was breaking through the web of uncertainty that had surrounded me. Beginning my long trek through the soft dust of the forest trail, I felt light and free, a feeling I had rarely known since coming to Goiás.

The afternoon was truly lovely, as was any day in the Great Forest once you had a chance to take a look at it. The farther

I got from the rushing river, the more lovely the still air and the benign sunlight seemed and the more grateful was the coolness of the shadows cast by the forest. So long as I kept moving, the tormenting gnats did not bite me. Now as I entered the deep forest, the deepening shadows smoothly enveloped me the way the gray depths of quiet waters embrace a downward-moving swimmer. The trees and saplings and bushes and grasses, tiered one above the other, were immobile on either hand, a gray-green wall, impenetrable, impassive.

There were big animals in the forest, I knew—jaguar, boar and others. How did they ever move through it, I wondered. The stillness seemed absolute; not even a bird's call broke the silence for a long while. Then I heard, on my right hand and behind me, a loud rustle in the underbrush.

It startled me, for I was half-dreaming a dream of perfect peace. The rustling continued, almost as if the animal that made it were trailing along with me. What, actually, would I do if a jaguar appeared, ran an unbidden thought. I was too far away from the river to call to the people there, and the one clearing between me and the big road was still some distance ahead. There were many tales in the backlands about jaguars trailing people for miles and miles and then attacking them.

Not very long before, the Aerovias pilot, Comandante Nilo Cuaresma, had been walking around his property just downriver from my land when his big trail dog treed what Nilo thought was a monkey. Nilo, in Goiás on a short visit, had a shotgun with him and cartridges loaded with light duckshot for the big wild ducks that occasionally visit our river. Nilo blazed away at the golden furry spot up in the foliage and instead of a monkey, a big jaguar fell out, wounded in the chest by the duckshot. Luckily the fall also stunned the beast, and Nilo managed to finish him off with his machete.

I was sure that I was not afraid, though it took a moment's self-examination to be sure I was sure. Now I heard a rustling slightly behind me on the opposite side of the road from the first noise and I paid it the doubtful tribute of switching the puny little .25 automatic from my handbag to a more accessible pocket in my slacks.

As I walked briskly along, half-seriously considering the rustling in the brush, I looked at the trees on either hand. Hunters say that the best defense against a jaguar is to climb a tree. But in the few hundred yards where I looked for a suitable tree to climb, I did not see a single one that was not too big or too little or lacking in convenient limbs to catch onto as you scrambled up from the cat's claws. Hunters also say that you can defend yourself against a charging jaguar with a pole—it's simple, they claim, you just hold him off with it. But my machete was miles away in Anápolis—what would I cut a pole with, and even if I had a knife, what would the jaguar be doing while I was hacking away at the sapling?

I decided that if a jaguar appeared, my best tactic would be to confuse him by walking toward him calling "Kitty, kitty" till I got close enough to pump six .25 bullets into his right eye.

No menace developed from the mysterious rustlings, which were probably caused by forest lizards, but the ring of an ax in the clearing ahead sounded good to me when I came within earshot of it. Before I reached the clearing, I met a man padding softly down the trail with a rifle over his arm. We murmured an exchange of greetings; I wondered why I felt no twinge of uneasiness about him, for with his rifle he had a potential advantage over me. The fact is, I never felt afraid of any *roçeiro* in the backlands, really afraid.

When I reached Davino's store, he hurried to fetch a tin basin of clean water for me to bathe my face and hands in. He also brought out coffee and sugar and gave it to the *caboclo's* wife to make coffee for us. The little activity of kindness and welcome warmed me. As the night came down, we sat on gasoline boxes outside the hut, leaning against the sapling wall, our heels digging at the hard-packed red earth while Anastásio, owner of the hut, squatted on his heels nearby.

I told them about the rustling in the forest and we discussed the mild local sensation of Nilo's exploit with the jaguar.

"Somebody up here was telling about a man coming home from work late one afternoon and a jaguar started trailing him," said Davino. "The man began to run and the jaguar ran. The man slowed down and walked and the jaguar walked. Then the man began to run, and he ran and he ran till he couldn't run any more. He stopped and looked around, and there was the jaguar standing a little way behind him, not even panting very hard. So the man sat down on a rock and burst into tears."

"And what did the jaguar do?"

"He went away."

When we finished chuckling over that, I repeated a "true" yarn I had heard at the Chacra, one I thought filled with quiet horror.

A *caboclo* was coming home at nightfall through the forest, went the yarn. Soon he noticed a jaguar was following him. He ran as hard as he could till he reached a river and dived in and swam under the water to a little island in the middle. He thought the jaguar would come over to the rocks after him, but instead he heard the animal dive in and swim on across to the other bank of the river where it hid in the brush.

The man either had to wait till dawn, when he'd have a better chance of getting by the jaguar, or be driven back into the forest. He shivered all night on the little pile of rocks in the river. At dawn he quietly swam downstream and crept through the underbrush to an open track that went right to his hut and he started running as hard as he could. When he was nearly to his hut he glanced back and saw the jaguar loping along behind him. He ran inside, jumped into bed and covered his head with a blanket.

"And then what happened?" Davino asked. "Did the jaguar get into bed with the man?"

"Well, it seems a neighbor saw him running and came over with his gun and dog to ask what the trouble was. The man said a jaguar was waiting on the edge of the clearing, and the other *caboclo* said why didn't they go and kill him. The first man wouldn't budge; more than that, he refused to get out of bed at all any more and lay there till he died about three months later."

The two men nodded as if it all fitted in perfectly. I added, "That part about his dying doesn't ring true to me, though."

"He died of *paixão*, Dona Virginia," said Anastásio earnestly. "Sometimes a *caboclo* just gives up and dies. I knew a man who went to bed and wouldn't get up because his little three-year-old girl died of snake bite."

"Some men had trouble with a jaguar when they were cutting the line back of your place, Dona Virginia," he continued. "One night a jaguar got to prowling around the camp, bawling and screaming, and almost scared the boys to death. They didn't get a wink of sleep all night. The next morning, though, they got it back on the jaguar when they found out he'd killed their pack mule."

"How—did they make a trap?"

"No, they buried the mule so the jaguar wouldn't get to eat it."

"Big joke on the jaguar," I observed ironically.

"It sure was," said Anastásio seriously. "They were laughing fit to kill about it when they came by here packing their camping things on their backs."

(When I wrote all this to Bill, who once owned a full-grown bobcat and was wild-animal wise, I got back full directions on what to do in an encounter with a jaguar. The first thing I did, in line with his common-sense ideas, was to order a heavier gun.)

The dark came down and the men built a fire in front of the store. A five-year-old boy who had been listening bug-eyed to the jaguar tales now began to talk to me. He lived across the road with his father, he told me. He was an exceptionally bright boy, full of imagination and manliness, and we began a fanciful negotiation for him to work for me. Before long his father, a hollow-chested young white man, came to fetch his son, and when he saw how we were playing, he offered to give the boy to me. He had no wife, he said, and he couldn't care for the boy, with all the work he had to do to hold his *Colônia* land.

At first I couldn't believe he was serious. But he quickly convinced me that he really wanted me to take and keep the little boy, that very night. I told him it was impossible, sad for the child and sharply reminded of the raw cruelty threaded through life in the beautiful country around me. Davino said in an aside that the woman had died in childbirth.

The jaguars and the other wild beasts were not the real terrors here. It was the fact that there was no cushioning for anything, no margin, no resource, no help. A man could not live alone here. He had to have a woman to prepare food from raw growths and grains, to cook for him, keep his clothes together, help him plant and harvest. They made love, children inevitably came and if anything went wrong, the woman was doomed. This man was trying to give away his son, although the boy was his one hope for help later on and for support in his old age. Soon, he might be forced to abandon the boy, as thousands of children are deserted by these poor people each year.

Davino piled on more wood to make the bonfire blaze up afresh, but the incident somehow robbed our firelight of its power to comfort away the chill of the great empty night around us. Before long we saw headlights coming down the big road and hailed the car. It was an extraordinary piece of luck, people whom I knew driving a fast car toward Anápolis, and there was room for me. I climbed in and we headed south.

5

As soon as I got back to Anápolis we plunged into a whirl of preparations for a wave of visitors. Roger Ward wrote that he was driving up from São Paulo in his jeep, bringing along Bill White, *Time Magazine* correspondent in Rio and a good friend of mine and of Susana's. The Bowens were expecting their friends Dr. and Mrs. Robert Platt, of the University of Chicago, together with their grown son and daughter and another young woman.

Through Brazilian friends met at the Bowens', Perla and Susana were now rapidly widening their acquaintanceships far beyond our immediate circle. I got busy arranging Liberty Hall for our share of the visitors; Perla and Susana already had one of the two big rooms and I planned to put Bill White and Roger in the other. I moved into a little room intended for a dressing room and inaccessible except through one of the big bedrooms. I made myself a private entrance simply by scrambling in and out through its low window, a stunt that gave me childish pleasure. Since the room partitions went up only a few feet above head level, privacy in the house was far from complete.

Long dark Roger and lanky blond Bill White arrived travel-worn and dust-dyed as red as Indians, but they came stocked with something hitherto scarce in Goiás—drinkable whisky. The two tall Americans were excellent foils for each other,

Bill's wit ready and quick, Roger's drawling and dry. I associated both of them with good times in Rio and Buenos Aires and was looking forward to their presence to offset the feminine majority in our little society. The Platt party duly arrived and for a few days we were all caught up in welcomes and celebration.

A fat hog was slaughtered and our two households gathered at the big house for an elaborate country feast built around spareribs. The men, still outnumbered, were badly outshouted also in our group of unusually articulate women, so at this feast, after a few drinks, I solemnly picked up a big golden grapefruit and offered it to Captain Bowen. "We award you this for patience above and beyond the call of duty in enduring so many females," I said gravely. The Captain, with a devilish gleam in his blue eyes, waved the fruit away.

"Don't give it to me, Virginia," he said. "I might throw it!"

After the dust of arrival settled, Roger busily prepared to move to Ceres to start his small brick factory. The Platts and the Bowens ranged over the country by land and air, and Bill White went with them, gathering information for his magazine. Perla and Susana continued to dash about with their new-found Brazilian friends. As for me, I still hoped that the newcomers would eventually find time to join me in some form of amusement; meanwhile, I washed dishes, marketed and chauffeured. My housemates were usually exhausted at night and we went to bed soon after supper, around nine or ten o'clock.

Finally there came a Saturday night, and now at last, I thought, we'd do something—go to a movie, anything. As I went to put our supper scraps in an outside garbage pit, I saw that a brilliant moon had come up in the sky. It was the kind of night when the rabbits dance in the light of the moon in little bare places on the tops of grassy hills; the whole earth outside Liberty Hall seemed to be stirring with invitation. I knew there was to be a country dance at one of the *caboclo* homes up the hollow and I could hear distant voices as the people gathered. Our little hell-maid had brought me word we'd be welcome if we cared to come.

Perla and Susana had already started going to bed, which suited me fine, for my plan was to mention the dance to Roger and Bill at the last minute, certain that the ladies would not arise from their rest to go with us. I climbed in through the window into my little room and to my horror heard going-to-bed sounds from Bill and Roger too.

"Hey in there! Let's go to the dance!" I called softly over the partition.

There was a pause and a groaning of springs.

"I think I'm going to bed," said Roger.

"I'm already in bed," said Bill White.

"A fine pair you two turned out to be!" I reproached them, more than half in earnest. "Here I looked forward to you for weeks and what happens? You go to bed every night at sun-down!"

Roger gave a mock groan.

"Do you want us to get up?"

"Certainly not! I wouldn't have you put yourselves out for anything."

I took a big swig out of a gift bottle of rum that I had been saving for hard times, and stuck my head out of the window. The gay tinkle of distant music from a guitar came to me now and I could hear cheerful yells and the occasional joyful pop of a six-shooter. I pulled in my head, in despair and frustration.

"All right for you two," I said to the partition between my room and Bill and Roger's. "I'm going to put up a dance hall in the City of Sin and I'll sit over the cash box with two big revolvers and see to it that neither one of you ever gets inside the door."

(The City of Sin was Barranca, the wide-open town divided from the well-regulated Ceres by the Rio das Almas.)

"It'll be different when White's gone," said Roger. "He's just a tenderfoot, you know."

Poor Bill, who had been caught in more than one cross-current that he didn't understand, now wailed, "But how did this get to be *my* fault? *I* was willing to get up!"

"That's all right for both of you," I said darkly, and rebelliously went to bed. Nothing, absolutely nothing, was working out according to plan. Not the big important things, not even the little important ones.

This incident was trivial, but a final division among our little society was in store. Not long after Bill White went back to Rio, an open disagreement developed between Perla and Susana on the one hand and the Bowens and myself on the other. Someone among the Argentines' new friends had told them that Susana had made a bad bargain in the land purchase, perhaps in hopes of selling Susana land themselves. I had bought land from the Bowens sight unseen and it was good land, better than I expected. I believed in the reliability of the men who had sold Susana's to her; on the frontier unexplored land has to be bought more or less on faith. After one short, rather confused discussion with Susana about it, I took the position that she was to do whatever she and Perla wished and thenceforth refused to discuss it further. It meant a break in one of the best friendships that I ever had, but I did it resolutely. ("I don't mind losing money," said Susana. "What I mind is losing friends.")

About this time I got an offer which gave me the idea that I might actually "go out" of the Goiás wilderness for a while. It came in the form of a letter from a friend of mine in the International Refugee Organization saying they wanted a press officer for Brazil and asking if I would accept the job. I told Susana that I might take it and this marked the definite end of our original plan.

The Platt party took their leave in the midst of all this. Roger, somewhat bewildered, prepared to withdraw to Ceres.

This dispersal was indeed a sorry outcome for a joint adventure so bravely planned, but the *sertão*, the backland, wages a strange war against civilized standards and as a group we had not managed to hold together against it.

Roger, moving to Ceres by stages, was sorry for me, I think, and his friendship was a help to me, simply because he would let me ride with him in the jeep. In the bumpy little vehicle I could get much closer to the country that I loved; I could see the whole life around us much better, the little plants by the roadside, even the weeds; I could have dragged my toes in the thick soft red dust as we jounced along. As we passed by at a distance, I always looked with great longing at the bold black mountain that loomed up behind Jaraguá, the old gold town on the road north. The mountain had been the scene of a local war over gold a long time ago and in its caves, inhabited now by jaguars, there were said to be old muskets and skeletons, and hidden treasures of gold nuggets.

One day I let slip a remark that was really a private thought spoken out loud.

"If Bill Mizelle were here, we'd climb that mountain," I said, remembering how Bill and I had explored Buenos Aires bit by bit till we knew the city as few Argentines did.

"Why don't you get Bill Mizelle up here, then?" asked Roger, not too sympathetically.

"He'd come if I said I needed him, I think," I replied, somewhat to my own surprise.

Though we were no longer sweethearts, Bill's devotion as my friend, expressed in his letters, was coming to be the one unchanging human tie in the foreground of my life. Roger's question made me consider whether I would ever, under any circumstances, appeal to Bill for support that he would give at once out of loyalty, and I knew I would not. I had always accepted so much that he gave, so much help, sustaining affection, patience, understanding. He had already taken five years away from his profession of writing to fight one war as a line officer in the Navy—it certainly wouldn't have been fair to involve him in setting aright my private campaign in the wilderness.

". . . But I don't think I'd ask him to come," I concluded after the long pause.

Whatever I did in Goiás would have to be done alone.

Once Roger was established at Ceres living in the Chateau

—the little house where I had once camped overnight with my tenants—the trips in the jeep ended. Roger plunged into his work and we saw little of him.

I still refused to discuss the land deal with Susana, though she made at least two overtures toward a kinder understanding with me about it. The break with the Chacra put her and Perla in rather a dilemma and they solved it by disposing of Susana's land and leaving. During their last days in Goiás, I could not bring myself to say very much to Susana and I deliberately avoided talking to her. There was a certain cruelty in this and I knew it, for silence has always been the sharpest weapon that anybody could turn against me. I had in the past envied people who could use it when I could not and always had felt at a disadvantage with them. Now I felt strong because, for once, I could keep my tongue still.

With an effort, I possibly could have mitigated the whole incident, but I coldly did nothing, a course entirely foreign to my nature. I can only believe that some of the intransigence of the country got into me. Captain Bowen had told me in São Paulo when he was briefing me on the *sertão* that it would kill you or make you fat. Since coming there, I had not seen a fat person, not one, though I had seen plenty who were obviously slowly dying. Perhaps the saying should run that the *sertão* will kill you or make you cruel.

The turn of events was not pleasant for the Bowens. Though we stood together in believing the land deal a good one—time has proved that it was a good investment—Joan and I had points of view widely different on many other things. Our friendship held only because we learned to wrangle childishly about our disagreements and then forget them. If she had not made consistent efforts to end these wrangles on a laugh, we might not have forgotten them. Increasingly I felt impelled to do things my own way, find out my own truths about the backlands, no matter what the cost.

I had lost all proper sense of time in the *sertão*. Weeks had seemed months while I was waiting for Susana and Roger to come and usher in our millennium, yet the weeks passed like days after they got there and our original plan started falling apart. When Susana and Perla left us and quiet descended once more on the Chacra with all our visitors gone, I hired a brown *caboclo* woman named Guiomar to live at Liberty Hall and cook, clean and wash for me. But it was too lonely to stay down there all the time and I gravitated back to eating with the Bowens in the evening. The little house, rearranged into a living room and a big bedroom for me, seemed sweet and attractive once more. It was especially charming to me when Guiomar built a big fire in my bedroom at night and left me a large can of hot water for my bath in a giant basin in front of the fire. Guiomar, who looked like a forty-five-year-old, weather-beaten Hedy Lamarr, kept piles of clean clothes ready for me and I luxuriated in changing my shirt, slacks and underthings two or three times a day.

The rickety old Plymouth, though in and out of the repair shop continually with broken springs and leaky hydraulic brake lines, now became my salvation. I began to spend at least half my time in it, with a chauffeur I hired because it was far too dangerous and exhausting for me to drive alone on the long trips.

My families of landworkers had set up a temporary camp under the big trees by the river and each day the six men trudged more than a mile up the forest trail to the site they had selected for the clearing. They had been at work there several weeks when I arrived at our store one day to find Davino in a very depressed mood.

"Dona Virginia, you know we're not making any money with this store," he told me. "I think we're going to have to give it up."

This was a staggering thought. Kindly little Davino, so worried, so plagued by the festering bites of the stinging gnats —he couldn't have dealt me a worse blow.

"But, Davino!" I protested, "we're marking this stuff up thirty to fifty per cent—we're bound to make money."

He showed me a near-empty cash box. "We could mark it up twice as much and still make nothing," he said mournfully.

"I'll prove we're making a profit right now," I asserted. It was absolutely necessary to get the pessimism out of Davino's mind.

For two days, I lived in the little dirt-floored store, sleeping on a straw mattress in the back of the Plymouth, while I took stock and ran a rough trial balance. We weren't doing too badly, but Davino was innocently enough using a good part of the store's cash for expenses in developing his lot. There was absolutely no question of dishonesty, but he was taking out capital, slowly liquidating us. I tried over and over to explain to Davino about turnover and to show him that we were indeed making a small profit. It was no use; the money was gone, so we weren't making a profit, as far as Davino could see.

"Let's divide the stock up and quit, Dona Virginia," he insisted. "This is not getting us anywhere."

"Well, there's certainly more than enough to give me back what I put in," I said, disconsolate.

Truck, pigs, friends and now even our little store, all had slipped away from me. Failure of the store would affect the farm project unfavorably, I knew.

The next day my driver, whom I had been boarding at the store, put a load of supplies into the back of the station wagon and we started in to the river. By now the forest track was deeply rutted and jutting roots and stobs threatened to tear the bottom out of the low-slung car at each trip. We crept in, usually in second gear, over the five weary miles, expecting every minute the fatal break that would strand us.

At the river we shouted for the canoe and piled our wares into it. The men laboriously paddled up to the new landing place where my families were camping under the trees.

The camp was attractive as we came toward it from the river. The underbrush had been cleared out of a big space under enormous trees that roofed it over completely, and the families had built six peaked, tent-shaped shelters out of unpeeled sapling poles tied together with vines and covered with rice straw. Manoel, typically, had planted his well-made hut right in the middle of the space. When we arrived at the land-

ing in the late afternoon, all the rest of the flock came down to
help us tote the supplies up the steep white sandbank of the
river. But not Manoel; a man apart, he sat in his gasoline-box
chair in front of his home, playing with his little son while his
wife pounded the husks off rice in a big *pilão*, a wooden
mortar made out of a tree trunk. Manoel had built his stove in
front of his thatched shelter. It was a platform of sticks on
which he had fashioned a hollow trough of mud, fitting the
iron stove top into the top of the trough. Properly fired, this
made a good and durable stove.

José's home stood just behind Manoel's and beyond were
those of Chico and Claudinho. The Feitosas had selected sites
a little inland and uphill from Manoel's and both their shelters
huddled at the foot of giant trees, as if humbly seeking protection. They had not built stoves but were cooking on skill-
fully arranged big stones.

All cooking and eating was done outdoors, of course, and all
washing, even of plates and knives and forks, in the river. The
shelters themselves were little more than roofs under which
to sleep and screens for a minimum of privacy—smaller and
less artfully made than the lodges of many tribes of Brazilian
"wild" Indians. They were crowded with beds, most of them
simple pole platforms covered by bags of ticking stuffed
loosely with straw. Under the beds were boxes containing
stored supplies and changes of clothing and their few personal
belongings. The tiny homes were without exception extremely
neat and well arranged, and no Boy Scouts trying for merit
badges could have maintained a more spick-and-span camp.

When I called the heads of the families together to deal out
the supplies, I had to tell them the bad news.

"S'hor Davino and I are going to give up the store," I announced.

The buck, José, who disguised a violent temperament under
a disarming grin, reacted first.

"Pah-h, I thought that wouldn't last!"

"And how are we going to get supplies through the rains?"
asked Manoel.

"Well, I could bring a stock up here and let somebody deal it out. Chico, since he knows how to 'sign.' "

("Sign" is their euphemism for "read and write and figure.")

As usual, responses from the others were slow in coming. We had fallen into our now-familiar pattern of council, I ensconced in one of Manoel's chairs, which he had set out for me, Manoel leaning back in another, his baby on his lap, and the other men sitting around us on low boxes or squatting back on their heels. It was quite natural for us to gather in front of Manoel's hut, since it stood square in the center of the camp, and his act with the chairs was part of a determined campaign on his part to require me to treat him as an equal, a partner in a contract—something he really didn't have to fight for, if he had only known it. I could see it gave him considerable satisfaction, as if he'd won a trick, to have our councils "happen" to work out with the two of us as it were on the bench. More and more he adopted the air of a spokesman and advocate for the group. I made up my mind that on the next visit, I'd sit on a gasoline box with the others, spreading a little equality among them for a change and leaving Manoel aloft in his chair.

"I'm behind in my work already, this foot I cut doesn't seem like it wants to heal up," complained Claudinho, who had wounded himself rather badly with an awkward stroke of the ax. "If Chico spends a lot of time on a store here we'll get further behind."

The two were still working as partners; it was a point to consider.

"We all got a late start," observed José. "If we have to build a storehouse we'll lose more time."

Chico, sweet-mannered as usual, had waited for the others to voice objections before airing his.

"Dona Virginia, we're all working together up here," he said hesitantly. "I don't . . . the boys might not like something I'd do. . . ."

Of course, Chico would have to exercise the traditional "hold-down" till the crop was planted to keep the men from drawing more than they needed, running up a debt greater than the worth of their work and possibly leaving. The hold-down is necessary not only to prevent loss of money but also of workers.

"You'll have to start bringing us everything—you're the *dona*," said Manoel. "We'd lose too much time going to Ceres to fetch everything back from there."

Manoel was right, of course, but he sparked anger in me with his dig implying that I had to be reminded of my responsibility. It was not just the blacksnake whips of the Old South stirring atavistically in my blood. As a matter of principle, if not of indoctrination, Manoel was as studiedly nasty as he could be and still get away with it. I could never show how it affected me, for that would have been a point of victory for him. He was out to prove that the owner, in this instance myself, was neglectful, dishonest, undependable, unreasonable, gouging, overbearing and so forth.

"Then we'll have to change the agreement all the way around," I said. "Our deal was that I was to pay you cash for clearing the land and advance money later if needed, so that you could buy your own supplies. But if I have to grubstake you, then we ought to do it the way everybody else does around here; I'll grubstake and you get seventy-five per cent of the crop and pay for your grubstaking in rice at the harvest."

In order to prevent future dispute, I asked Chico to write out this agreement in the back of one of my account books and had him and Claudinho sign it. The others made a mark, all but Manoel, who faded into the forest background while we were going through this little formality.

Chico and José rowed me back across the river where my driver was waiting and he eased the Plymouth out over the rough trail. As it grew darker, the headlights helped, since we could see stobs and roots better. We spent the night at the store, somewhat forlorn in the atmosphere of disintegration reigning there.

My driver at this time was Waldemar, a slight, talkative,

weak-chinned little white man whose soft treble voice going on and on as we drove the long dusty miles had a certain flute-like note in it. Waldemar loved to drive in spurts, speeding up, slowing down for a pothole, racing the engine, braking at once, speeding up, on and on and on. He liked the wrong side of the road, as many backlanders do for some strange reason; but often he unaccountably wandered all over it. Once he had us so near the edge of a chasm that I actually had to grab the wheel. One night he stopped the car to put oil in the crank-case, pulling up square in the middle of the road, as is also customary in the backlands. First he lighted matches and held them down inside the oil- and gasoline-soaked old engine. The car had already caught fire on the road once when Santinho was driving it, so I insisted that he use a flashlight. Then an enormous truck loaded with a hundred sacks of rice which we had passed some miles back appeared over the horizon be-hind us, thundering down on us at cannon-ball speed. I yelled to Waldemar to get the car out of the road, but his reactions were so slow I had to scramble under the wheel, kick the starter and buck her over to the side myself. At that, the big truck barely missed us.

Waldemar said of me afterwards:

"Dona Virginia is a very nice lady, but she's a little nerv-ous."

I listened sympathetically to Waldemar's love problems—he wanted to marry a sixteen-year-old girl in Minas Gerais, to whom it seemed he hadn't even written in a year. But a widow in Anápolis had offered to buy a truck and set him up driving it and Waldemar knew she meant matrimony. "You think that pretty little sixteen-year-old would still marry you after you've been away a year without even writing to her?" I asked. "Oh, yes, Dona Virginia," piped bandy-legged, bat-tered, scrawny little Waldemar with the supreme confidence of the Latin male. In return for listening to him, which I could not in fact avoid, Waldemar entered wholeheartedly into helping me find fatback, brown sugar and other scarce supplies for my forest band. His friendships up and down the big road now came in handy.

When Davino broke the bad news to me about the store, I did not return directly to Anápolis, where I knew it was difficult to find fatback and *rapadura*, the brown brick sugar the *roçeiros* preferred. Instead I decided to have Waldemar drive us north toward the edge of the big forest where there were old homesteads and *fazendas* that might agree to supply us regularly. Somehow or other, Anastásio, he from whom we rented store space, got in on the party; it is very easy to acquire a retinue in the *sertão*, especially for trips. Anastásio was not supposed to receive pay for his "assistance" on the trip, but in the end he cost me dearly, since I had to feed him and tip him. Favors and friendly gestures, I learned, always cost high in the end, at least twice as high as paying for the same services.

For many long miles beyond our turnoff at the store, the land was rich, the forests thick and the valleys deep. But finally the country flattens out and there is open land, the less fertile *campo*, interspersed with patches of second- or third-grade forest made up of small softwood trees. After an early morning drive to and through this country, we came to a little river with which I fell immediately in love.

This river was so clear and sparkling now in the dry season it looked like bubbly-water in its rocky bed. Just beyond it stood a small inn, the neatest, cleanest, sunniest in all Goiás. No pigs in the kitchen here, rather flowers in the patio, bright against whitewashed walls. The brick floors were soft pink from much scrubbing, and the spotless walls cast blue shadows along a tile-roofed gallery bordering the patio. I glanced into an unoccupied bedroom; it was clean as a pin, sparsely furnished as a nun's cell, airy, inviting.

I made friends with the couple who kept the inn while Waldemar scoured the neighborhood for pigs. The woman was washing clothes in the sunny, flowered patio with two smiling, gentle-mannered helpers—servants or daughters, you could not tell which. They were easy, unhurried; there was such an air of contented, happy domestic activity, cleanliness and peace here that I could scarcely tear myself away and go back to my own world of petty difficulty, in which both major and minor cogs kept slipping and slipping.

Waldemar and Anastásio came back, reporting failure of course, and we set out toward the south again, canvassing the country farm by farm. We found only a few bricks of brown sugar and some sun-blackened cow meat, which we took back to the store for lunch.

I was worn out from the days of travel on bad roads, the unrelieved diet of greasy rice, soupy beans and heavily sweetened coffee, and I told Waldemar to head for home. We were over the big divide and on the home stretch when we decided to make a midafternoon stop at an ancient *fazenda* where Waldemar had once worked.

With some pride, Waldemar took me in and introduced me to the lady of the house, Dona Maria. I liked this handsome young woman on sight, she was so open of countenance and kind in her manner of welcoming me. I particularly remember her big flashing eyes and the gold loop earrings she wore, like a gypsy.

Dona Maria was running an enormous cattle ranch at this moment because her husband, Arnaulf, though much beloved locally for his generosity and friendly nature, had a weakness: when drunk, he hated soldiers. Months before, he had gone on a spectacular spree in Anápolis. When three young conscripts serving as traffic police stopped the truck in which he was careening through the streets and asked to see his driving license, he pulled a revolver and shot all three of them dead before they could get their holster flaps open. This made a total of five soldiers that he had killed, I was told. He was now in hiding. "*Êle sumiú,*" people said. "He just disappeared"— many thought to some tenant's house on the estate.

My hostess and I did not speak of this, naturally. She served me coffee and marmalade on delicious home-baked bread. I told her I had heard what fine stock she had and she took me to see the hogs. I was admiring these enormous snub-nosed beauties when we heard a truck stop out in front. In a moment one of her lanky, leather-chapped cowboys came to say that somebody was asking for Dona Virginia.

"What's gone wrong, José?" I demanded as soon as I saw who it was. Hitchhiking to Anápolis, José had seen my Plymouth parked outside and had stopped here. I knew at that moment why ancient rulers had the heads of messengers bearing ill news chopped off virtually on arrival. Discouraging such announcements was probably the only way they could ever get to spend an afternoon in peace.

"Dona Virginia, you'd better go back up there to the *mato* in a hurry," said José excitedly. "That Claudinho has just laid down and quit and Manoel went to Barranca yesterday and isn't back yet and I've broken every ax I had. That Ezequiel is getting lazier all the time and me and Chico and Emílio can't clear the whole piece of forest by ourselves."

There was nothing else for it. I had to turn around and go all the way back and it seemed much farther this time than it ever had before. We stopped in Barranca to search vainly for the right kind of axes and as we drove out of town toward the farm, I spotted Manoel standing by the road, waiting in the dusk to catch a ride.

"Get in, Manoel," I said none too cordially. "I'm surprised to see you here."

"I came here to get some medicine for my son," he replied, his face like a stormcloud. "I walked half the way to get here and it looked as if I'd have to walk all the way back." He climbed into the Plymouth.

"I thought S'hor Davino had some medicine left at the store," I said. "Is it all gone?"

"I want my boy to have some good medicine, and you don't have to worry about me coming down here to Barranca to lie around drunk on *pinga*, either. I've got plenty of work to do, I want my boy to know how to read and write when he grows up and not be a stupid donkey like all these other *roçeiros*."

"You're going to take up land in the *Colônia* next year and when he's big enough, he can go to *Colônia* schools," I said. "What is the medicine you walked twelve miles for?" "Biotônico, *senhora*, the best there is." I had never heard of this patent medicine then, but months later when I was the luncheon guest of Olavo Fontoura, whose vast pharmaceutical empire is built on it, it was served to us as an *apéritif*. I told him even the backwoodsmen swore by it and asked him what was in it. "Eet ees the Es-spanish fly," he said with a grin. Spanish fly, one of the world's most notorious aphrodisiacs.

We eased the Plymouth into the forest trail after dark, Waldemar fluting his interminable tales of trucker derring-do, José listening admiringly, Manoel silent and scornful by his side on the back seat. At the camp, I called an immediate council and this time I plumped myself down on a low gasoline box. When Claudinho limped out of the shadows I told him to sit in Manoel's second chair, beside Manoel. This turned Manoel's subtle seating arrangement trick against its inventor. Grouping me with the majority, it made Manoel seem less like a self-appointed spokesman for the group, and more like an accused man in the dock with Claudinho.

"There seems to be some little difficulty here and I thought I'd come back and see if I could help out," I said. Some people think it is best to talk to the *roçeiros* one by one in these situations and politick among them, but I felt the direct approach would protect me from the eternal whisper behind my back, "Yes, Dona Virginia said *that* to you, but what she said to *me* was . . ."

"What right had José to go running down to Anápolis after you, Dona Virginia?" began Manoel, ever seeking cause for contention. "I mean to take care of my family and have my rights respected and if José doesn't like that, let him prove how good a man he is!"

This was sheer bombast, but José made an angry movement.

"Manoel, we're just not going to have any foolishness here," I said, cutting José off from speech. "The first thing the men want to know is when you're going to make up the time you've lost. You're all supposed to put in equal time, as you agreed."

"Is everybody going to make up lost time?" Manoel asked belligerently.

"Everybody wants to try to stay even. That's how everybody's rights will be respected, speaking of rights."

"I'll work a day for one of the others when he has to go to Barranca for medicine for one of his children."

Always the dig from Manoel. And if he worked a day for one of the others, wouldn't that put his own tally another day behind? It took higher mathematics to keep up with Manoel's "deals."

"Work one holiday or two Saturday afternoons," I suggested.

Manoel considered it. "We'll see," he said. He knew the others were bound to want a day off sooner or later and that the account would even out.

"Now, Claudinho, do you need to go to the hospital at Ceres with that foot?"

"I do not, Dona Virginia. It's not the foot so much, I'm just so far behind I almost can't drag myself up and down that trail twice a day."

Claudinho never failed to irritate me, for he was like a softwood tree, all pith at the center. But how well I knew what he meant. Nagging pain over days, falling behind the rest, discouragement, the others' silent scorn . . . Brazilian country people, when discouraged or heartbroken, sometimes do take to their beds like the man in the jaguar story and die of *paixão*, which is, as nearly as it can be translated, grief or shock. If Claudinho collapsed on us, I'd be in a pretty pickle sure enough.

And poor old Ezequiel, hunched up silent and miserable on his box. He knew he was far behind too; he simply did not have the physical strength to keep up with the others. They had bravely started out saying they'd do all the tree felling together, but in fact they were expecting each man to do very nearly an equal share. If we could get Ezequiel through the stage of tree felling, maybe he could keep up with the help of his two growing sons. I looked at them also, skinny boys huddled beside their father.

"Look, Claudinho, there's only one way out. I'm going to hire some outside help for you and Ezequiel and charge it against your accounts."

This was approved of by all of them; it took the pressure off the two weaker vessels and assured the stronger men they would not be penalized for their strength. The risk was transferred to the owner, who had to advance more money.

About axes; I asked Emílio to lend José an ax until I could send some to them from Anápolis. And now about the extra workmen—who, incidentally, meant more supplies to be brought in, since we had to feed them.

Chico said a homesteader along the forest trail had two cousins with him who wanted to earn some cash. Though it was late, I asked him to go with us to see them. We crossed the wild river in our wobbly canoe, started up the creaking old Plymouth and crept through the tunnel of the night woods till we came to the clearing, a patch of brilliant starlight on our left.

Once the deal was arranged, I insisted that Waldemar continue on to Anápolis, though it meant driving most of the night.

Speed-up, slow-down, ride-the-brake-down . . . Waldemar's staccato driving, jerking my head back and forth, made dozing out of the question; besides, I wanted to stay awake to be sure that he did. Flute-flute-flute went his nasal tenor monologue . . . Usually on night drives such as this, I enjoyed watching for the swift foxes that jumped out of the bushes to dart across in front of us or race the car for a few moments. It was fun to pop at them with my little automatic, although I'm sure I never even scratched one. Tonight my little gun stayed joyless in its holster, however. I began to dream about the inn beyond the sparkling river.

This small river, the São Patrício, was not turbulent and frightening like the mighty Rio das Almas, which charged into the Tocantins and finally, far, far away, into the great Amazon. In the little stream a bather not too expert at swimming could feel safe. I grew up in a country where wild rivers cutting cruelly deep into the earth each year took their toll of lives among my young friends, who dived off their high banks into underwater traps of tangled root or flood-shifted sand. I mistrust big rivers for their power and their treachery and feel happy only with the little ones.

The inn itself was the most peaceful spot I had found so far in this far frontier where man's onslaught against the forest was bruising its way forward with raw vigor. The country around the inn was open, spacious. I remembered the smile of the woman who ran the inn; she was kindly, easy.

As Waldemar rocked my head back and forth with his jerky tap dance between accelerator and brake pedal, I was thinking: "I'll just vanish away like Dona Maria's husband and go and stay at the inn." One of the great panaceas of the backlands is to disappear, hide yourself away, "*sumirse.*" I could hear people asking, "And what ever became of that American woman, Dona Virginia?" And the reply, "Oh, *ela sumiú!*" It was a happy fancy, and comforted me all through the chilly night.

When I stumbled in at the Chacra, bone-weary, I was greeted with the news that we were expecting another visitation from the great world outside: Alfredo de los Ríos, a Chilean-born naturalized American, was coming to Goiás to look for land for his millionaire brother to buy. "Oh, no!" I said to myself. "Not another merry-go-round like the last one. I'll go to that inn, I'll go, I'll go!"

"I hope he doesn't turn into a fiasco like the Argentines," I said aloud, deep in the pessimism of the overtired.

But for once my fears were groundless. Alfredo's unexpected coming was to bring a new turn to the story and happier times in Goiás.

6

THE next evening, clean and rested, I went up to the Bowens' to have a sundown highball before the pleasant wood fire in their comfortable living room and there met Alfredo de los Ríos.

Our visitor's name translated into English meant Alfred of the Rivers but his element, it came out early in our conversation, was the sky. He was one of those bred-in-the-bone fliers who began piloting small planes before instruments had removed so much of the fortuity of flying, and who continue out of the compulsion to seek the release they find only in flight. It was difficult for me to guess Alfredo's age as I studied him that first evening in the firelight. I suppose he must have been in his late forties. His hair was gray, but he obviously had in him that strain of Castilian blood that may silver a man's head even in youth. Even if I had not known he was of pure Spanish descent, his appearance would have told me, for his pleasantly bold nose and firm chin in profile looked like that of Alfonso XII on Spanish coins, a modified version of the Bourbon profile so often seen on the Iberian peninsula. Below middle height, rather chunky, he seemed very much alive, though he was calm and reposed, his face unlined by past stress or present worries.

He told me once later that he felt just as he had when he was twenty and I'm sure it was true.

Since he was naturally modest, it was rather hard to get him started telling us about his exploits. As a young man, he had barnstormed around the United States in a rickety plane taking up the yokels at so much per ride. He worked for New York's Spanish-language press, then went back to flying, representing the manufacturers of small planes, and in a quiet way had made some notable long-distance flights in the tiny planes that he loved. He was the only American citizen who had ever received a private pilot's license in Brazil. The Brazilians gave it to him in sheer astonishment when he dropped out of the sky at Rio one day in the Culver Cadet he had flown from the United States.

A Culver Cadet, I was told, is one of the smallest airplanes made. Powerful for its size, Alfredo's Culver could carry an unusually large quantity of gasoline, enough for eight hours of flight, I believe. According to Alfredo, it could carry "one and a half persons," which meant two small adults. Since Alfredo was no featherweight, the plane was actually overloaded whenever he carried any passenger at all. The Culver needed a longer take-off run than most small planes; its wings were stubby, it was really a baby of a plane that looked unbelievably small on the ground. Even the Brazilian bush pilots, who will fly anything in almost any condition, used to shake their heads in wonderment when they saw it.

After dinner we got Alfredo started telling us tales of his flights and the clouds and the spaces above, and it entertained and diverted me as nothing had for a long time. The first flying that I ever did was in 1941 and 1942 when I spent months in a leisurely flight around South America to do research for my second book. Flying was slower then and the long hours I spent in the clear, sunny air, seeing for the first time the unimaginable beauties of the southern continent's forests, plains and mountains, comprised the first sustained happiness I had ever known in my life. I not only saw another continent, I entered another world and experienced a broadening of the spirit within. It was like acquiring a new faculty. I seemed to learn to understand the concept of eternity; I saw the unimportance of man, the impertinent ant, as he looks from above and yet I realized his fearful might in having dammed great rivers, tunneled the high mountains and built huge cities to change the face of the earth itself. Since then, I had spent a great deal of time in South American skies, always with a certain recall of the original exaltation. Alfredo's tales of his adventures evoked happy images, visions of the grandeur and beauty of the earth when seen from the heavens.

Alfredo's coming altered the tone of our lives at the Chacra. Ever since I had arrived, a fever then running through all Goiás had affected our conversation and our talk had turned on land, land profits, rice profits, corn and hog profits, and of course, the golden opportunity to plant coffee and make big profits from it. Most people in Goiás, regardless of whether they themselves had either capital or land, spent their spare time figuring up on the backs of envelopes how rich they could get in a very short time on rice or land or some business venture.

Almost from the first, this kind of talk had made me unaccountably nervous, and finally I grew to hate it. I hated it because it stirred in me a spirit of competition, made me feel that time was pressing all around me and golden chances dancing just beyond my finger tips. Also, from my own experience with the truck, the store and the pigs, I was beginning to learn a few of the bitter truths underlying the surface promise of the frontier. Its profits were gamblers' profits and the odds were long against you.

Alfredo, entirely uninterested in making money, brushed aside the lures of gain held out to him and would always lead the conversation on to the far places of Goiás, beyond our horizon, beyond the blue mountains. The unknown distances drew him irresistibly, and I began to follow him around like a child, listening to the backland lore he drew out of people, with my own farm project on the River of Ghosts temporarily pushed to the back of my mind.

Far to the northeast, we were told, there lay a fabulous upland, called the Chapada dos Veadeiros, the Deer Hunters'

Plateau, stretching for leagues on top of a sheer wall of cliff that rimmed it and made it accessible only by airplane or muleback. Largely unexplored, this upland contained a great area where pure crystal rock gleamed in geometrical formations in the thin sunlight. Here you might kick against a chunk of semiprecious stone lying right out on top of the ground—the soft jewels, purple amethyst, yellow citrine, brownish-yellow topaz and deep blue aquamarine. In my mind's eye, I could see a world aglitter, white, remote, cold except for the fire the sun might strike from a facet of crystalline rock so clear it scarcely needed polishing.

"Could some of that rock be quartz crystal?" inquired Alfredo of an old man who claimed to have hunted in the area.

"Oh, yes," was the answer. Quartz crystal, produced in commercial quantities only in Brazil, is indispensable in radio, electronics and many other scientific devices without which our Western civilization would be set back a century.

"Are there diamonds there?" I put in, visions of all the treasure troves of the world glittering briefly in my mind's eye.

"Certainly, *dona*, there're diamonds all over that country."

"What about gold?" asked Alfredo, descendant of Spanish conquistadores who plundered the New World for its yellow metal.

"Oh, yes, there's probably gold up there too."

Reports of the wondrous upland intrigued me, but Alfredo was far more interested in the almost completely unknown parts of Brazil which lay not far away to the northwest. This region is marked "Unexplored" on honest Brazilian maps even today, for it is the land of the savage Chavantes, who have resisted all efforts to conquer or woo them for scores of years. Once there was incessant warfare between them and the daring small parties of Brazilians attempting to get into their lands. For a long time now, the Brazilian government has forbidden the use of force against them and has been trying to win them over. Till lately, the best the Indian agents could do was to maintain an outpost near the edge of Chavante territory and leave good-will gifts for the Indians—clothes, tools and trinkets.

(The Brazilians, who like to tell jokes on themselves, say the Chavantes are quite choosy and bend the gift machetes double to test them, with the result that the ignorant savages are armed with only the finest imported steel blades. The Brazilian-made machetes they usually leave broken behind them.)

The Indian Service had an outpost on the Island of Bananal which he could visit, Alfredo was told. Bananal is a river island, a big one lying between two branches of the Araguáia, and the Chavante territory begins just across the west branch.

"On Bananal, S'hor Alfredo, all you have to do is walk a few yards out into the forest and you see all sorts of animals," a bush pilot told us. "There are black jaguars over there, lots of them, and in the Araguáia River that runs by the island, there's a big fish that saves men's lives when they fall into the water."

"What do you mean, is it a *nego de agua?*" Only the day before we had heard tales of this legendary inhabitant of Goiás rivers, a mysterious something shaped like a man. It is my theory that the name is a corruption of *negro de agua,* "black man of the water" in old Portuguese, and may be a species of manatee such as grows in the Amazon river system.

"No, *senhor!* It's a big fish, but it pushes its food out of the water to eat it and if you fall in, it'll push you out too."

"That's a tall tale," I said. Afterwards I learned of the sea legend that the dolphin will push a drowning man out of the water—and there are river dolphins in the tributaries of the Amazon.

"*Ai, tem muitas coisas lá, além do Roncador, além do Vão do Sono,*" said the Brazilian. Yes, there are many strange things over there, beyond the Snoring Mountain, beyond the Vale of Sleep. . . .

This was more than Alfredo could resist; he began to plan a trip to this outpost back of the beyond. I, too, longed to penetrate its mysteries, needless to say.

Along with his adventurous spirit, Alfredo had the rare

ability to savor the small things of the day, I soon learned. He was sleeping at the Bowens' and used to get up very early; one morning I came up the path from Liberty Hall to find him standing out in the Bowens' front yard gazing up into the leafy trees that shaded the house.

"Sh-h-h," he warned. "The little monkeys . . ."

I peered nearsightedly up into the foliage.

"Where?" I whispered.

Finally he spotted them for me, a pert family of the most amazing small monkeys, who were putting on a circus in the treetops out of sheer joy of life. We watched for a while and their silly gaiety came over to us to make us lighter in spirit, gayer too.

"You know, Alfredo," I said, as we went in to breakfast, "I've been here for months now and you're the first person who has paid any attention to those monkeys in the trees. And we've had some big brains visiting here."

"You're all missing the point of Goiás," answered Alfredo gently. "Why is everybody in such a rush?"

"Well, it's sort of hard to explain. There's so much to be done and it's so difficult to *get* anything done."

"But what do you get out of it?" asked Alfredo. "You could rush and worry yourself into a nervous breakdown in New York City."

(And for more pay, I thought to myself.)

Alfredo's serene presence slowed down all our lives somewhat. Joan, full of nervous energy and worried about the business, used to rush us off to town after breakfast. "Come on, Ginny, the Captain's ready to go. Come on, Alfredo, we're leaving. . . ." Alfredo, who always politely waited to be last in the bathroom, began to appear to lag behind, and the Captain and I watched with some amusement the little byplay as Joan attempted tactfully to speed him up. Finally one morning she dealt briskly and openly with the situation as Alfredo went into the bathroom.

"We're leaving in fifteen minutes, Alfredo," she announced cheerily.

"Joan, I can't be ready," answered Alfredo calmly, wielding that tremendous weapon, the firm and unanswerable refusal. We did not leave in Joan's fifteen minutes and the tempo of our breakfast bustle slowed down somewhat thereafter.

Alfredo also turned my thoughts back toward writing again. As he made ready to fly over to the outpost on the big river island of Bananal, we heard over the grapevine that the Indian Service was about to succeed in the attempt to establish friendly contacts with the Chavante Indians after decades of peace overtures. We both thought there might be a magazine story in it. Alfredo proposed to investigate the possibility on his first trip there and suggested that we coauthor the article.

Joan, the Captain and I went out to see Alfredo off at the flying field on the morning he took flight for the Mato Grosso. He had filled two used gasoline cans with aviation gas bought from the bush pilots, and had soldered caps back on the cans; he now put them in the seat beside him. I was somewhat worried to notice that one of the caps was leaking, but Alfredo, though he was smoking a cigarette, did not seem to attach any importance to it. Joan, who had flown with him several times, was anxious for me to have the pleasure and kept wishing that I could go along on this trip.

I had never been afraid in a big plane, no matter how rough the weather, and fully expected to enjoy flying in the little one. But something inside me said "No!" to the idea as strongly as if I were being urged to walk over a land mine. I was greatly relieved when Alfredo decided it would be too risky to take me on this first trip.

The day after Alfredo left, I rounded up Waldemar and loaded the Plymouth and struck out for the north, conscience-stricken about having been so long away from the farm. As Waldemar and I drove in over the forest trail holding our breaths as usual for fear of the fatal snap in the old Plymouth's underworks, we met Rodrigues, one of the men I'd hired to help Claudinho and Ezequiel. To my dismay, Rodrigues said that José had chased him away from the camp after he had been there one day.

I paid Rodrigues what I owed him and went on to the work camp, dreading what I might find there. With Manoel always ready to be nasty and José turned bully, the situation could easily get out of hand. José, younger than Manoel, less intelligent, his energies and ideas not channeled for good or ill in any one direction, was like a package of explosives and I knew I'd have to handle him with care.

In camp, I first of all gathered the families around and divided out the supplies. I showed them a lard substitute I had brought from Anápolis, hoping it could replace the hard-to-get hog fat, but none appeared even mildly interested except Chico and Manoel.

I asked Emílio if he'd like to try it.

"Dona Virginia, it just seems like my food wouldn't taste right without hog fat," he answered after a long moment of soul pondering.

"This lard is a great deal better for the *fígado*," I said, playing my trump card. The *fígado* is the liver, to which all South Americans, backlanders included, attribute many of the vague ills that come to them as a result of eating too much pasty food or from bad diet in general. It is their endemic complaint, like "nerves" among Americans.

"I'll try a can," said Manoel.

"And you will too, won't you, Chico," I asked.

He was too polite to refuse.

I turned to José. "José, you're forward-looking—why don't you try one too? It can't do you any harm." I wanted to draw a little circle and take him in before I broached the subject of his troublemaking.

José, expecting a call-down, for he'd actually threatened to brain Rodrigues with a rock, had been sullenly silent till now. He brightened up.

"All right, *senhora!*"

I distributed the cans of lard and we put down the charges in our respective books, Chico officiating as recorder.

I called José aside. "You know, José, there's a lot of work to be done up here, and I want it done on time so you men can have a good year," I said, determined to prevail through reason. "But how are we going to manage if you run off the workmen I send in here to help you catch up?"

José flared up defensively.

"Dona Virginia, that Rodrigues, he had *pinga* here, and didn't you say there wasn't to be any drinking in camp? That Rodrigues is no good, he was already beginning to fool around with the women! Ask the others, ask them!"

"I came to you first. I don't like to go behind people's backs. But look, José, how are we going to get this work done, even if you were right?"

"That boy that came with Rodrigues, he says he'll stay on and finish out Rodrigues's work. He'll tell you I did right, too!"

This was a great relief, since it freed me from having to scour the country for another man, who might turn out to be as bad as Rodrigues.

"I tell you what, I'll speak to Chico if you want me to. But answer me this. Haven't I always tried to do the right thing by you?"

José cast down his eyes, like a child called to account by teacher.

"I guess so, *senhora*."

The *roçeiros*, at the bottom of a terrible pyramid, think and speak much of "the right thing," "the right way," for the moral law is virtually the only law they can ever invoke to protect them. Many times they use the adjective *"direito,"* right or straight, as we would use "good." *"É um homem direito"* means "He's a good man." *"Está direito,"* they often say when we would say "all right" or "very well" to indicate assent.

"Well, I always try to be *direita*," I continued. "And I want you to promise me one thing: don't pick up any rocks in this camp to hit people with. If there's trouble, I'll see that it gets straightened out myself. Will you promise?"

José smiled now, again like a child, one who has been let off an expected punishment.

"All right, Dona Virginia, but you be sure to ask Chico, because I *was* in the right."

We went back to the little circle waiting under the trees. I told them all good-by, one by one, with the ceremonial handshake in which their horny fingers always seemed cold and limp. When I got to Chico, I asked him in a low voice:

"Did Rodrigues have *pinga* here?"

"Yes, *senhora*."

I turned to the group.

"None of us wants *pinga* drinking here, but José has promised me there'll be no more talk about bashing in heads with rocks. José agrees that we'll settle our problems another way. Isn't that the right thing to do?"

There was a murmured assent and I took my leave, hoping that my efforts to spread sweet reason would stick. When they ferried me over the river to where Waldemar was waiting with the Plymouth, I told him about the incident and said I hoped I could keep the camp peaceful till they burned over the clearing and each separated to his own plot of ground.

Waldemar said someday one of them would turn on me. "You don't know these people like I do, *dona*," he warned me. "You oughtn't to go over there to that camp all by yourself. That José's a bad actor—he'll pick up a rock and hit you with it if something doesn't suit him. You better let me talk to those men with a gun on my hip. Then you'll have no more trouble there."

This was the backland pattern, the old pattern of the *jagunço*, the gunman enforcer.

"I don't think I could do that, Waldemar," I said. "I'm not afraid of them. I'm afraid they'll fight among themselves, if anything; I want the camp to hold together till the trees are cut." But it was unpleasant.

It was late when we got to Ceres, and I decided to stay overnight with the Sayãos. When we got back to the Chacra, I had been gone for two days.

"Alfredo's missing," Joan greeted me as I walked in.

"Alfredo who?" I said stupidly; the idea that it could be

the Intrepid Aviator was so preposterous that it bounced off my mind. I couldn't take it in.

"Alfredo de los Ríos, of course," she said, somewhat shocked at what she mistook for lack of feeling in me. "And Santinho had a dream, he saw Alfredo's face hidden in a cloud of smoke."

"He's only a day overdue," I objected, still refusing to entertain the thought. "He'll be in tomorrow."

But Alfredo did not come the next day as I had predicted. We became seriously alarmed. Captain Bowen went to Goiânia to see our friend the governor, Gerónimo Coimbra Bueno, who hastened to lend him an official plane and pilot to take him to the island outpost in search of Alfredo.

The Captain's flight really worried me, for I had far less confidence in the borrowed pilot than in Alfredo. Old Vitalina, the Bowens' Indian cook, was full of dire forebodings about these multiple flights; the voices of doom were all about us, the bright sunlight a mockery as we waited anxiously for news from the two men. The spirit of the backlands is catching. The day the Captain left for Goiânia, I was sure I heard the little Culver Cadet circling the town in the dusk. I even went out to the airport to meet Alfredo. At the field, I was told no plane had flown over and none afterwards came in. I don't know how I made the mistake and I kept the weird incident to myself, fearing to add to the superstitious uneasiness about us.

On the second day after the Captain left, he and Alfredo popped cheerfully out of the sky in the little plane. The Captain had just missed Alfredo at Bananal, but they met at Goiânia and came home together.

Alfredo, on first arriving at the wilderness outpost, had found himself involved in an epoch-making event, and he had simply and quite understandably stayed to enjoy it. This was one of the rare peaceful meetings between the Indian Service men and representatives of the Chavante Indians, actually a preliminary meeting that was to pave the way for a really spectacular ceremony sometime later marking the "pacification" of the Chavantes. Alfredo had made fast friends with the Brazilian authorities and had gotten permission for us to take exclusive photographs and write the story for American magazines. He had arranged to take the Chavante chief up in his plane, he said, and I privately wondered what would happen to us on the ground if they didn't get safely back. The history of Brazil is dotted with Chavante "pacification" ceremonies that ended up in a massacre of the "pacifiers."

Out of experience in magazine writing, I insisted that we should try to get a fairly firm commitment for the piece. In no time at all, Alfredo and I had ideas for a whole series of adventure articles. Alfredo had taken photographs for publication and he had an excellent camera. We planned to write together and sign with a double by-line.

When we discussed working together on these additional article ideas, I discovered that, in Alfredo's mind, the series had expanded from Bananal and Goiás to all Brazil and indeed, all South America. He had a yen to fly into the unknown part of Colombia, the land of El Dorado, the Golden Man, and of gold and emeralds and head-hunters. Like me, he had always been fascinated by the lost worlds that exist in the hinterland of Venezuela on that country's tremendous tablelands. There were a dozen places on the great continent filled with mystery and romance for each of us; eagerly we made tentative lists of them.

The plans snowballed and almost before I realized it, we had decided to go to the United States for article assignments. Alfredo suggested that, for effect, we fly home in the Culver, get a larger plane to ferry back, then try for a time record between Miami and Rio and São Paulo. I had heard nothing from the International Refugee Organization about the job they had offered me when Susana was in Goiás, so I felt free to go.

Planning for this new adventure into the unknown now occupied my thoughts to the exclusion of everything else. The work at the farm was organized and I felt sure I could get someone at Anápolis to look after it till the harvest, almost a year away. I had realized the farm could not give me immediately the happiness I had expected of it; its development would be a long, slow process, beset by hardship. The farm lapsed into unimportance, the inn by the river was forgotten, the sparkling river no longer called me. A larger and a farther beyond was beckoning; it would take me from my disappointments and difficulties, and I welcomed the prospect of the new escape.

7

ONCE I had agreed to the new venture and allowed the worries of Goiás to lapse into unimportance, I enjoyed an interlude of quiet preparation like the one that had preceded my move to Brazil.

Not long after his return from the island of Bananal, Alfredo had the mechanics at the airfield start taking down the motor of his plane to install new pistons. Each day I drove him out to the field in the station wagon so that he could supervise the work. I usually took along my travel-battered portable typewriter and worked also, writing letters to the States paving the way for our return there. The Brazilian Air Force sergeant attached to the field very kindly let me set up my typewriter on a gasoline box on the unused side porch of his bungalow.

During the long hours that I spent working at a leisurely tempo at the lonely backland airport, life slowed down. Finally there came moments in the sunny day as still and vivid, and as deep and soft-wrapped around me as long-forgotten afternoons of childhood in Tennessee when a strong June sun had brought out the pungency of the clover in the pastures and the restless, angry winds of my home country were for a season quiet. In the blaze of noon, pools of heat quivering over the red earth of Goiás had the same mesmeric effect on my becalmed senses as the remembered shimmers over the deep green of the clover fields. Sometimes the changing drone of one of the field's small air-taxi planes as the pilot gunned his motor for a take-off evoked the patterned rising and falling hum of the big bumblebees in the Tennessee clover.

Often Alfredo and I would return to the Chacra in the early afternoon to go for a walk over the rolling countryside beyond the Bowens' home. I have always been a walker and I enjoyed this very much. I also shared with Alfredo an enjoyment that I had had before only with my long-dead father and with Bill Mizelle—the sport of target shooting.

Alfredo had a good target pistol, a .22 Hi-Standard, built on a .45 frame, like one Bill had had. I had my .25 Walthers (the golden gun) and a new .38 Colt Police Positive. This revolver, really too heavy for my hand, was stiff with newness and its ammunition was very expensive, so we usually shot the .22. I had practiced a good deal with Bill in Argentina and was a somewhat better shot than Alfredo. Bill, a modern man in the good sense, had always been proud of my skill and had coached me in ways to improve, but with Alfredo I soon observed that it was best not to shoot too well. He seemed to retire from the game if I appeared to get ahead, and I made a point of not doing so, though it took some of the fun out of the sport to have to be so careful about my shooting partner's ego. It was a curious minor echo of the Latin's deeply ingrained conviction that he must always shine in comparison with a woman, an attitude that Alfredo on the whole seemed to have grown beyond.

After the day Alfredo called attention to the antics of the tiny monkeys in the trees at the Chacra, we always watched for them. One morning I ventured to tell him how much it had meant to me to recapture with Bill in Argentina something else lost since childhood, this habit of enjoying the little things going on around me. Bill had always called attention to a cavorting puppy on the street or a baby asleep in a carriage and he would pause to speak to the big fat self-satisfied cats that live in downtown Buenos Aires (they always spoke politely back). Often when I met him for lunch distressed and indignant over some event in the political battle then raging, he'd take me to the Plaza de Mayo to calm down by watching the silly pigeons strut around. It always helped restore my perspective to see the absurd love dances the little males performed, puffing out their shiny feathers to impress the utterly indifferent females, as if bowing from the waist out of a weary sense of social obligation. I learned that much of the strain could be taken out of the day by a moment's pause here and there, to feel quiet amusement at the pigeons, to note once again how tranquilly the small clouds always moved in the exquisite pale blue of Argentine skies. It was a wider sweep for the mind's eye, a multiplication of life.

And now as Alfredo and I roamed in the still sunshine over the old pastures and the scrubland back of the Bowens' home, he joined me in keeping a keen watch for birds and rabbits and the small game of the countryside. There was surprisingly little of it, but there were plenty of enormous ants busy cutting up leaves and transporting cyclopean burdens to their tall earth mounds. Watching the ants, we discussed what would happen to any real sluggard who followed the Biblical admonition to observe and copy them, and we agreed he'd probably go home and take to his bed in an access of *paixão*, like the man frightened by the jaguar.

On our walks we also used to pass the earth-floored, earth-plastered huts of the backlanders who live in that region, an ingrown people descended from the Portuguese and the Dutch who first explored Goiás. Their poor little dirty towheaded children, bellies ballooning, gaped at us blankly. We never saw them at play and never could get a smile or response out of them. The mothers, dirty, overworked, nearly always pregnant, gap-toothed, usually goiter-swollen at the neck, would pause in their primitive, slow-motion housekeeping and pass the time of day with us, polite, impassive, withdrawn.

The country around the Chacra began to seem less hostile than it had when I first attempted to make friends with it by myself. But I never felt that it welcomed us.

My new companion, fast becoming my friend, was extremely easy to talk to, especially about matters you'd never dream of mentioning. I have noticed that most people in our action-loving civilization do not like to turn a subject over and over, but shy away from the process as "philosophizing" or "digging in too much." With Alfredo, however, I never felt I was risking making myself a bore no matter what I might get strung out talking about. You could even mention Heaven without feeling guilty of indelicate exposure.

One night when we were on our way back from an after-supper walk in the bright Goiás moonlight, I told him how I had been curiously certain he was not lost on the Bananal flight, had in fact been so obviously unworried about him that Joan almost lost patience with me for it. I said I so associated him with flying, which in my mind meant soaring above the earth into sunlight and clear skies, that I couldn't imagine a somber thing like death happening to him.

"It's odd you should say that," he replied after a moment's musing. "I used to be afraid lots of times, but I'm not any more. When I was on the way down from the States, I got lost in a thunderstorm over the lower Amazon Valley and flew a long time without really knowing where I was. There had to be a big river somewhere in the direction I was headed, and I knew I could follow it and find the seacoast and a town with an airport. As my gas went lower, I thought, 'Well, I guess this is it, but it's all right.' It seems strange to me even now, but I smiled and felt almost happy."

We were following a wagon track over the brow of a hill and there in the valley below us we saw the black shadow of the Bowens' house with its guardian stand of trees. Bright kerosene lamps within the living room sent sparkling pinpoints of light through chinks in the handmade tiles of the roof. It looked from where we were as if stars had fallen down on the house.

"I haven't even thought about death in years, until lately," I said, watching the sparkles of light. "I used to think about it vaguely some years ago when I was trying to pull myself together and get out of an unhappy marriage. But it wasn't really dying I thought about. I just wished I could dissolve, so I wouldn't have to make the big effort to untangle my life."

"Sometimes you don't get over things like that," said Alfredo.

"Oh, I did, completely. It's as if it had happened to another person."

"That's fortunate. . . . But then, you're a strong person."

I never liked to be told this, because it usually meant that somebody was about to dump a load on me far beyond my strength to bear.

"I'm no iron woman, Alfredo," I said. "And I've had bad things happen to me, just as most people have. My parents were divorced while I was growing up, then they both died and I had to support myself. I've been short of money and I've been sick when I was all alone and I've made mistakes. . . . It all hurt, plenty. But you have to strike an average. I've also had lots of good times, wonderful friends, a chance to develop, maybe more love than I deserved, as much 'success' as I wanted. . . . I've just had one disappointment that was not a selfish one offset by good things. That was over the fight against Perón in Argentina."

I had not talked about Argentina for a long time; emotion always arose in me when I did and then I talked too much, too vehemently. Here, with a companion of quiet mind, suddenly I wanted to tell it over, to recapitulate, and I briefly did.

"Once you've been through an experience like that," I said, "your personal troubles simply fade into unimportance."

"You probably took it harder because this one issue came to mean a sort of compensation for what you call 'personal disappointments'," offered Alfredo.

"It was a lot simpler than that," I answered. "In Argentina you couldn't think about yourself when you saw a whole people using such courage against a vicious dictator. The whole world was fighting over the same thing, but the Argentines were doing it absolutely alone. Nobody was dropping them radio sets and guns. And what they were trying to get is just about what I was born to, just by being born in the United States. Why shouldn't they have it—is there so much difference between them and us? I don't think so."

"Why do you think the men in Washington changed around as they did?" Alfredo asked.

"I think there were several sets of people involved, with several sets of motives. The big excuse was, we had to have 'Hemisphere solidarity' in the face of Russia. Yet saving the enemy's neck in this part of the world couldn't possibly help us against one somewhere else. The thing about the press corps was the last straw—maybe the rest of the correspondents were all just as disgusted as I was, but reacted differently. It was enough to make anybody want to take to the tall timber."

I was thinking of the dilemma of the men managing the American news services in Buenos Aires. Their operations depended not only on sending news to the United States, but on earnings from contracts to deliver news to the Argentine papers, and they were continually harassed in this by the government. I was sure they'd received instructions to "keep the bureau open" which meant trying to get along with Perón, something possible only if you tried to please him. Now I wondered whether some of the special or staff newspaper correspondents who came last might not have been told to "keep the bureau open" also.

"The worst thing was almost having to fight my own side, the correspondents, there at the last," I added.

Alfredo appeared to be turning it all over in his mind. "Do you know the Gita?" he asked after a while.

I had to shake my thoughts loose from Argentina and cast around for a moment to understand what he meant.

"You mean the Bhagavad Gita? I've read it, but I don't recall too much about it."

"It's worth rereading. I have the book, let's go get it."

"Fine," I said. "I'd be glad to get my mind off the whole stupid business. I've had too many Argentines ask me questions about it that hurt."

We detoured by the Chacra long enough for Alfredo to fish the slender volume out of his baggage. When we arrived at Liberty Hall, Guiomar and her beautiful three-year-old woods-colt baby were both asleep in the little bedroom where I had stayed while Susana and Perla and Roger were with us. The woman roused up and replenished the fire in my living room and prepared coffee for us. We settled down to read the Gita by the harsh white light of an Aladdin lamp. I knew that Alfredo meant to develop some thought out of it pertinent to my Argentine experience and I let him bring it out in his own way. He suggested we take turns reading aloud the ancient Hindu scripture.

As the story opens, two great families, nobles and kinsmen, are drawn up against each other to do battle, five worthy princes arrayed against a hundred who are seeking to usurp their rightful power. Arjuna, chief of the five, orders his charioteer to drive him along between the two armies, so that he may look them over before giving the signal for his men to attack. What he sees chills his soul, for to gain victory he must slay many kinsmen and old friends.

Arjuna's charioteer is an incarnation of the Lord Krishna and to him the perplexed leader now turns for guidance. Should he give the signal for battle or renounce it and retire to the forest to lead the peaceful life of a hermit?

Krishna bids Arjuna stand up for battle; Arjuna's hesitation comes from egotism, he says, for the Lord is the Doer and man only the instrument. Arjuna must follow the path cut out for him and fulfill his nature, which is to fight.

The troubled prince asks what is to be gained if in winning he destroy kinsmen and old friends.

"Having spoken thus . . ." runs the parable, "Arjuna, scorcher of foes, said to Him, 'I will not fight' and fell silent." I could see why Alfredo thought of reminding me of the story.

Arjuna must fight, says the Lord Krishna, representative of the Divine. It is his place to fight, no matter who may be slain nor how the battle end: for the wise grieve not . . . the wise grieve neither for the living nor the dead.

Here we paused. There was no need to labor the point. It was clear enough.

"You think I should go on with my work and not 'take it all so seriously'?" I said. "I've been told that before, but somebody *has* to care about every important thing that happens anywhere and to know about it. How do you think a correspondent can do a job, day and night for years, always under pressure, always struggling for clear facts, for his own perspective, unless his heart is in it? It was the deliberate policy of Perón to confuse everything, always to make the worse appear the better part and it would have been only too easy to follow his lead. But those were *people* I was writing about—not chess pawns or a set of census figures. I had to care enough to work hard enough to keep the story coming out the way it was happening, and to resist the pressure."

Alfredo made a little gesture as if to grant me that.

"But in the end, you took it all so seriously you had to quit, didn't you?"

I considered this and the moments ticked on. The fire crackled, quiet reigned. Grieve not for the living or the dead. . . . I thought about my friends, especially the ones who had been tortured by the Argentine Gestapo. I thought about one man who kept on long after most resistance had gone far underground, remembering his fine eyes, his clear brow— and how he was imprisoned and beaten and tortured.

I shook my head.

"No, Alfredo, your Gita's not for me. Since 1943, I must have written half a million words for American newspapers about it all—and that's 'fight' enough, I think."

"Well, if you ever want to go back to political reporting while we're on our trips, it'll be all right with me."

"Let's not change anything," I said firmly. "I want to write about beautiful places and happy people—if we can find them."

This was the first of a number of long talks that Alfredo and I had on our rambles. He gradually told me, in outline at least, the main adventures he had had, flying exploits, disappointments over women, and excursions into the realm that I can only call the semimiraculous. Alfredo had been brought back from death's door once by a Mexican witch doctor, and this impressed him far more than any achievement of modern science. Self-exiled from his native environment and religion, he apparently had won what I have called his "serene manner" through a conscious effort to adapt himself to Oriental beliefs turning on denial of emotion and sensation. When he gently attempted to proselyte me, I tossed Christian theology or Biblical quotations at him, as a minister's child always will in these discussions, and observed that it shook him. Rather ruefully, I wrote to Bill that Alfredo was trying to lift me into a higher plane, but that it might work out the other way: I, who loved the earth so well, might pull him back to terra firma.

Just at this stage of my idyl of friendship with the Lone Flyer, I got a letter from Bill in answer to one of mine telling about the new project, and it brought me up short. Not long after Alfredo's return from Bananal, I had written to my sisters Mildred and Frances at home and to Bill a long account of my plans to fly with Alfredo, saying I knew it was risky and we might fall into the sea or something, but that I was perfectly happy about it and they weren't to worry. My sisters had ceased by now to wonder at any new venture of mine. But from Bill came another kind of reply.

This letter of his began with vivid word pictures of the life around him, as usual. But toward the end, in commenting on the new adventure, he said he doubted if he'd find anyone else to fit into such a life as we used to have. He wished me luck and happiness with Alfredo. "As for me," he wrote, "I am spoiled for the kind of woman of which there is only one." It was his first comment on our parting.

Though I had always presented Alfredo in my letters as a man about whom I could never feel romantic, it was obvious that Bill believed I was falling in love with him.

I had to consider the thought. Any companionship between a man and a woman where so much sympathy exists is a potential courtship—who would deny it? But I was not the one for Alfredo, of that I was sure from the first moment I seriously considered the idea. The truth was that from my years of living among the Latins, to whom I am temperamentally close in many ways, I understood him far too well.

Alfredo, sensitive and intelligent, had been born into an older order of the Latin civilization, a society in which the one true, pure love of a man's life is always for his mother. The wife is selected as an ornament to the family and as a mother for the next generation, and no fidelity is owed her. This is supposed to have something to do with the "more passionate" nature of the Latin male, but I believe there is another underlying cause: the centuries-old system of using marriage as a ladder up which a young man climbs to better himself economically or socially or as a means through which families bring or hold fortunes together. Ruled by the tradition that a man may, or must, chase any number of women just so long as mama and papa approve of his wife, the Latin man finds it hard ever to combine sacred and profane love for one woman. Custom and youth fire the *latino's* first licenses, and then he gets caught in a vicious spiral. The split between the spiritual and the carnal is so profound within him, he is seldom able to reconcile them, though as he matures he may feel a deep dissatisfaction with this part of his life. The result is a truly compulsive and rather pathetic woman-chasing, in search of an assuagement he can never find.

Alfredo, impelled by the tradition and his own youth to keep busy with more vivid women during the years when he might have found the Madonna-bride his soul now longed for, had come to fear he had missed love altogether. In our talks in the moonlight his musings on this part of his life ran as far back as the innocent girl of sixteen whom he had seen only twice on visits home to Chile; it might have been she, if he had only lingered to find out, his trend of reminiscence implied.

No, I was not falling in love with Alfredo, for I wanted nothing to do with men whose emotions had been tangled

and scrambled before I ever saw them, whether by old traditions, their parents or other women (or by the war or by
having been spanked too hard by the doctor when they were
born). The unforgettable phrase in Bill's letter pulled me back
toward him, as it could not fail to; its suggestion of exclusive
fidelity was imperatively appealing to my nature. But even if
the image of a younger man of my own country—a man full
of health and promise and blessedly balanced within himself—
had not been there to make it more difficult, I'm sure that I
would never have wanted anything from Alfredo except the
affection of a friend. I wrote to Bill at once and told him that
I was making no new ties.

The fact is that the overtones of finality in my "farewell"
letters had a completely different origin. I expressed it ex-
plicitly in those letters, which still exist; I had come to believe
that at some time on the flying adventure with Alfredo I
would be killed.

I did not have any particular notion about when or how
it would happen, except that I had the feeling it would involve Alfredo's plane. It was a very logical possibility, for the
ship was small and the forests and mountains and plains we
proposed to fly over were vast and wild. It was a new feeling
for me; I had never before thought about getting killed at
all, even when doing stunts just as risky. I had walked around
the streets of Mexico City and Buenos Aires while gunfire was
going on and ventured with a strange guide through the dark
alleys and gullies of Asunción, Paraguay, to get the story of
the anti-Morínigo maquis' fight against the dictator there.
These were certainly exploits hazardous enough to make anybody renew his life insurance. The thought of death that I
had now in Goiás was unaccompanied by fear or dread; I
simply recognized it would be there, awaiting its chance. I
went so far as to ask my sister Mildred (who writes for *The
New Yorker* and other publications as Bowen Ingram) to
make engagements for me at home with a small number of
people to whom I wanted to express thanks, or regrets, before it was all over.

It may be that the false alarm over Alfredo when he was overdue on the Bananal flight was the start of it all. Or perhaps it began even before that, when the backlands ate into me to the point that I grabbed my gun, ready to use it, the day the trucker almost ran us over the side of the road into the chasm. I dreamed afterward of an actual killing, as I have said. It is not so far, perhaps, from dreams of dealing out death to thoughts of dying.

However that may be, I was happier now than I had been for some time, in spite of the curious dark cloud that I now recognized in the prospect of my gay gypsy flying life with Alfredo. I was almost as happy as I had been during the last months in Argentina when I was planning to come to Goiás, another period when my past had been put behind me and an untried future was still ahead.

8

IF ALFREDO and I could have continued our pleasant companionship till we started flying and writing together, I probably would have gone through with our plan without hesitation. But as soon as his ship's new pistons had been broken in, he told me he intended to go to São Paulo to try to get a larger plane for our exploring-writing venture, and I waved him off at the airfield.

For a week or more, I lived quietly at Liberty Hall with Guiomar, my star-crossed fading backland beauty, and her pretty little fatherless baby girl, accidental embodiment of the star dust that had beclouded Guiomar's good name.

Guiomar was a sturdy woman of the *roça*, used to the heavy toil of the clearings. I paid her well, so theoretically she was better off doing my light housekeeping tasks than ever before in her life. Maybe she had too little work to keep her interested or perhaps she missed living close to other human beings as the poor live in their crowded huts even in the most lonely places. Anyhow, now when I turned my attention to it, I found that Guiomar spent most of the day woolgathering around the house. When I went into the kitchen to ask her as gently as possible about some neglected detail, she would clap a hand to her brow and exclaim dramatically, "*Aii, Dona Virginia, ó!* I think there's something wrong with my head!" Then she'd tune up to cry while her three-year-old stared big-eyed at me from among the pots and pans on a low ledge by the tile stove where she perched to keep out of the way.

Guiomar's tears irritated me almost beyond endurance, but the child's gaze made it mandatory for me not to show it.

To "*chorar*," literally, to "weep," which means enlarging volubly on your troubles to defend a failure, is the technique used by many Brazilians to meet difficulties in their "non-materialistic" civilization, and it is one hard to resist unless you can turn it off with a heart of stone or "cry" back, as they do among themselves. Guiomar simply carried the tactic of defensive self-pity one step further than the rest and really wept. She never improved her work one whit and I dared not fire her, for I truly felt sorry for her and dreaded the scene it would cause. Gradually I quit saying anything to her at all, to keep from having to hate her when she browbeat me with her tears.

In spite of the minor emotional crises that took place in the kitchen until at last I let Guiomar have her own way, I enjoyed a degree of real peace in these days. The old charm of Goiás began to creep back over me as it had never failed to in interludes of calm. In a letter to Bill I described a moment in the early evening when I walked the few hundred yards from the Bowens' house to my home. I was always glad when I could record a compensating experience, for often I had written him about my accidents and disappointments.

"There was the moon, just out of its shell, looking down on me in my little hollow between the hills," I wrote. "Over to the right there was a big bank of clouds. Venus, which shines so bright here you often mistake her for an automobile light on the horizon, began playing hide and seek. She would peep out one minute, then back again. The cloud bank didn't seem to be moving, but it must have been.

"Higher in the sky, above a hilltop, old Mars had his wattles red. All the other stars were timid still, since it was early and in the half-light. Somewhere over behind the place, on one of the mysterious wagon roads that lace the country, an oxcart with singing wheels was traveling along, sending its melody over.

"Just across the valley, one of the tenants was baking bricks or making pottery. The red glow of the flame sent up its particular fervor of color. You could hear the earth breathe."

It was a moment of truce, when the harshness of life in Goiás did not overshadow the country's loveliness.

I continued to eat supper with the Bowens each day; otherwise I could not have stood the loneliness, which the lachrymose Guiomar did nothing to relieve. About this time Eric Seddon, an English friend who had visited us, sent me a whole case of a new kind of liquor that I liked very much. It was called Menelik's Rum, and it must have been made out of sugar cane, though it was unlike any other drink known on land or sea. It was dark and thin like sloe gin and flavored by a medicinal herb very faintly reminiscent of both ginger and cinnamon. It was strong; I once made a cold fire blaze up by throwing half a glassful over logs in the fireplace and tossing a lighted match among them.

It was the only medicine that ever worked for me against the night emptiness of Goiás. To be alone and cold sober in that geologically ancient part of the world after the dark had doused its warmth and rich colors was to foretaste the chill indrawing of the blood that the first man ever marooned on the moon will know. A good stiff nightcap of the Menelik's also gave power over both the future and the past. For a brief half hour while I bathed in my enormous tin basin by the rosy light of the big wood fire, the worst difficulties of my life would unreel through my mind as the most wonderful adventures anybody had ever lived. And when I plumped into bed, to watch the firelight shadow-dancing on my white walls for a few last delicious moments before sliding into a bottomless sleep, I was sure I would write again; the very next day I would start putting down all the marvelous things I had learned about the world.

The Menelik's also could cushion shock. Once on my way home, while caught up in a rum-inspired moment of moon worship, I wandered briefly off the usual path to perform a minor necessity and without noticing it paused in an ant bed. These brutes, in surprise and alarm, swarmed up into my clothes, as I discovered a moment later. I popped into my room and met the crisis calmly, although it would have sent me into a shuddering panic if I had not been well fortified by the Menelik's. I simply stripped off everything I had on, shirt, slacks, panties, shoes, socks and head scarf, and plunged them deep into the big can of hot bath water awaiting me by the fireplace. The next day I got a bit of my own back on Guiomar by saying nothing at all to explain this odd behavior, although she came out of her haze long enough to wonder why all the clothes and dead ants turned up in the bath water.

The strange drink, which I was never able to buy either in Goiás or the coast cities, did not make me giddy as alcohol usually does, and never gave me a headache. It was a pity the solace of it was denied me at all times except when I was alone with the Bowens at the Chacra. A foreign woman might wear pants and pack a gun or even accept a polite "Es-scotch" at a formal party. But if anybody ever saw me drinking straight rum, I would lose face enormously. This I could not risk, since the respect I could impose by my own behavior was my main protection in the back country.

About ten days after Alfredo set sail, he wrote he had "arranged" for a bigger plane, a four-seater Luscombe, for us to ferry from the United States. He had agreed to try to fly from Miami to São Paulo in four days, thereby breaking the small-plane record for the flight. My future, in Alfredo's hands, was expanding: it would be the first time a woman had ever made this flight in a small private plane.

Set down on paper, this somehow failed to thrill me as had our talks about exploring the mysterious places of South America like the remote Venezuelan highland where they say gold nuggets and emeralds lie out on top of the ground. I had no clear idea what Alfredo's commitment meant in terms of effort and risk.

Alfredo wrote of other plans that I could understand and they appalled me. He blithely proposed to submit, on speculation: (1) articles in English for American newspapers, (2) the same in Spanish for South American papers, (3) articles for general magazines, (4) articles for aviation magazines, and (5) material for an aviation guide. I had flown around Latin America as a writer at least three times, stopping over in each country, and I knew it would take the full time of one of us even to keep a good series of newspaper stories moving steadily out. I could see very plainly that Alfredo's program would grind me to a frazzle.

These doubts nibbled at my hard-won interlude of pleasant calm, so I folded the letter away and put it out of my mind for the time being. I sent supplies to the farm and heard that the men were working steadily and well. Things were going along so nicely that I ventured to accept an invitation to go to the Sayãos' in Ceres on a pleasure visit, something I had not as yet indulged in here in the backlands. With Leah Sayão and a big blond young man to whom she was engaged, I started north in the Plymouth one afternoon. The young man, Raul, drove us.

It was a happy kind of day, a cloudless day in the middle of the dry time when the upland air has a very faint coolness in it unless you are right out in the blaze of the thin Goiás sunlight. We were in a good mood and Raul outran the dust, driving the old Plymouth faster than she had ever gone since I'd had her. There was not much traffic on the road, for the harvest was about over.

As we wound through the grazing country between Anápolis and the mountain divide, I noticed that the strongrooted Jaraguá grass of the pastures was still green, though paler than when it first came out fresh and lush under the rains. And as we wound up the long slopes of the divide and plunged once more into the welter of beauty that lay beyond it, I found a new adornment had been added to this countryside: the flowering trees were in bloom.

"It is so beautiful that it is as hard to describe as the body of the beloved," I wrote to Bill in Argentina early the next morning. "It is a hilly country, but the hills are rounded. The vegetation is now of the plains, now of the forests. The forests now are filled with flowering trees, purple-flowered *ipés* and yellow-flowered. Other trees on the hillsides are covered over with white blossoms. As you drive down the dusty road, the roadside growth is a vivid green overlaid with a strong orange-red where the dust has settled on the vegetation. In front, in the distance, are incredible soft blues and purples and greens. Yesterday the evening sky was green. This morning, the mists over the frondy vegetation where palm trees have been left standing in the cleared land made a fantastic dreamlike picture, too unreal to be anything but enchanted."

I did not put it in my letter, but this region that had captured me anew with its splendor in the time of the flowering trees had not failed to strike at me while my guard was down, as it nearly always did, like a cruel lover. Leah, Raul and I were speeding gaily down the very best part of the big road, a stretch recently graded and graveled, when a piece of rock flew up from under one of the front wheels and pierced the old Plymouth's oil pan. This was the end of the Plymouth. After I finally got it towed to Anápolis, I decided to send it to São Paulo to be rebuilt and sold.

The old car's final accident was a severe blow to me. My expenses were mounting, always going beyond my highest expectation. The new disaster forced me at last to face my account books and when I ran a trial balance on them and consulted my checkbook, a cold chill went through me at the way my money was melting away.

The truck, on which I still owed money, was in the repair shop for life, it seemed. When it finally was repaired, however, I could sell it through the Bowens' truck agency and my balance after paying the debt on the truck would run the tenants through till the harvest, I calculated. Even so, my most hopeful estimates told me it would take my last thousand dollars to make the trip to the States.

I kept on expecting to hear something more from Alfredo, or for him to show up. I was hoping he might have a suggestion on the problem of finances. But Alfredo still lingered in São Paulo and friends there wrote us he had found a Brazilian circle interested in spiritualism and had taken to attending séances. He would have been much better employed in Goiás looking after the state of mind of his partner-to-be, for close behind the chilling thoughts about money came another intrusion, a rival offer.

I received a letter from Dumon Stansby, chief of the International Refugee Organization in Brazil, repeating their earlier offer of a job as their information officer. He said their Geneva headquarters had approved hiring me and asked if I were still free to accept. He would soon fly to Goiânia with an official party, he wrote, and suggested we could meet then and talk it over.

I could not decide how to answer. I had become accustomed to consulting with Bill during my years in Buenos Aires, and needed help with my decision. I turned to Captain Bowen, whose judgment had proved sound time and again. The Captain was noncommittal at first, but at the end of our consultation, with the characteristic blaze-up of his blue eyes that came when he grinned, he let drop one of his pearls of true wisdom.

"Get on the payroll, Virginia," he said.

In a few days Alfredo dropped out of the skies. He obviously expected everything to be as it was when he had left me weeks ago. With quiet satisfaction, he elaborated on his plans for the record-breaking flight. He said the distributor had applied for permission to import the Luscombe, and that we had to wait till the permit came through.

I was a coward about marring his happy, if hazy, dreams for our writing program by asking sharp questions about money. But at last I told him the IRO wanted me to do a press job in Rio for a few months, and that I thought it might be a good way to get capital for our venture. Alfredo's cheerful buzz of planning stopped now. He made no comment, as if money had little reality for him, but offered to fly me to Goiânia to meet Stansby. It was his way of leaving me free to make up my mind, I'm sure, but it was an ill-advised tactic with me at the time.

A day or two later, we took off from the Anápolis airfield to go to the state capital to meet Stansby's party. And now I learned what it was like to fly with Alfredo.

When we first took off in the Culver, I felt exactly as if I were riding a tricycle out of a high window. The sensation stayed with me.

My first experience in small-plane navigation was no more reassuring. In late August the backlanders start to burn over their broad pastures and the still air grows hazy with smoke. Though we flew quite low, the details of the landscape below us were vague.

Flying by compass, we were due to sight Goiânia in a very short time—it was only about thirty-five miles away. But the burned-over pastures with their big white spots of ash looked like clusters of houses from above and made recognition extremely difficult. We did not find Goiânia where Alfredo expected it to be. He had just corrected our course several degrees to the east to compensate for what he calculated to be a wind drift when I happened to spot a glint of water over to the west—the river near Goiânia. We turned back west and found our way through the haze to the airfield. Alfredo took it all calmly, but it seemed to me as if we'd almost been lost. I could not keep from wondering what would have happened if my eye had not caught the faint glint of the river.

Stansby's party had already left on a flight that would take them to the *Colônia* the next day and we could catch them there. We stayed overnight with friends in Goiânia and the next morning took off into hazy skies for the *Colônia*, over a hundred miles to the north.

This time we followed the road from Goiânia to Anápolis

and the *Colônia*. Since I knew the route, I had to spot land-marks for Alfredo's contact flying. Between Goiânia and Anápolis we came to a place where a branch of the road bent away to the right.

"Don't we follow that way?" Alfredo asked me.

"No, go straight on. That branch turns off to the railroad."

"Are you sure?"

"Yes, I've driven the main road lots of times."

Silence.

"This road ahead is much narrower than the one that turned off," observed Alfredo finally. "It almost peters out up there in that patch of trees. Are you sure it's the right one, Virginia?"

"That branch is wider because there are so many trucks using it to haul goods to Goiânia," I said. The railroad at that time did not reach all the way in to the state capital.

"All right, then, if you're sure that's the one."

Silence. I tried to remember if there was another branch to the right before the turnoff to the railroad.

"You are sure, aren't you?"

"I'm sure, Alfredo." I was not scared, but uncomfortable and miserable with the responsibility and uncertainty.

Suddenly the plane gave a violent lurch, its wings wobbling up and down.

"What's wrong?" I demanded, grabbing my seat belt with both hands.

"Nothing. I was just saying hello to that truck down below. I guess this is the road, after all."

I could see myself out over the big blue shark-infested Caribbean.

"Is that land over there, Virginia?" he would say.

"Sure it's land, it's an island right here on the chart," I'd reply.

"But can you see it, are you sure?"

"Sure I'm sure. . . ."

I guess I'm sure. . . . Am I sure? Of course I'm not sure . . . how could I be *sure?* This fancy afforded me no pleasure.

At the *Colônia*, I met Mr. Stansby and he told me he wanted an intensive press and information job done in Brazil, and then in other South American countries. He offered a year's contract instead of the few months originally discussed, and I told him I'd let him know soon if and when I would come.

When we took off from the *Colônia* field in the little blue plane to go back to Anápolis, Alfredo had a pilot's decision to make: he could use the long runway and go across the wind slightly or take off into the wind on the short one, a strip not as long as the distance the Culver really needed to get her stubby wings air-borne. With a little smile, Alfredo zoomed her right down the shorter runway and off the ground, lifting her up far short of the run she was supposed to have. The tiny plane staggered as we sailed off over the end of the airstrip, which terminated at a miniature cliff, and the fields at the foot of the low bank tip-tilted under us. I thought the grass and trees would come on up and slap us, but the plane righted itself and away we buzzed, Alfredo still smiling his happy little smile.

I was a novice small-plane woman and knew nothing about the art at which Alfredo had so long excelled, so I could not judge his decision about the runways. But I had heard the matter debated by the men at the field before we took off. I knew the length of the short runway and the run needed by the Culver. I knew also that the Lone Flyer, as if in sheer bravado, had taken the ship off the ground even before he had used all that he could have of the short runway. And from that time on, I was afraid of Alfredo as a pilot, as well as of his plane. My mind made itself up then and there that I would take the job with the IRO.

The next afternoon, Alfredo and I walked over the hills back of the Chacra and we found a miracle there, strange succulent little flowers growing right out of a rocky hillside where no rain had fallen for long months. It had recently been burned over and someone later told me that the ash combined with heavy dew might have brought forth this amazing flowering, unlike anything I had ever heard of. We went from tiny flower to flower, exclaiming over their small perfection and wondering how they came to be. When we paused, swept round with the beauty of the rolling hills and the open sky and the delightful discovery of the magic flowers, I told Alfredo I thought I ought to go to work for the IRO, for a while at least.

I said that if I could go to Rio for six months, till the rains and the hurricanes were past, I could save my money and get together another stake for our joint venture.

Alfredo reminded me how I had forsworn world problems and political tangles. He recalled the talk when I had assured him I wanted to do nothing more than write about "happy people."

I told Alfredo I wondered whether or not I *could* turn down a request to help the refugees, people who preferred exile to living under communism. I also went back to our past discussions and reminded him of his Gita, which says you must put away selfish desires to realize the Self.

Alfredo could not deny his own doctrine. He knew he had lost, though I am sure he did not know why. He had been pleased over the prospect of making a living by flying with me and writing about the out-of-the-way places. I think he was disappointed or impatient at one time because I could not fulfill his need for a Madonna-in-a-niche, for it would have suited him very well to find his two solutions in one person. But flying was his real passion and my writing experience would have enabled him to live entirely by flying. It was hard for him to give it up.

I began to enlarge on the hope of accomplishing something real to help the DP's, and he cheered up; like any good man, he was the more willing to set aside a cherished design of his own if it would actually help distressed people.

I was relieved to win freedom so easily, and was anxious to get away. I wired the IRO I'd report in a few days and started setting my business affairs in order. I found an agent to send supplies to Fazenda Chavante through the rainy season, due to begin in late September and continue for about six months.

The Bowens agreed to sell the truck when she was finally rebuilt, and to send the Plymouth to São Paulo for body work after all the mechanical repairs were done.

On my final trip to the farm, I arrived at camp so early in the afternoon that I had to go back to the clearing to find the men.

I fought my way up the forest trace through a leafy world where the light came down cool and green-tinted as if through still water. In the distance I could hear the ring of the men's axes against hard wood. In tune to their strokes they were singing a backland melody, *Asas Brancas* (White Wings), a nostalgic minor music completely unlike the samba or the hypnotic drum music of the coast. It was strange to hear them; this was the only time I ever heard the *roçeiros* sing in the forest.

When I got to the clearing, I found there a most tremendous anarchy of mighty fallen trees. They had crashed in every direction and their upright branches and green leaves mingling with those of the thick cut underbrush were like high surf threatening to engulf me. I had to teeter along the big trunks of prone trees, zigzagging, to get to the far side where the men were working. Many of the felled trunks were so big I had to swing myself up onto them by a branch. Then I had to push through tangled vines and thick foliage like a swimmer making slow headway in a frothed-up sea.

The forest was thicker, the downed trees bigger, the banks of the stream I had to cross steeper and the whole scene wilder than anything I had ever seen or imagined. I was completely disoriented; I could not tell north from south and if I had not had the plangent strokes of the men's axes to guide me, I would have been lost. It was almost impossible to imagine that such destruction as I saw around me had been wrought by six men with axes in only a few months. It seemed incredible that I owned all this and had ordered the havoc done, for it dwarfed and overwhelmed me.

I called the men together and told them frankly that I

had to go out to the coast to work for a few months in order to get new capital.

Chico, Ezequiel and Emílio took the news with characteristic acquiescence, nodding in silence. Claudinho merely gaped at me.

"The *senhora* leaves us to turn *granfa* down on the coast, eh?" said Manoel, his bitter smile curling his thin lips. *Granfo* (or *granfa*) is backland slang meaning "refined person" or "high-hat rich." Manoel meant "big bad rich."

"I wonder where you think I got the money I've advanced to you so far, Manoel. It certainly didn't grow on these trees up here," I answered with asperity of my own.

"But, Dona Virginia, who will send us our supplies?" demanded José. To my surprise, he showed real distress. He had taken pride in his co-operation in the camp since he had given his promise not to fight any more, and had done well.

"That's all attended to," I said confidently. "Anyway, I'll be back to check up on everything from time to time. Everything will be taken care of."

"It will not be, *dona!* We'll starve up here in this *mato* if you leave!" José was accusing in his tone. I had worked to gain his confidence and now it depended on my staying nearby.

"José, believe me, it's all arranged for," I said firmly. "I *have* to go."

I saw that it wouldn't do just to walk away when they were in this mood, so I decided to spend the night and try to reassure them further. I fought my way down the trace once more to the camp, where I rested my weary legs all afternoon while the women worked around me.

That evening by the campfire I explained once more that I had arranged for an agent in Anápolis to send them supplies through the rains; the money was guaranteed. I wrote down a list of things they needed and we balanced our books. Chico put his child on a fluffed-up straw pallet on the ground and insisted that I sleep on a sapling platform bed in his thatched tent.

It was hard for me to get to sleep that night, for the ridges of the pole bed pressed into my body and I had many things to think about. Deep in the still night I heard once again a sound that always awed me, the tremendous rending crash of a forest tree falling because its dying shallow roots could no longer uphold its great weight. The rapids of the River of Ghosts muttered nearby, seeming to whisper secrets of the wild land. I knew I was infinitely remote from everything familiar, yet curiously enough, the sense of being among people who depended on me and on whom I depended made me feel for a brief night safely shielded from harsh surprises.

The next morning the stirring of the small camp huddled under the giant trees was engrossing to watch: the women making fires in their primitive stoves and the men and children who emerged one by one from the sleeping shelters into the misty outside air all followed a simple choreography as old as nomadic life. Together we sipped tiny cups of heavily sweetened black coffee, the only nourishment even the woodcutters would take until their cold lunch of rice and beans at eleven o'clock.

After breakfast I shook hands all round. Manoel was mysteriously absent, as he often was at handshaking time.

"I will return soon," I said. "May everything go well with you. I'm sure it will."

"*Se Deus quiser*," they murmured. "If God wills it."

"Until then."

"Until then, *senhora*."

Chico and José rowed me over the river and I walked out to the big road before the sun grew hot.

I was fairly lucky this time and caught a series of rides that got me to Anápolis about sundown. The Bowens' gasoline post was already closed and the only way I could get out to the Chacra was to hire one of Anápolis's horse-drawn taxis, the two-wheeled buggies in which the town's whores rode sedately around in the daytime taking the air and advertising for trade later on. I felt a mite self-conscious till we were well out of town, but I had made up my mind to let nothing keep me from reaching home that day.

The old driver and I slowly jogged the six miles behind an undersized backland horse. We watched a pale green and gold sunset fade out in the west and saw mirrored above the horizon ahead of us the fan-shaped pink glows of brush fires burning in the north. The great vault above us gradually turned an unearthly color, the dull purple of its thickening haze faintly powdered by a last touch of daylight. When the afternoon breeze fell the backlanders had set fire to their dry cut timber and now while the wide darkness spread over us from the east, vast reflections of red on purple began to arise from the burning clearings.

Soon the dark closed down the final thin silver streak of light in the west. All around us the gloom thickened, menacing in aspect. The distant flames raged higher against the night sky, as if from the mouths of tremendous fiery furnaces. It was like Judgment Day.

I could always be affected by this country and had first thought of coming here because its varied splendor cast a spell on me. I had lived with it now. When I first tried to make friends with it as a newcomer, it had blandly rejected me and closed me out. On the memorable afternoon when the Captain and I struggled so desperately with the balky Plymouth and the hell-pigs, it had covertly mocked me for my temerity and ignorance. Today I was on the run, driving my affairs ruthlessly to get away from it. And today all around me the hills, the sky, the countryside, seemed to be in agony, caught up in a torment of murk and fire. It was on far too grand a scale to have any direct reference to me and yet I felt an anguish in it.

I was wild to get away. Alfredo had not accused me of desertion nor had any of the roçeiros except José, but I was not entirely sure I was doing right to leave them. Yet I had to go; I quailed before all the perplexities and risks I would be faced with in staying. I insisted to myself that my leaving was only temporary and consoled myself with the thought that my agents here in Anápolis, with money guaranteed, would look after my tenants better even than I, the novice.

The next day or two saw my business finished in slapdash haste. I gave Guiomar an extra month's pay and gritted my teeth while she embraced me in a freshet of grateful tears. Packing a few clothes not ruined by the red backland dust, I consigned Liberty Hall and its furnishings to the next comer. The Captain had been very ill during this time, so on the morning I left, Alfredo took me to the airport.

Alfredo enjoyed the freedom of the airfield, and he boarded the plane with me and strapped me into my seat. He bent over me to kiss me good-by, a brother's kiss.

"I'll fly down to the coast soon," he said. "I'll see you in Rio."

"We'll fly together in the spring, Alfredo," I promised. "Take good care of yourself."

The DC-3 was ready to go. Alfredo left me and the door was bolted behind him. The motors roared. I waved to my friend as he backed away toward the low white administration building where a small crowd stood watching the departure.

Our pilot wheeled us around and we taxied down to the far end of the field. Turning once more to run past the building, we started the take-off, a moment I always enjoy for the feel of power that runs through the plane and into and through me as we gather flying speed. Thrilling to the mighty machine that was bearing me away to a new phase of life, I was still impelled to search for Alfredo among the group now waving their final good-bys.

We were going too fast for me to distinguish him—already we were parted. I saw his tiny blue ship, hateful bug, on the ground; the next instant, our air-borne plane, turning away, tipped the horizon down. The wide, thinly-hazed bowl of Anápolis tilted down, the tall white tower of the town's one big building gleamed. Then we had turned away toward the southeast and in that moment it was all behind me.

9

A FIVE-HOUR flight raised São Paulo, where I changed to a plane that put me in Rio by midafternoon. My sudden appearance out of the wilds somewhat bewildered Mr. Stansby, the IRO chief, who was later to be equally nonplussed when I unaccountably vanished once more into the same mysterious hinterland. He outlined my assignment and I immediately set to work to find out everything I could about the IRO's press problem. I was lucky to find through friends at the IRO a most pleasant place to stay, sharing an elegant small flat near Copacabana Beach with Irene da Costa Carvalho, a Brazilian young woman of quality.

For the first day or two, I was like a child at a circus, savoring the minor delights of civilization—cold drinks, varied food, magazines, books and, above all, cleanliness. Then with all thought of Goiás put aside for the time being, I concentrated on my job.

The IRO's Brazilian office was an embassy of the United Nations set up to secure Brazil's co-operation in the biggest single task the UN had undertaken up until that time. Its task was to resettle millions of people unwilling to return to their Communist-dominated homelands after the Second World War, and this involved tremendous housing, feeding, and training efforts in Europe as well as world-wide diplomatic negotiations with countries asked to accept the Displaced

Persons as new settlers. Then the refugees had to be moved to their new homes by train, ship, and plane. When I joined the IRO it was operating the largest ocean-crossing passenger service in the world.

A trickle of DP's had started coming into Brazil about a year before. From the first they had had a furiously bad press, especially in Rio, the capital, where it hurt most. Poring over newspaper files, I found the main slurs were (1) the DP's were "useless" people, (2) they were "rebellious" labor and (3) they included many communists. (This latter rumor, we discovered, was propagated by the Brazilian communists themselves in an effort to dupe anti-communists into opposing DP immigration.)

To correct these misconceptions, I began to assemble evidence to disprove the charges of uselessness by gathering case histories of DP's who were performing valuable services in Brazil—and we got together a wealth of proof. I obtained statements from Brazilian employers praising DP's as workmen and technicians. We began to arrange interviews in which DP's told local reporters of their suffering under communism. We invited Rio newsmen to visit our offices, our ships and the reception center for arriving DP's. The response was immediate and favorable. The IRO's bad public relations had started because there was no information officer to explain our work, and as I put our case before them, the Rio papers began to back us.

It took me weeks of absorbed effort to get my new job started and I lived from day to day, thinking as little as possible about Goiás, which I had not left in a happy state of mind. I considered this period in Rio merely temporary, for I still intended to fly with Alfredo, with Goiás as our permanent base. For a time, the requirements of my job and my desire to forget my upland defeats plunged me into an intense interest in the city of Rio de Janeiro. Rather than closing me out as had the *sertão*, Rio seized upon me and drew me in.

Brazil's capital is a city in the grand manner. It stands on an enormous blue-purple bay and has pearl-white beaches and dramatic blue-green mountains all around and through it. Its long beaches are lined with gleaming ranks of tall apartment houses; in its downtown business district tower some of the most daringly designed big office buildings in the world. All this makes a bold first impression, but the true key to Rio's complex character can be found best by peering closely down between the big buildings and the upthrusting mountains. It is well to begin by noticing the city's mosaic sidewalks.

As the Rio sidewalks are painstakingly hand-wrought of tiny irregular black and white stones set in changing patterns, so downtown Rio itself is a mosaic of small blocks, narrow streets, odd-shaped squares where whites and blacks live and work side by side. Space is divided and subdivided there, even the "big" stores are small. Along the narrow side streets you see shop after shop each only a few feet wide though reaching deep into its building. These shops keep their entire fronts open during the day and customers bargain therein as in an Oriental bazaar.

Moist the year round and wept on by misty clouds for months on end, Rio is a city where age comes quickly to everything, but deals gently and lingers long. And with it there comes, and lingers, a unique smell, a lightly sweet-sour rancidness, the aroma of the back streets of the beautiful tropical seaside city of Rio.

Though the coast Brazilians practice putting things off as a supreme art, life in the fantastically beautiful city of Rio, Afro-Oriental odalisque of the Western Hemisphere, is not slow and lazy. On the contrary, Rio's narrow downtown streets are jammed from morning till night with a restless stream of people and noisy, honking cars. The vast majority of those who work and shop downtown live in suburbs five to fifteen miles distant and at the day's end this leads to a most amazing phenomenon, their sudden mass flight by automotive vehicle.

Around five o'clock Rio's many ramshackle taxis turn into jitneys and with thousands of big and little busses begin to streak down the Avenida do Rio Branco, the one wide street traversing the business section to the broad beach boulevards that lead to outlying suburbs. Everyone who has a private car loads up with co-workers or neighbors and joins in the mad rush. Empty jitneys and busses careen wildly back to town, to dash out once more with a new load. For nearly an hour and a half, jitneys, small busses, giant busses and private cars, all jam-packed, thunder through Rio like a stampede of wild animals on the African veldt.

A special exaltation blotting out all normal humanity seems to enter the bus drivers who take part in this daily mass race and they treat their passengers like so many newly-netted fish. Brazilians have profound contempt for the machine and the Rio drivers appear to enjoy the daily chance to beat their vehicles to death as if in a ceremony of communal revenge. Giant busses in their hands become fearful juggernauts. While I was in Rio an attempt was made to stop the big busses from racing each other after a luckless passenger, in boarding one, was thrown onto the hood by the driver's quick getaway. He clung there for miles while the other passengers inside screamed protests, but fell off and was crushed to death before they could prevail on the driver to stop. There were other instances of bus accidents equally weird.

By 8:30 P.M. downtown Rio is a ghost city. The small shops put up wooden doors. The big ones waste little electricity on show-window illumination. The streets seem dimmed out and only the occasional grind of a streetcar or an optimistic news-boy's cry echoes through them until the return stampede begins the next morning about eight o'clock. The morning rush, spread out over more time, is somewhat less savage, but the cars race terrifyingly fast.

Rio de Janeiro, intended by nature to be a superb playground, misappropriated by man as the capital of a great nation, is a city where *macumba* candles, the offerings of despairing lovers practicing witchcraft, are seen marking high tide on the fashionable beaches at night; where intricate police formalities may leave a murdered man lying all day on the street just as he fell, candles set at his head and feet by pious strangers, crowds eddying around him; where a hundred people of all shades from black to white regularly leap and writhe hysterically for hours through the tropic night, worshiping the white magic of São Jorge in a loft next door to one of the ultramodern office buildings.

Someone once said the Brazilian coast civilization went from savagery to decadence without any intervening stages. Many of the things you see in Rio incline you to this belief. Gradually you come to understand why the Brazilians have an old ambition to move their capital away from this city which is as magnificent in color and beauty as the great bay around it. They know better than anyone else that if it is bewitching, it is also bewitched, and that it has, like the restless South Atlantic surf caressing its long beaches, a dangerous undertow.

I am accustomed to sliding easily into the life of any Latin American city but in Rio, first of all, I had to wrestle with the tricky language, which few Brazilians pronounce clearly or spell alike, and which was difficult for me even though I knew French and Spanish and Catalan, a Romance dialect rather similar to Portuguese. The psychology of the coast Brazilians, I already knew, was different from any other in the Western world, and I studied it in fascination. Though the Brazilians themselves boast of a strong African heritage, both British and Americans who knew pre-communist China say they are like the Chinese, only more complicated. And of recent years, the business world of the big cities, where most foreigners receive their schooling in Brazilian ways, has been made even more complex by the introduction of a new element, the Brazilian working girl.

Brazilian women are on the whole kept carefully imprisoned in the harem mentality. When young and slim they are delightful, doe-eyed and beautiful as houris, and they have a capacity for tender affection and a sense of play not usual among other Latin women, who have more steel in them. Brazilian women are not encouraged to be even mildly efficient. They are born to adorn, to bear children, to have negro servants if they belong to the class that wears shoes, and to be helpless under the domination of the nearest male, whatever their class.

As can easily be imagined, these lovely beings bring considerable havoc into the business world.

They do not, in their souls, like business (as who can blame them?) and the one thing they really put their hearts into is saying "No".

Call a man's office and ask to speak to him.

"*Não está, senhora*," says the sweetest feminine voice in the world. "He's not in, ma'am."

"When will he be back?"

"*Não sei, senhora*," answers the voice in dulcet tones that scarcely disguise satisfaction. "I don't know, ma'am."

"Can I leave a message?"

"*Desculpe, senhora*," says the voice, dripping honey. "*Chame em vinte minutos!*"—"Pardon, ma'am. Call back in twenty minutes!" This comes on a rising note of triumph.

By a great unwritten law among the working girls of Rio, twenty minutes is the period of time after which everything is going to be possible. It often takes about that long to get a local call through, so I imagine the period has been settled on because it would give your man time to come back to his desk and leave again before you can get another call through. It is really the girls' polite way of saying, "To hell with the whole thing—you and the boss and all of it." It makes certain you will fail to get anything done quickly except by great good luck. This helps break the nerve and soften you up; it discourages you from causing more work in the office you called.

I learned it was quicker and surer to walk or taxi over to see the person with whom I had business. I was always on the girls' side, but they made my life almost unendurable at first.

As time went on I learned gradually that once an American gets past the mild constant bafflements of the telephone system and the secretaries and comes up against the Brazilian men themselves, it is necessary to make two radical adjustments. First, you have to revise your American understanding of courtesy; second, you have to reverse your American approach to time.

Among the Brazilians the practice of kind manners is paramount and universal. It covers their civilization with a patina of charm. But to comprehend Brazil, you must realize that Brazilians use gentle and sympathetic manners in dealing with people no matter what the purpose or end of the dealing may be. They understand this perfectly among themselves and apparently get satisfaction out of observing the ceremonial courtesies, win or lose.

Many Americans with commercial projects to promote in Brazil have learned that Brazilian "contacts" will entertain them lavishly and talk over their hopes and plans for hours, days or weeks without the slightest intention of doing business with them ever. The Brazilians do not mean to be misleading, they are merely fulfilling traditions of hospitality. At the same time, they rarely close important deals without first going through fairly elaborate social preliminaries. It can be very confusing.

If a Brazilian may be friendly in manner and not become friendly in a practical sense, he may also become a business enemy from one day to the next and never show it. They say the Chinese will cross a street rather than meet an enemy face to face; the Brazilians save themselves the trouble by refusing to admit open enmity, even though you may have bested them by trickery. Their custom of appearing to turn the other cheek is an excellent way of staying close by till they see a chance to get their own back—and they will cheerfully wait years if necessary.

The Brazilian approach to time is so strikingly different from ours and so uncongenial that we brush off their do-it-tomorrow spirit in practical affairs as the effect of indolence and climate. I learned by many a lesson large and small in Rio that nothing could be more mistaken. The Brazilian custom of delay in business is on all levels a practical technique of living, a part of their personal economics.

The small percentage of Brazilians who control capital

keep most of their money spread around in various high-paying enterprises. They are under no pressure of need in undertaking new ventures and therefore can force the man with the smaller margin of time to grant them concessions. Time waited is money made among them and outwaiting the other man is a major tactic in their amiable banditry.

Among the small middle class, the overworked, underpaid clerks and petty officials, delay protects a system of favor-granting, I discovered. When affairs are chronically retarded, it is a real favor to speed up the particular bit of business of a friend or a friend's friend. Gifts and favors to repay such speedups, even money gifts, are not looked on as bribes. Everyone maintains the fiction that they are genuine expressions of appreciation, hence the importance of "friendship" as a face-saving cover-up. Salaries are low and static, but as a man widens his connections, he can in effect get added income in gifts and favors as if they were fees or gratuities.

The great majority of Brazilians are of course below the middle class and their do-it-tomorrow (or do-it-never) spirit is something else again: a form of passive resistance developed out of the survival instinct. This is true among other dispossessed peoples too, of course. The master in Brazil traditionally wielded absolute power, even of life and death, over the man and the latter's ability to avoid effort was his only protection. Patience, sweetness and gentleness are the disguises the ill-fed, disease-ridden lowly Brazilians drape over their systematic, ingrained passive noncompliance, and they are artists at it.

Their resistance is very difficult to overcome unless you are prepared to act ruthlessly and even then your effort may go for nothing. The messenger at the IRO always used to plead he had an errand for the chief every time I needed him. I was dealing with rigid press schedules and if the messenger could not take my notices to the newspapers, I had to go myself or send my secretary, which seriously delayed our work.

One day when the messenger with all courtesy again told me he could not help me, I looked him straight in the eye and said, as roughly as I had ever spoken to a subordinate: "One of these days, I'm going to see to it that you deliver something for me, if I have to go to the chief and stake my job on it. I'll see that you deliver one thing for me, just once!"

I thought he would burst into tears, a grown young man. "But Dona Virginia, I *like* you! There isn't a nicer person in this whole office—I'd *love* to deliver your messages. It's just that . . ." Blah, blah, blah, the old story of delays in traffic, long waits in official anterooms and this, that and the other.

I stalked away without answering. I was morally certain he took his own good time on every trip out of the office, drank innumerable *cafezinhos* and was carrying on a courtship or two along his routes. Yet his soft answer to my wrath impelled me to tell him later that I should not have blazed out as I did. This consolidated his victory and he never bothered about me afterward, naturally.

The ingrained habit of passive resistance to effort, developed as an art of survival, had made the underdog in Brazil to an extent impervious to money lures, I began to learn; they do not respect the cruzeiro to the extent that they will necessarily deliver more and better work for more pay. The small top-dog class of Brazilians, on the other hand, can afford their own kind of "nonmaterialism" because they have stacked the cards of their system heavily in their own favor; they can reap low-taxed profits of from forty to four hundred per cent annually without too much strenuous effort. Hence in Brazil, as they often mention, many of the tensions of the "dollar-chasing machine age" are not in evidence.

This lack of obvious tension and the universal practice of kind manners give life on the Brazilian littoral a very attractive surface. But the pain of the Brazilian underdog's life eventually seeps into you there and their passive resistance makes the very conduct of life emotionally exhausting. Today their bent for conserving or avoiding physical or mental effort, developed for survival, has outlived its usefulness. These people are not happy living on the crumbs of Brazil's table and the rigid hold-downs from above are cracking, yet their own long tradition of passivity is helping stagnate them. Their outlived defensive technique is dangerous today, since it makes them susceptible to the -isms—fascism, communism, what have you—which promise to hand down benefits through a state party in which the people all have nominal membership but need exercise no real effort of control.

I had a better chance to understand Brazil than the average foreigner, I believe, because I knew many other Latin countries, as well as the negroes and my native South, where somewhat similar characteristics have existed. But what helped most of all, I think, was being a woman accustomed to business. The truth is that Brazilian men, with their kind, gentle manners, employ in their practical affairs the winning approach with which men in our civilization mask the aggression of sexual seduction. Curiously enough, in this Brazilian society where the male is lord of all, the men themselves consistently parry each other's honeyed, masked aggression by the use of the kind of wiles which Americans associate with women. The widespread use of the appeal to sympathy in business affairs—"weeping"—is a case in point. The accent on gentle manners is itself far more "feminine" than "masculine," as we judge traits.

But do not be deceived; though the surface manner may appear soft and "feminine," the effect is masculine in the extreme. The Brazilian coast civilization has a terrible strength to force the outsider into its mold. The soft appearance appeals to all the softness in you and once you yield, you are caught. I know more than one American who after a few years there has become afraid deep in his heart to return to his own country, which he comes to think of as having an extremely high-pressure pace. The Brazilian littoral is like the Venus flytrap, the insect-devouring flower which with its rare beauty lures flying visitors to light upon it and in the end assimilates them.

My absorption in the Rio scene spent itself as the pervasive unhappiness of the city's ill-nourished people became apparent to me. One night while walking along the ultrafashionable Copacabana Beach with a Brazilian friend, I heard soft guitar music behind the boarding surrounding an excavation for one of the luxury apartments into which have gone so much of the profits from Brazil's latter-day urban boom. Through a crack we saw sitting around a flickering light a group of workmen, mostly negroes, who were obviously eating and sleeping in the dank hole they helped dig during the daylight hours. My companion half-indignantly said it ought not to be allowed. The Brazilians have a song about "*O Pedreiro Waldemar . . . constrói um edifício e depois não pode entrar*"—Waldemar, the homeless stonemason, who builds a building and then isn't allowed to enter it. To me, this song sums up the story of opulent Rio and the vast majority of its people.

The city closing in on me turned my thoughts once more back to Goiás. When Brazilians asked me to tell them about that mysterious hinterland on the edge of which their civilization has been hesitating for three centuries, I longed to be there with a sick longing. I did not want the Goiás of my first impossible imaginings nor the disturbing reality from which I had fled. But I grew homesick for the pale gold upland sunshine, so deceptively bright, and for the long vistas and the crisp air of the dry time. I wanted a new dream in the same setting.

Another discomfort gradually forced me to think more about myself. I had hurt my left arm and shoulder while climbing through a heavy wire fence in Goiás, and though the doctor who gave me the physical examination for the IRO said the pain would fade with time, it did not go away. It was always worse at night and made sleep difficult. Irene Carvalho, endowed with intelligence and heart, had recognized me at once for what I was, an international waif, and she was so kind to me that I could not for some weeks tell her the hard bed in the flat we shared was aggravating the shoulder pain. (The Brazilians like hard beds, they claim.

The women say they are cooler and the men reportedly prefer them for the violent kind of love-making which is their national sport.)

We got a softer mattress and the pain improved. But one day someone turned abruptly in a crowd and accidentally hit me just above the left breast. The pain now came back and to my alarm centered in the breast itself.

Irene was engaged to marry a young Spanish doctor named Xavier Puig y Serra who had a brilliant record in cancer research. One day I casually asked Serra what kind of an operation they performed for breast cancer. He said they removed the whole breast and part of the big chest and arm muscle. It conjured up a horrible picture of mutilation.

I had to keep very busy, continuing to put in eighteen hours a day for the IRO. No one with a heart could resist the human appeal of the refugees, among whom every second man was a hero and every single person part of a millenary epic. The first phases of my press work in Rio were successful far beyond our hopes. We had a genuinely important running story and the reporters welcomed our aid in helping them cover it. Soon I was able to start visiting editorial writers and we began to get editorial support from the best papers. Next I had to think of extending my press activities to the other Latin American countries, especially to Peru, Chile, Bolivia, Argentina and Uruguay. Before long my days became a race to attend to the multiplying demands of my job and my nights uneasy sessions with pain.

To almost any woman nowadays, pain in the breast would spell the possibility of cancer. My mind did not dwell on the thought of cancer, for if I had it, I had it; nor did I think about the possibility of death as I had when I was planning to fly with Alfredo. I assumed that any cancer would be extirpated and cured, but it was the cure I dreaded, the mutilation.

Though I'd had a share of pain and illness in my life, I had always had a very strong body. Physical endurance for work, for travel, for overcoming obstacles and my own mistakes, had been my only operating capital. No matter how hard I drove my good equipment, it always renewed itself; long periods of overwork and stress might exhaust me, but a good night's rest, a sunny day, a happy time, would bring back my sense of well-being once more and with it joy of life. I had learned to curb this upwelling, for people around me, going their usual ways, were seldom prepared to fall in with my sudden holiday moods. But the knowledge that within me existed a spring of energy I could count on was my bank account and my insurance. I connected it with wholeness, which mutilation would take away from me. The mutilation would make me another person than myself.

It would mean the end of love. I had always been sure my life would come right in that respect and now the sustaining conviction would have to go. I could imagine a man remaining loyal to a beloved wife who might have the operation, but it was difficult to envisage a beginning with a woman already so maimed. It presaged the worst thing that could possibly happen short of death—condemnation to permanent loneliness. I did not think I preferred to die; but I would have to get used to the idea of becoming a different person, a woman resigned to living in a desert, before I risked hearing the sentence.

I kept putting off the day.

In November, Larry Keighley, roving staff photographer and writer for *The Saturday Evening Post*, wanted to do a picture story on the "old settler" DP's around São Paulo and I went there to help on it. I knew there was an excellent American-Brazilian doctor in the city and made up my mind to go to him just as soon as the story was finished.

Not long before, a letter from Bill Mizelle had mentioned "going down a long black tunnel with a low black roof" in his life, the only direct admission of unhappiness he ever made to me. This kind of journey is one everybody has to make sometime. ("It doesn't really hurt you," I said to him afterwards, to which he replied, "It doesn't do you any good!") I suppose most people go through periods like that more than once in their lives. Those are the times when you seem to have left your past behind you, yet feel you have no future, only a gloomy present. It is like the limbo of the ancients, or an outer circle of Hell.

The DP's and the job at hand kept me afloat for the time. I had never worked on a magazine picture story before and in spite of myself, became very interested in the elaborate process of preparing this one. Mário de Moraes, a Brazilian in charge of our resettlement in São Paulo, had a broad grasp of his responsibilities and seeing him at work with the DP's made up for a score of the small-souled Brazilian bureaucrats who clogged progress at Rio. Patriotic, full of heart and intelligence, hard-working and patient, Mário was one of those Brazilians who could make his country great today, instead of in the vague tomorrow, if he and his kind had the sort of international backing that the communists and the fascists have. Even within the limits of IRO work, he was doing wonders for the refugees, whom he often helped over their worst crises with money out of his own small salary.

Guided by Mário, Keighley and I visited many DP's in factories and at home. We were both amazed and touched to see at first hand the gallant efforts the refugees were making in the new and difficult country. Most of the families had been turned loose less than a year before with only ten dollars for each person and no knowledge of the language. They were working at low-paid factory or manual jobs. Yet many of them, in less than a year, had already achieved neat homes of their own, tiny wooden buildings which they had helped each other build out of scrap lumber on ground bought on the installment plan. They had made their own furniture, decorations, often even their kitchen utensils. (I always noticed the hand-decorated religious mottos on their walls.) Almost without exception, they were now helping refugees who had come later.

Keighley made scores of photographs of the urban DP's, but we both wanted to see how they were faring in the country. The nearest coffee plantation where a group was established was at Jaú, far inland from the city. Governor Adhemar de Barros lent us an airplane in which to visit them and Olavo Fontoura of the Biotônico fortune gave us his personal pilot. Thus I came to be at the aforementioned luncheon where Olavo revealed the secret of his famous patent medicine's popularity—"Eet ees Es-spanish fly."

On the trip to Jaú, we flew low over the fabulous coffee region of São Paulo, and what I observed was a shock to me. Under its thin veil of coffee trees, the red soil of São Paulo, legendary for its richness, was bare, baked, cracked and gullied. As we drove through the country around Jaú after landing, we saw entire plantations, millions of trees, slowly dying. I had been told the coffee trees were aging and I knew they exhausted the soil. But nobody had told me the broader truth: the fabulous red soil of São Paulo had been completely neglected, as proved by the widespread erosion and cracking. It was not being exhausted so much as raped. The land between those trees could have been plowed and planted with soil-renewing cover crops, if chemical fertilizers were too costly, and the cover growth would have helped hold back erosion. The coffee growing practiced here had not been agriculture at all, but crude open-pit mining of the soil. Many of the plantations would produce for a while yet, five, ten, fifteen years; but what are fifteen years in the life of a soil that should have been good for many decades more?

Everywhere I looked, I saw deserts-to-be, below me and ahead of me, in my own life.

On our return, we cut our time rather too fine in leaving Jaú, and as we came in over São Paulo in the twilight, the control tower at the airport advised our pilot the field was closed by one of the region's sudden fogs. The pilot did not have enough gas to seek another field and proceeded in against the interdiction.

There was complete silence in the plane as we came in over the city at telephone-pole height and set down in a mist as thick as the one Alfredo and I almost got lost in going to Goiânia. I could admire the pilot's coolness and magnificent skill; beyond that I had no reaction. Out of a desert and into a mist—the progression seemed natural enough.

One lifting of the fog around me came in these days in a brief conversational exchange with Larry Keighley. I must have mentioned cancer in some connection, because he said a friend who was a cancer specialist once told him people could worry themselves into cancer. This ray of doubt on my self-diagnosis gave me the courage to make a date with a doctor immediately.

While I was winding up my assignment in São Paulo, Joan Bowen came there for a visit, bringing news from Chavante that only added to my worries. She told me that José had tried to get all my tenants to leave and when they wouldn't, he had slipped up to the clearing one night and set fire to it before it was quite dry.

"But *why* did he burn the clearing, why didn't he just leave?" I asked her, bewildered.

"He wanted to force the others to go. He said they'd all starve up there in the rains. He took his family and vanished and Claudinho and his brood went with him."

José, violent in his every reaction, childlike, simple. I had established confidence with him all too well, for his act smacked of vengeance for the imagined betrayal of my leaving. But at least I was rid of Claudinho, though at a high cost.

When a clearing is improperly fired or burns before it is dry enough, too many of the small branches and limbs survive. Even after a proper firing, there is much work to be done clearing away the smaller branches that cover ground and make planting irregular and difficult. The big trunks of course lie till they rot.

"Is it pretty bad?" I asked Joan.

"We sent some men up there to help clear away the small branches so they can plant better."

I knew I should go to Goiás, but I could not pull myself together to face the physical effort. I asked about Alfredo. He had moved to the hotel in Anápolis and was making short flights around the state, Joan told me. He was still waiting for the import permit for the Luscombe.

On the last day I was in São Paulo, I went to see the doctor and summoned up courage enough to tell him I was afraid an accidental blow had caused "something serious" to develop in my left breast. He gave me a thorough examination and assured me there was no abnormality present.

The news should have been a tremendous relief, but instead of feeling a proper surge of joy, I remained emotionally numb. I could see the sunlight again, but I couldn't feel its warmth. My old depression seemed to be sitting just up above me, like one of Alfredo's thunderheads, ready to come back down like a black cloud at any moment.

When I went to the airport to return to Rio, I happened to meet Mr. Cross, in whose home Joan had been visiting. I had barely said hello to him when my plane was announced for departure and I began to say good-by.

"Too bad about de los Ríos, wasn't it?" said Mr. Cross.

I was not sure I had heard aright in the chatter around us. "What about Alfredo? Has something happened?"

"He crashed up there in Goiás, in the Corumbá River, and was killed instantly. I've wired for details."

I was utterly dumfounded. It had never seemed possible that Alfredo could come to harm in the plane—he was the Lone Flyer with the charmed life. I had to hurry to leave.

"Please let me know!" I called over my shoulder.

I climbed into the waiting DC-3 and found a seat with a friend. I had been in a daze for what seemed like a long time and I stayed in one. I had described Alfredo in a letter to Bill as "a man with one hand firmly grasping the gold bars of Heaven." He had vaulted over, without taking leave of any of us.

Alfredo dead. So strange, when I had been so sure that I would die in his plane.

It was curiously appropriate that the news of Alfredo's

death became real to me on an airplane. He had entered my life as part of a picture of flight through sunny skies. We had walked together in the sunlight and the white moonlight under an arching sky; we had planned a future mingled with the sky. He had told me he was not afraid of death and my lack of sharper grief did not seem disloyal. My first emotion when emotion began to come was wonderment, tinged with exasperation, at his rashness in throwing his good life away in the stubby plane.

"Alfredo, how could you!" was my thought.

The flight from São Paulo to Rio took only a little more than an hour. Within two hours after I heard of his crash, I was at home reading Alfredo's last letter to me.

His four-page hand-written letter was very like him, serene, calm, full of plans. He had taken to doing occasional taxi flying as a convenience to his acquaintances at Anápolis— he liked to study the region anyway, he said. He had flown a man to Ipamerí to see the country horse races there. During the races, he wrote, Brazilian bush pilots in small planes had buzzed the crowd and landed and taken off in the middle of the race track. "There's going to be a bad accident around here some day," he wrote in disapproval. He said he intended to fly to the coast soon to try to get action on the permit for the Luscombe and would see me then.

Kindly, serene Alfredo, the little hero with his anguish well buttoned up inside. How apt now was his admonition, spoken through the words of Krishna, *Grieve not for the living or the dead.* I still could not grieve for him, for I did not connect his disappearance with anything like death as I had encountered it when my mother died rebelling against leaving her young children. It seemed, literally, as if he were just in another state, like the state of Goiás, only one not defined on the map. As if he had flown to Chavante-land and were happy there.

I soon received a letter from Goiás with more details. Alfredo had taxied a man from Ipamerí, where he was staying a few days, to a town called Cristalina. Against warnings, he had started his return flight with a very narrow margin of daylight. He became lost when the haze closed in and wandered for hours, till eight o'clock at night. I could imagine it perfectly after our flight to Goiânia.

He told me once you could not get lost in Goiás because the region was boxed by rivers and all you had to do was fly till you found one. He had successfully ditched a plane in water years before and I think may have made a mystical connection between his name and the certainty of help from rivers when he was in trouble. This time his talisman failed him, for there were big rocks in the river. He hit them, and was instantly crushed. My prayer was that as he flew on and on in the murk, searching for his river, he could still smile as he said he had when he was lost over the Amazon Valley.

The people of the town of Burití Alegre, near where he fell, buried him with a shred of his blue plane, "in the best coffin," I was told.

My letters written a short time afterward say this: "I am positive that if I had not taken the IRO job, I would have died with Alfredo. Now I have a sort of added lease on life."

Part of my sense of reprieve may have come from relief over the breast pain, and from its accompanying fear of mutilation. But the foreboding of death itself had been specifically connected with Alfredo's plane, and his accident released me from the obligation to risk it when my promise to him fell due. It did not seem wrong for me to be glad I was alive, but an uneasy regret developed on another score.

I was sorry about our inconclusive good-by. It always disturbs me profoundly to go through an important last parting and not know its finality, for I have a strong need to exchange terminal generosities when there has existed the least degree of love, even the indefinable affection of friends. It seems imperative to close emotional accounts properly, no matter how raggedly I may have kept them as they ran along. The permanent wound is not so much loss, which is normal to living, but failure to exchange final expressions of forgiveness and last blessings.

The Brazilians seem to have a similar instinct. At the end of a visit, whether they have been hosts or guests, they will often say as the very last word, "*E desculpe, eh?*" They mean, "And please forgive anything not just right."

I had a chronic ache in my shoulder and worries over the far more important problems of the refugees; I did not want this new dull sorrow over Alfredo. I tried to analyze the regret away. What terminal forgiveness did I need from him? The answer was easy: he had been very much alone and I should have told him I could understand his interior drama, even if imperfectly. When a person is in an arid stretch of life and in unfamiliar surroundings, even the small kindnesses dealt out by strangers as common courtesy take on importance; how much more a friend's expression of sympathy.

Out of my nostalgic sadness, *saudades* over Alfredo, a doubt was born. Would he have taken the last foolish flight with its uncalled-for risks if he had not been adrift in a void, without one close tie or one comprehending person nearby to serve as mooring? I told myself nothing could have swerved him from his end in the river. Vividly I remembered how Joan, herself a forceful personality, could not deviate him one whit from his course even in so small a matter as getting to breakfast on time. Death had been all around us up there in Goiás looking for someone, I reflected; Captain Bowen had nearly died just before I left. The Lone Flyer had given death too easy an opening.

The thought about the Captain was unfortunate, for in its train came a memory of the way the people around him had closed ranks to help him fight death—Joan, the doctor, the Indian cook Vitalina, even Alfredo and myself, who together had made a wild dash to town for help one night when Joan thought her unconscious husband's heart would stop. I failed to convince myself that destiny had directed all our lives; the conviction of free will was too strong a mental habit. The misgiving that I might have deserted Alfredo in a time of special need came to mark the thought of him with an asterisk of self-blame.

One bright sunny day the blue sky above a glittering, frolicsome sea, the gay white sands of Copacabana Beach, the dainty trees lining the streets there, all reminded me there is much more to the world than the family griefs of the species man. Weary of sadness, I suddenly solved my dilemma of responsibility and regret by dismissing the whole subject.

I buried the dead Alfredo. My attention turned to plans for a flight on IRO business to Peru, Chile, Argentina and Uruguay.

Argentina. I had been happy there many times, with Bill. Even in the midst of turmoil there, I had discovered with him for the only time in my life a kind of joy that did not turn heavy and slip through my fingers, bruising them. The remembrance returned again and again, to flicker around the edge of consciousness in the restless times at night, like a dancing star.

10

IT was not easy to get away to my oasis in the South. After Alfredo's death I gave up all idea of leaving the IRO in the spring. Our work broadened daily and I was called on to help solve resettlement problems. The change in press comment brought about by our rudimentary press activities helped the mission and the DP's, but I gradually learned the root of our troubles went far deeper, to the leaders of the Dutra administration itself.

Their policy was to make us sweat for every DP we brought in and make us pay for everything they possibly could. It arose from one of those profound misunderstandings so tragic when they happen among friends. The Brazilians had given the United States and the United Nations far more war support than any other Latin American country and they thought they had earned the right to about a billion dollars' worth of postwar loans for national rehabilitation. Several medium-sized loans were indeed working through the international banks. But for any big over-all project, the banks wanted specific plans and guarantees which the Brazilians considered injurious to the national honor.

I could see both sides of the difference, though I believed the two sets of leaders, for their countries' sakes, should have found a way to reconcile their views. Nobody could favor handing the Brazilians a billion dollars to spend helter-skelter.

178 BEYOND THE GREAT FOREST

Yet a firm hint from the United States in 1945 had helped influence Brazil to turn out its entrenched dictatorship and set up elective government. I felt strongly the United States should reward the loyalty of its best Latin American friend and encourage it to perfect its elective government. Not only would this be an honorable role, but it would strengthen a bulwark against communism and Peronism in South America. Our policy-makers, however, had neglected to do this and the Brazilians, under their traditional smiles, were deeply resentful.

From years of reporting on Brazil, I knew how bad its plight was. Its inadequate railroads were falling to pieces; the whole country had fewer miles of paved highway than the state of Tennessee. Its creaky power plants were long outgrown; only São Paulo had a good supply of electricity. Its food production was falling, and the landworkers were crowding into the towns and cities.

But what about glittering São Paulo, the fastest growing city in the world? This ultramodern capital of the temperate coffee-growing region, ever bustling with energetic newcome European blood, is really an enclave in the rest of Brazil, one that in appearance at least makes startling contrast to the tropical, Portuguese-influenced civilization dominating in so large a part of the country. São Paulo has enjoyed its long boom largely because two world wars, a depression and fifteen years of official import controls have cut off foreign imports of made goods and the city has become manufacturer for the nation. It is not an unmixed blessing. Though coffee money rolls back through São Paulo, not too much of it seeps down to the workers' level. Hordes of migrants press constantly on the city, keeping wages low. The manufacturers, in a protected market, turn out small quantities of high-priced goods and reap fabulous profits. Their industrialism is entirely different from ours, in which highly paid workers use intricate machines for mass output at low prices. Theirs is the European type of industrialism in a form which seems to an American as antiquated as medieval handcraft. The low-paid workers of São Paulo know nothing of the better American system and the communists teach them to hate all capitalism in the name of the only kind they have experienced. The more I dealt in the realities of Brazil, the more I was convinced it would be best by far to settle the refugees in strong groups on their own land. It was good to learn our chief was discussing a small program along these lines with the governor of Goiás. We all began to look toward the new country in the interior as the land of hope for our people.

In mid-December it at last became possible for me to visit the other countries where I had to set up our regional information network. The last-minute rush of getting away was exhausting but luckily the plane carrying me across South America to Lima, Peru, was weathered in for several days at Santa Cruz de la Sierra, just west of the mighty Andes wall. The Pan American guest house was comfortable and the break very welcome.

I suddenly realized how strange it was that fate was taking me back to the scenes I had deserted. One afternoon when I was walking along Santa Cruz's deep-gullied streets, which became little rivers in the heavy rains, all at once I met a ghost. It came home to me that the red earth I was slogging through was the very heart of Bolivia, and the ghost I met was a former self, the bride of doomed causes.

In early 1944 the clique of Argentine colonels and German Nazis who pushed Perón to power had also engineered an uprising in Bolivia. Their puppet regime, led by Gualberto Villarroel, desperately needed United States recognition. In my *Washington Post* column I repeatedly wrote that this would be against our national interest, pointing up the Bolivian incident as a turning point for the whole region. The *Washington Post* was very important because it was read by members of Congress; for this reason, Latin American politicos, in trying to change my views, had used every method of persuasion from mild threats to crude courtship.

I saw then for the first but not the last time how the extreme right and the extreme left were both bringing pressure to favor clique-rule in Latin America.

The United States recognized the power boys on their promise to be good little democrats, which promise they honored soon after by messily murdering most of the opposition leaders. Bolivia endured bloody rule until 1946; then one day the people of La Paz swarmed into the presidential palace and took the tyrant Villarroel out and hung him to a lamppost.

The old questions roiled in my mind. How could the leaders of the greatest democracy on earth sponsor such regimes? Had they honestly believed anything good could come from such bad men? Why had our government so often tipped the scales to favor some clique-ruler in Latin America and failed to give timely aid to governments attempting to practice democracy? Why did we not at least encourage those leaders who would be pro-American? At the time of the Bolivian crisis, I knew such men had been available, not perfect men, but better than the Nazis. I remembered how much of my life-force, my only treasure, had been spent in swimming against the stream in these matters. It was hard for me to reconcile myself to such a painful expenditure of effort when it went for nothing.

These were the corroding thoughts I had once fled from to the backlands, and I still had no answer for them. I picked up a handful of the damp Bolivian earth and felt it with my fingers; it was not alien earth to me, for I had shared in its battles. It was red and rich, like the soil of Goiás, although more sandy. Can the earth heal, except when it falls on a coffin lid? Now came vivid remembrance of the red soil of Goiás and the blue distances that once had promised me peace in which to see my way forward. I had made my adult peace with Heaven when I asked to be confirmed in the Episcopal Church in 1944. But still I needed to find a clearer path on earth.

My role in Goiás, I reflected, had not been filled with dignity. I had beaten ignominious retreat to a new project every time harsh reality contradicted my fixed dream there. And now I seemed to be preparing my escape from the IRO; my growing conviction it was not right to bring DP's into Brazil as we were doing it smacked of new retreat.

On this memorable afternoon I began to think I had done wrong ever to leave Goiás. When my IRO stint was done, I would go back and straighten it all out, I resolved. In the meantime, there was the promise of a respite in Buenos Aires.

The rain clouds lifted from the mountain pass one day and we flew through and over the broad Andes to Lima. Both Lima and Santiago de Chile were a whirl of work for me, of making new friends and planning with our officials how to apply my services to local problems. At last I took flight for Buenos Aires and I cabled Bill Mizelle my arrival time. I did not know how it would be with us, yet I looked forward to seeing him.

I was in line awaiting a customs check at Morón airport when I spotted Bill coming through the crowd beyond the wire barrier, my eye caught by the characteristic, rapierlike quickness of his erect, athlete's body. Every brown hair was in place, his white collar gleaming, tie exactly tied, his suit neat—a man whose person, like his personality, for some blessed reason never got mussed. His thin face, with nose bold and chin strong, was serious, almost stern; his quick, assured movements as he sliced through the crowd made the milling people seem lumpy and doddering. If he had been a stranger, I felt, I would not have wanted to get in his way.

He caught sight of me now and waved and smiled, his whole face changing to become sunny. My spirits lifted on a flood of pleasant associations. (What a wonderful word, "pleasant.") When I first met Bill, he was the only person in all the troubled world around me who had the extra something in him to stay light-mannered in adversity. Often at first I had had to force myself to seem lighthearted with him, but ended by automatically feeling much happier just to be in his company.

"You got here!" he said through the high wire fence.

"Hello!" I was free to leave the customs table now and walked over to him. Our fingers touched briefly through the wire.

"I've got a cab waiting. Are all your bags through?"

"I just have these two and the typewriter."

The wire gate opened and I handed him my baggage checks. Now life would be properly managed in competent hands. We had a cab, we would have a porter, things would move briskly along. The petty snarls of everyday practical living that had so often tripped me into annoyance and overshadowed larger satisfactions would be handled rapidly and effectively, and I could begin to smooth out.

Bill guided me to our cab, and directed the stowing of the luggage.

"I found a service flat you can take if you like it, on Corrientes, near where you used to live," he was saying. "Do you know yet how long you can stay?"

"At least a month. The flat sounds ideal. I may have to go to Montevideo later, but I'll come back afterwards. There's a lot to do here."

"Oh, fine. But you won't have to be in Monte over Christmas, will you?" he asked.

"No, I'll be here for Christmas and New Year. Won't you get a vacation soon? Maybe you could go over to Monte when I go."

We were in the cab, driving to Buenos Aires, which is miles from the airport.

"I'm pretty sure I can," he said. "Do we want to go to the old beat-up Belgrano Club again for New Year's?"

We had danced the two past New Years in at the very British Belgrano Club in the suburbs. Two years before, unable to get a cab home, we had taken an owl streetcar and wandered for hours in a fantastic transportation jam which at one point unaccountably stranded us at a cemetery.

"Let's go," I said. "Maybe we'll have another adventure. I've got a new long dress for the dance."

"You've got on a new pretty dress now."

"You've got a new suit. I like it."

In the exchange of trivia, we were weaving back our old closeness. It was the same, yet not the same. I knew him better, from our letters, but I was not at all sure of myself.

"Where would you like to go tonight?" Bill asked. We always made a great business of planning our evenings. Later we would go into long, thoughtful discussions about our news and people we knew and Bill would give absorbing reports about other friends, such as the pigeons in the plaza and Marilú, the office cat who saw spooks. It was a way of catching the present, making it satisfactorily real.

"The old Mariwal, maybe, if you'd like it." I named one of our favorite restaurants, a Viennese-waltz sort of place. "Do they still keep their tabasco sauce in the safe?"

"I don't know," he said. "I haven't been there lately."

We were quiet for a moment.

"The Currans and Bill McCall were on the plane," I said. "Did you see them?"

"We waved at each other. . . . I had a couple of dates with a girl named Irene Day and Tom Curran asked me to a cocktail party and he said, 'Bring your girl,' meaning Irene. I told him, 'I can't, Virginia's in Brazil.'"

This surprised me; we had always been very noncommittal about each other to outsiders. But it pleased me. It was a way of saying there was nobody else. Our hands slipped together easily and naturally, solidarity re-established.

"Let's do go to the old beat-up Marryvarry!" I said, suddenly elated. Marryvarry was a special name for the Mariwal Restaurant and part of a private language of catchwords and phrases we had evolved for the fun of playing on words as well as to annoy the secret police who used to listen in on our telephone conversations. "I'll dress up. . . . It's such a pretty day!"

The last phrase was our incantation against all the bothers and worries of the world, a slamming of the door upon them, an invocation of happiness.

"Let's mote around town after dinner and go dancing if we want to." Bill finished out my thought. "It's a wonderful day. . . ."

I knew everything was going to be fine. There'd be no digging into each other, no need for lacerating self-revelations about our separation or recriminations or anything painful. Easily, without any strain, the separation would be blotted out.

The IRO staff at Buenos Aires were congenial and we worked together well. The Argentines were bringing in fairly large numbers of DP's and our main concern there was to avoid publicity. I counseled this, for fear the Peróns might want to use us for propaganda purposes, which would hurt us with other Latin American countries. Or Evita might send around for a "contribution" to one of her "charities," the polite blackmail grown familiar in Argentina.

On investigation, I found many DP's there were well started on new lives. Perón was making better use of our scientists and technicians than most countries. But doubts assailed me. What would happen to these people later? Obviously they would be pressed into a mold by the dictatorship or they would suffer; their old choice would have to be made again. I doubted very much if many of them would resist again. We were snatching them from the clutches of one tyranny to deliver them to another.

I believed our refugees would be better off in Uruguay and Chile, where self-government obtained. Chile was already taking some. In January, Bob Rossborough, then in charge of the Buenos Aires mission, went with me to Uruguay to try to open the way for a program there.

Bill got his vacation at this time and went along with us. He and Bob got along well. Bill ended by helping me informally on IRO press business in the daytime, while the three of us explored Montevideo's lighter side by night. A month later, we all returned for another week end in Uruguay, and this was my farewell to the South for a while. The good times were over and on the last Sunday night I saw Bill off on the night boat to Buenos Aires in a rather solemn mood. Rossborough was staying in Monte after us and when I went back to the hotel I had a good-night drink with him. Bob was a bit curious and he probed my affairs a little. We had become friends and there was no ill intention in it.

We began talking about his ideas on marriage. I said I'd have to be very sure about my own mind for marriage before I ever attempted it again. I should feel the need of many guarantees of happiness in so hazardous an undertaking.

Bob made a switch. He remarked that it was high time for Bill to get married. I caught the unspoken part of his thought, ". . . to some nice little girl who will make a home and have babies and not go flapping around all over the place in airplanes."

I said to Bob it probably would be better for Bill to start a home and silently I agreed to the unspoken part of his thought also. Maybe I had done wrong ever to come back to Buenos Aires. As for myself, I knew I had big, unfinished business in Goiás. It had been wonderful, visiting in Buenos Aires, like a glorious holiday; I had had the best of it, no responsibilities toward Bill, no worries. It had been so utterly pleasant, until Bob suggested a "problem."

The inference that it was doing Bill no good to continue his attachment to me year after year was disquieting, and the next morning when he called from Buenos Aires to say good-by before my plane left, I came as near to showing I was upset as I ever had. I was wondering if I ought not to bow out, for good this time.

Bill had developed an uncanny ability to read my mind, even at a distance. When I got back to Rio I received a letter from him asking me to promise I would not fade away into the backlands or somewhere without a word. Promises had never been necessary between us but I agreed.

During my absence from Rio, plans to settle DP's in Goiás had developed rapidly. Governor Coimbra Bueno was taking steps to start a farm colony on state lands.

Also, a man named Hugo Borghi had started a large farm development in eastern Goiás and had asked for DP labor. I was delegated to make a brief trip to Goiânia for the IRO and to return by Formosa, where Borghi's land was, to see if it would be all right to send DP's there. Since I had to go to Anápolis to catch the cargo plane servicing Borghi's place, it was agreed I could take a Saturday afternoon and Sunday for a quick trip to Fazenda Chavante.

My life had somewhat resembled a slow travelogue for the past four years, but of late it had speeded up. In one December day I had left Rio de Janeiro's purple bay and blue-green mountains, had circled the white, ultramodern city of São Paulo with its raw red earth all around and arrived in Santa Cruz de la Sierra, where I was centuries back in deep Bolivia, pressed down by rain clouds and overhung by the Andes, mightier than the Alps. Next I was put down among the stately palm trees, timeless wooden balconies and still airs of Lima, queen of the vanished Spanish Empire. Then great wings carried me above a tremendous desert, as in the Arabian Nights, to Santiago de Chile, remarkable for its cheerful poverty and keen air and the tall Andean wall nearby. Soon I was transported to the broad and gleaming city of Buenos Aires, with its romantic little bars and glitter and bustle and the ghosts of the good fight we fought there. . . . Next I crossed the tawny Río de la Plata to Montevideo, always calm and serene in seeming. Then São Paulo again for one day, then Rio, then Goiânia, of all places.

And now, like a woman in a dream, I was flying back into the shallow upland bowl of Anápolis.

The Bowens met me on this Saturday afternoon and we planned an early start to the *fazenda* the next morning. There were changes. A French couple, Jazz and Gazu Antoinette, whom I had met in Rio, were living in Liberty Hall. Roger Ward was gone, sold out and returned to his job with Boeing. The French people had bought his land. A contract had been let to pave the streets of Anápolis (miracle!).

And things were still the same. People still were saying the national capital would be moved to Goiás soon. And they were still figuring their possible profits from land and rice deals on the backs of grubby envelopes.

When early on a Sunday morning I set out once more on the long drive to Fazenda Chavante, the world which had been spinning around me like a badly-edited travel film came to a full stop. All at once, the gentle hills and the far distances summoned me toward quietude.

As we left the sprawling sun-baked city of Anápolis behind us, the pleasure of my sight in resting on the ancient rolling hills and their valleys subtle with morning shadow was like that aroused by hearing great music or an assurance of steadfast love. As we drove rapidly along, the distance blurred details which otherwise would have caused pain. Huts unfit for animals to live in became mysteriously right for their setting and the lithe, soft-voiced backlanders who pass in them such brief, uncertain lives became part of a panoramic slow-motion ballet of infinite mannered charm.

The hills rising to low mountains as we went along were themselves integral to the story, a changing background that acted on the people to vary their pattern of life and their postures. For me a crescendo always came when at last our vehicle labored to the top of the range and there burst into view the magnificence of the rich forests and the broad plains and the miragelike mountains far beyond.

A Spanish legend says the mountain to which Satan led the Christ for his great temptation in the wilderness was in Spain, near Barcelona, and they call it Tibidabo, "All these things will I give thee." Once you free the story from the conventional Biblical geography, it might just as well have happened on Brazil's highland divide. Only a Divinity, looking northeast from the mountain ridge here dominating the remote beginnings of the tremendous world-apart that is the Amazon Valley, could resist the imposing power of its beauty.

A few miles beyond the ridge, when I could see more

clearly the blue mountains to the northeast, I said to myself:
"The place is there, there!" Once again I seemed to have safe
haven in my grasp. Once more I believed sanctuary could be
found in my forests along the Rio das Almas, in the direction
of the blue mountains.

There was new life stirring in the upper country, for the
long harvest was about to begin. New inns were going up
along the big road. We passed trucks bringing in dark-skinned
migrants seeking work in the harvest and land in the *Colônia*.
We saw the roadside camps of others who had come by foot
from as far as Bahia, a thousand miles away.

There were changes at Barranca also, new houses everywhere and a new concrete bridge a-building across Ghost
River. We stopped for cold drinks at the café of my slightly
cross-eyed friend, Donato, with whom I had become ac-
quainted when I stopped there on trips to and from the farm.
He and his tiny wife seemed glad to see me. They were telling
a story of Dr. Sayão's.

"They say this Joaquim went to Dr. Sayão and said, 'Dr.
Sayão, what am I going to do? Last week I went to visit my
mother in Anápolis and when I got back, there were new
houses built on three sides of mine, right up against the walls.
This morning when I woke up, there was another one built
right up against my front door! How am I going to get in
and out of my house?' Then Dr. Sayão said, 'Joaquim, I guess
you'll just have to get yourself a ladder and scramble over
the other man's roof!' " They swore it was a true story of
fast-growing, uncontrolled Barranca.

The boom spirit was in the air. Many of the new buildings
housed bars and there were side-street *pensões* where girls
lived in rowdy prostitution, along with petty criminals and
crooks from all over the region. Rich pickings from the growing *Colônia* had drawn them there, making the wildcat town,
Barranca, like one of the old frontier towns of our West.
Dusty trucks replaced horses at hitching posts and a radio
loud-speaker blaring dance music reminded you it was the
twentieth century. But the spirit was the same, as any devotee

of Wild West movies could tell at once. To me it often looked more like a movie set than a real town.

As we drove on toward the farm, I looked with curiosity at the tall mountain rice growing on the steep hillsides around Ceres. It was silvery blue-green and the heads were long and heavy, like big wheat heads, only not bearded. When we turned into our forest trail, we could see many markings where new clearings were to be. The road was deeply gutted with wheel ruts, but I didn't care. The Plymouth was far, far away, in São Paulo being rebuilt so that I could (might) [did not] get my money out of it.

I idly asked the driver at one of our stops what had become of my former driver, Waldemar; I like to know how every story ends.

"Oh, he married that widow at Anápolis," was the answer.

A *caboclo* nearby spoke up.

"Didn't he get killed in that shooting up at Sant' Ana?"

The driver shook his head doubtfully.

"Wasn't it a wreck he was in? I believe something did happen to him."

Exit Waldemar. In the backlands you get shot or maybe it was a wreck or you die of malaria or maybe it was syphilis or pneumonia. At least you don't have to worry about growing old. I was briefly sad for Waldemar till I reflected that if he got killed in a wreck it was no doubt his own fault and he probably took better men with him.

We stopped at Davino's home a few hundred yards from the river. It was a mansion hut, bigger than most and tile-roofed. Davino was there, with his bedraggled little wife and pretty towheaded girl children, all of them dirt-stained and cruelly bitten by the stinging gnats. I went in to say hello and Davino served the ceremonial cup of coffee.

Changes at the river port surprised me. Trees had been cut on the *Colônia* side and there were several huts standing about, one of them a "store." The port was quite towny.

When we crossed in the dancing canoe, I found changes on the other side too. A new track ran up through the

Bowens' clearing parallel to the Frenchman's line. About a mile inland, opposite to where my clearing was located, a path cut through the woods to it.

When I emerged into the Chavante clearing, I was all at once utterly lost, turned around, disoriented, as I had been the first time I came there, before the burning.

It was a big strange hole in a forbidding forest; the giant trees stood all around like palisades or a prison stockade. The silvery-green rice came up to my shoulders, the heavy, paling heads bending gracefully over. As I toiled along a "path," I stumbled over concealed stumps and had to climb over huge logs every few yards. These obstacles bred impatience in me. Why didn't they clear the main path into the farm? Then I remembered that neither the wheel nor the saw was used in daily life on Fazenda Chavante, nor any other tools except axes, crude brush hooks, hoes and sickles.

The first house we came to was Manoel's. It was a well-built pole hut covered with rice straw. Inside it partitions of split saplings divided the house into three tiny rooms— entrance, kitchen and sleeping room. Manoel's wife was there, but he was not. After we exchanged civilities I asked her to send for him, and went on.

Several hundred yards farther on I came to a big open space where Emílio had built his home. Emílio and his family emerged from the dark interior of the hut to shake my hand, their work-hardened palms limp and cold against mine. There was a big log in the shade of the house and we perched along the natural bench to take coffee out of thimble-sized enamel cups. We conversed.

"How have you passed the rains, S'hor Emílio?" I asked after a while. "There was some trouble with José after I left, they tell me."

Pause. "There was trouble, senhora."

"Was it bad, the way the roça burned?"

Pause, and then: "It was bad, senhora."

Ezequiel and his wife appeared through the grain and after shaking my hand, sat with us on the log.

"What about the harvest? They say the rice looks good around here."

"It looks good, *senhora*." The answer came slowly, in rough unison.

"Are you two going to have a good crop?"

The men fell into ruminative silence. Ezequiel began working his face, prelude to speech.

"The *senhora* can be sure of one thing, she won't lose money on me," he finally got out.

We had been over this ground once already. Also, I had glimpsed Ezequiel's account book the night before and the only thing I was sure about was that lose money on him I would.

"And how did you fare through the rains?" This was the crucial question, to which I had been leading by steps.

Silence.

"I'd like to hear about it," I said.

Emílio stirred in the shadow of his hut. "We managed, *senhora*," he said.

"Did you get enough supplies?"

Silence.

"I was just wondering how things came through."

More silence. Then Emílio repeated, "We managed." Ezequiel gave a deep assenting sound, a long drawn-out "Eh-h-h-*h*" that rose in tone at the very end.

I only had a few hours here at most and at this rate I would never learn anything definite. In saying so little, the men had implied so much.

"I'll arrange money to help with the harvest," I said. "I hope to come back about the time you finish cutting the rice."

One of Ezequiel's fuzzy-headed, spindly sons guided me across a deep-banked stream to the little knoll where Chico had built his house. Chico's wife was cooking out of doors, with only a roof above the stove. His hut, sheltering his household furnishings, was flimsy and I wondered how they had kept dry in the rains. We went gravely through the handshaking and I accepted another *cafezinho*. We talked a while.

"Chico, you know all this is new to me and I have to depend

on you to help me keep up with things," I said finally. "I'm anxious to know how you got along here during the rains. I have the impression there were some complaints about supplies.

Chico studied the ground, not answering.

"Didn't the food supplies come through?"

At last he said: "They did not always come through, *dona*. They say the river washed out the bridge at Ceres."

This was true; for about a month the only way to cross the flood-high Rio das Almas had been by canoe.

My heart felt heavy.

"Did you actually do without food?"

A long pause, and then: "We got by."

I would never find out what had happened!

"Was there sickness?" I asked, still trying.

"There were some colds. Nothing serious."

Thank Heaven for that.

Chico thought our rice was promising. I told him I had heard the general crop was small because the late rains had failed. It would probably make the price go high.

"*Se Deus quiser*," said Chico, and he meant "God grant it."

Alone I returned toward Emílio's, scrambling down the steep bank of the little stream they had named Chavante, the brook where the whole community got their water and did their washing. Everything I had seen in the clearing was raw and forbidding, like the scene of a mighty knock-down fight, as indeed it was. It was harsh beyond description; the very earth between the growing rice looked wrong for culti-vated earth. Around the clumps of rice it was lumpy, streaked with ash and filled with the light debris of the burning. In other places, where the waters of the heavy rains had stood or run, it looked too packed, too slick.

I had never known anything like this, only hills and fields and streams and woods that had been cared for or at least tamed. It oppressed me. Many backlanders believe there are spirits in the forest. They will not leave a tree standing near their huts for fear an evil one will hide behind it. Even their

Christianity is often mixed with belief in the ancient earth spirits. I could comprehend this, for an alien presence seemed round about me here.

It would never do not to take the ceremonial *cafezinho* with each family, so I went to Ezequiel's hut. There I met for the first time Ezequiel's daughter, Maria, whom Joan and I had paid a small salary to teach a school for the children on our places. She had become the chief figure in a drama, I had been told on the way to the farm. Her cash salary from the school had caused envy. Wagging tongues had shadowed the girl's good name and her suitor, a landworker on a neighboring place, had broken off with her. Maria had offered to go to Ceres and have a doctor examine her for virginity and when this suggestion was not accepted, she pulverized a piece of broken glass and ate it.

The ensuing excitement had been tremendous, naturally. It ended with Ezequiel and his wife and Maria and the suitor all walking out to the big road to catch a ride to the hospital in Ceres, where Maria was given treatment.

Maria apparently had come through it without serious consequences, for she was plump and healthy-looking. The romance was patched up, I had been told. I did not know whether to admire the girl for what might have been a clever trick or to pity her for the great suffering she must have gone through to want to take her own life. The trouble upset the school and led to its abandonment.

My last call was at Manoel's, on my way out. When I approached his home through the tall rice, I saw him in characteristic pose, sitting in one of his cherished chairs, his young son on his lap. We shook hands, then he fetched the other chair and invited me to sit. He asked his wife to bring *cafezinhos*. He was polite, detached, restrained in manner. We talked generalities for a while.

"How is your crop, Manoel?" I inquired at last.

"More or less, Dona Virginia, more or less."

I ventured a few more questions and got equally uninformative answers.

"Manoel, why did José do what he did?" I asked. "I was disappointed in him. I thought he'd make a good man here."

Now came the old sneer, bitter and strong.

"José didn't want to starve up here in this *mato!*"

"You know I arranged for food to be sent. Didn't the bridge go out?"

We contemplated the tall rice beyond the bare space, not looking at each other.

"So they said. It's always something, *dona*, always something."

"It hasn't been too easy for me, either," I said, after a short silence. "I made the best arrangements possible."

"My family didn't starve," said Manoel. "In spite of . . ."

He didn't continue on and say whether it was in spite of the bridge going out or in spite of José's predictions or of my failure to foresee a break in the communications during the rains. This illiterate backwoodsman was a master of the subtle thrust. If you were in the right, you were invulnerable against him. But if you were on uncertain ground, he would find a way to cut it from under your feet.

I saw we would get nowhere.

"Manoel, I've got to go now. Thank you for the *cafezinho*. Do you need anything for the harvest besides the money I promised?"

"I *need* a big cloth to thresh the rice on." His emphasis implied there was a great deal of difference between his needing something and his getting it.

"Very well, I'll see about it. Until later, Manoel."

"Until later, *senhora*."

Their horny hands were always so limp and cold in mine.

I hurried away, hurried, hurried. With every step that took me away from the hostile clearing, I breathed more easily. Ghost River, yellow and swollen with rain, muttered angrily in the narrows above our landing. The new little community on the *Colônia* side of the river port suddenly seemed forlorn, hopeless, lost. As we drove out through the tunnel of forest trees covering the trail, the shade cast there seemed not only dark but dank. Only when we reached the highway did my near-panic begin to ease.

We stopped to eat at Córrego Sêco on the return trip and the greasy food sat heavily on my stomach. On the long return drive to Anápolis, my left side, which had improved immensely in Buenos Aires, began to ache miserably. For half the night I could not sleep, though I was utterly exhausted. My thoughts went around and around. My life, it seemed to me, had been going in aimless circles ever since I first began to refuse the jumps the backlands put in my way. I had turned from one new avenue of escape to another, till finally, in Bolivia, I had come to see that I should start all over again in Goiás.

But it did not seem possible after my visit to the clearing; there was too much against me there. Since my return visit to the Fazenda Chavante, I felt as if I were spinning, like a runner who had run to give himself the momentum to leap up and climb over a high wall and who, at the moment of clutching the wall, had found it was paper and burst through it to stagger and spin on, out of control.

In the morning, I had to get up early to catch the plane for the Borghi settlement, and this I accordingly did.

Hugo Borghi, a Brazilian of Italian blood, had bought or taken option on a tremendous acreage in eastern Goiás where he was setting up a complete agro-industrial community. The products of mechanized farming were to be processed and packaged there and delivered by air freight to Borghi's own retail outlets in Rio and São Paulo. Borghi intended to build houses on cleared land and sell the plots to farmers, who would, of necessity, become suppliers for him. He already had a cargo service using U.S. surplus-property DC-3's in the highlands and it touched his Formosa settlement, which was some three hundred rough miles by road from Anápolis.

For three days I was shown over Borghi's huge operation, riding by muleback part of the time and flying in a tiny observation plane the rest. The beginnings I saw were very ambitious, but I was aware that the rich vegetation of Brazil covers the ruins of many brave beginnings and I wondered what would happen to our DP's if they got marooned here as day labor. When money grew tight, they would feel it first of all. They would have to walk out, new additions to the landless millions roaming Brazil. I decided to advise against sending them here. (The project has since come to a full stop, I have learned.)

On this visit, a new, strange and interesting scene helped me put my personal perplexities out of mind. When you are among Brazilians, even the most serious business has its zany moments. Once when I was returning from an observation flight, an *ema*, a Brazilian ostrich, nearly wrecked our small plane by running under us just as we landed. Immediately the pilot and I piled out of the plane and onto an already over-loaded waiting jeep, to pursue the swift bird wildly around the jungle landing strip until he darted into the woods. Why we made the dangerous and futile chase I do not know. It was instinctive and reckless and somehow satisfying.

My visit to this raw outpost seemed to cap a series of incidents growing more and more unreal. Two months previously I had landed at Montevideo one morning with Bill and Bob Rossborough, picked up the telephone and arranged for us to see the president of the country the next day on IRO business without stopping once to think this was certainly some kind of a speed record for arranging an interview with a chief of state. Quick changes and sudden contrasts had dulled my power to recognize the unusual. Here at Formosa I met a man—horribly scarred—who hunted jaguars by following them into a cave armed only with a torch and a spear, and I was blithely arranging to go along as spectator on one of these suicide hunts when a change in airplane schedules upset the plans. If anybody had said, "By the way, Dona Virginia, we have a young dinosaur out here that we're trying to break," I would no doubt have answered with a big smile on my slap-happy face, "Oh, wonderful! *Please* let me ride him!"

There were five persons on the cargo plane that took us from Formosa to Rio—the pilot and co-pilot, a relative of the governor of Goiás, an inspector of the Bank of Brazil and myself. An overcast developed during the five-hour trip and the pilot went above it to about ten thousand feet, where we swam along in a light haze, the motors throbbing with a smooth rhythm. The sun had wheeled overhead and was sinking behind us when we sighted the taller peaks of the mountain chain behind Rio de Janeiro thrusting through the overcast in a jagged irregular line. Soon after, we all knew we must be near the coast itself and over an invisible nest of lower peaks in and around Rio. On my first flight to Brazil in 1941 our plane had broken through an overcast north of the city and floated like a leaf settling down over the green-purple mountains and the dramatic purple-blue bay. Unforgettable against the rich colors, which were so like those of an iridescent Brazilian butterfly's wings, stood the enormous Christ of Corcovado, spread-eagled against the blue-purple-green glory as a gleaming cross of white. I waited to see this uplifting sight again but it did not come.

We remained in a world of light, the sky a thinning blue, the clouds just below us white as new snow except here and there where they reflected gold and pink from the sunset. I noticed the sun coming around across my window time after time and realized we were circling.

Around and around we circled, in a wide, steady sweep. My two men companions went into the cabin. Around we circled, majestically, and I watched the sun, red and enormous now, sink closer to our white horizon. Our white cloud-floor, trailing up wisps here and there, was like those scenes in movies where a heavenly aviator-guide comes to take departing souls to a better world. So light, so gay, the scene was; I thought about my life and was sure it had been a very good life because I had been lucky enough to see so much of the wonder of the wide, wide world. I thought also how lucky I had been to find at last the sweetest kind of assuagement for the need for love and I believed I had myself learned to be kind in love; I was proud of that. On we swept in our wide circle.

I knew we must be in trouble, but I didn't stir to go and find out what it was. The scene outside my window was entrancing, the red-gold sinking sun appeared to roll slowly around us. Once, the clouds underneath us thinned and I thought I glimpsed city lights at the bottom of a blue well far below, but the plane wheeled on.

We must have been circling for three-quarters of an hour when the sun left us and the dusk of the tropic night seeped up from the darkening cloud bank below.

I had a fleeting vision of Alfredo silently appearing in his little blue plane to take me away, but it was only the fancy of a fancy. Gone now were the wearisome details of living; I seemed slightly drunk on a light wine pressed out of everything lovely I had ever known. The governor's relative, pale green in color, came out of the cabin to warn me to fasten my seat belt, but this I had already done. He said the radio had been out for two hours. The pilot had been waiting for a hole to develop in the clouds below, but none had come and we had to go down.

As we slowly wheeled around on our last wide circle I thought that if we hit a mountain it would all be over in an instant. If we grazed one and toppled into the sea, I should have to try to keep afloat although I am a very poor swimmer. I took off my mosquito boots and my leather coat, to give myself more freedom in the water. I was sitting by one emergency door and the governor's relative strapped himself in near the other.

The plane tilted, with the night thickening all around us, and plunged softly into the darkening cloud. As we turned and sank, the sound of the motors changed, became lulling. The soft downward motion through the deep gray mist and the deepened hum of the motors came into my senses with an inexpressible sweetness, as sleep comes softly after the most ardent and most tender love.

How long it took us to float earthward through the overcast I do not know, for the last moments of it were a pleasant grayout for me, as if I were meeting the final release halfway. The sound of the motors sharpened again as we came out of the cloud, not against a mountain, but far out over the night-black sea. In the distance could be seen the glow and then the sparkle of lights—the earth once more.

The sparkle of the lights was lovely, but I felt no relief for I had felt no fear. As our now thoroughly rattled pilot came down at Rio's short Santos Dumont airport, he made such a steep approach I thought he'd spatter us all over the administration building. He managed to pull up, however, and soon I was climbing out into the soft warm moist night air of Rio. News of our trouble upstairs had got around, since we were well overdue, and Borghi himself, complete with entourage, was there to meet us. I slipped away and took a cab to Copacabana and home.

On the long seaside drive from downtown Rio to Copacabana Beach, I gradually made my own delayed landing back on earth. Except for rare good luck, I realized, I should even now be dead, like Alfredo, crashed against one of the peaks thrusting up like fingers around Rio de Janeiro. I remembered the peacefulness that had come over me when the plane sank gently into the misty darkness and for the first time in a long while, I felt something close to genuine dismay. Here with the earth friendly about me, I was not uneasy because of the danger of immediate death I had passed through, but because I had drawn so much sweetness from it.

When I got home I told Irene and Serra about our close shave and laughed about the way the governor's relative had turned pea-green. It was very funny to remember his pop-eyes trying to look unconcerned out of a face that color.

"You will do thees crazee thing too many time, Virginia," said Irene, who knew how Alfredo and I had flirted with haze-danger on our trip to Goiânia and about the return from Jaú. "One day you will crash down the same as your Chilean friend."

"Oh, I've always had flying luck," I protested. "Nothing can happen to me."

I did not like being compared to Alfredo, whom I had come to consider a sort of suicide. I needed to settle down in one place for a while and catch up with myself, that was all.

11

The city of Rio de Janeiro is not the place for an American to get his feet back on the ground. My renewed sense of defeat after I visited the Chavante clearing had affected me curiously; it had set me swinging far wide of my own temperament's orbit and I knew I should pull myself back. But the soft-mannered people around me, with their constant encouragement not to worry, were an influence against my making the effort.

The difference between the Brazilians and me was this: if I yielded to their civilization's gentle but constant pressure to let things slide and abandoned my own bent for seeking solutions, then I would let go altogether. But the Brazilians' penchant for postponing crises is a way of yielding little skirmishes to win larger campaigns; they smile and avoid forcing issues, yet underneath their complaisance seethes a fantastically subtle wire-pulling for advantage.

Although it had never bothered me before, the climate of Rio seemed to turn against me now and the sedative heat of the rainy season slackened my mainspring of resolution. As if this were not enough, the brand-new building into which the IRO had recently moved—providing us with the best quarters to be found for the price—had begun to lean. With pessimists warning darkly of collapse, it was far from stabilizing for me to work nine stories up in an office where some of the floors had visibly buckled and a dropped pencil might go creeping off by itself as if it had a grisly little will of its own.

If you can manage to hold yourself together through the wet, hot months of Rio, you are lucky, but not safe. For at the end of the heat, when your fiber is already weakened, comes the Rio *carnaval*.

In Rio's unique carnival the African darkness always lurking just beyond appearances in tropical Brazil at last comes out into the open. It begins with a literal invasion of Rio de Janeiro by the dark people of the *favelas*.

The *favelas* are shacktowns built on Rio's wastelands, especially on the abrupt mountains that rise in and around the city. For fifty-one weeks of the year the dark poor live a life apart in these shantytowns, entering the city proper in the daytime to perform its menial tasks and hard labor. In Rio's mountaintop slums, which command an extravagant panorama of natural beauty, the witch doctor is king. No one dares go up there from the city below except occasional squads of Rio's tough, spindly-legged little policemen. But at *carnaval* time, the *favelas* pour down, their people descending in small, crudely costumed groups, each group with a little band playing battered horns and trumpets and homemade drums.

At first, as if in timidity, they ride around on streetcars, chanting the chosen carnival samba tunes, and then, growing bolder, they start jogging through the streets with a simple, loose-kneed dance step. Fortified by raw rum and the ether content of the cheap perfume they spray lavishly on each other, they can sustain this primitive dancing for days.

As the *favela* groups grow ever more numerous, costumed dancing parties begin to pour out from the warrens where live the middle class and the poor of the lower city. Business slows to a stop and soon the city seems to melt together, all color and class lines gone. At night there is a rough sorting out, for the rich have their own elegant costume balls and the middle class their preferred cabarets. But the spirit of the *favela* penetrates everywhere; like somnambulists, the dancers pack together and jog slowly up and down to the monotonous, blaring repetition of the same two or three *carnaval* tunes. The deep night covers sporadic private saturnalia, but that is part of Rio's everyday life; the novelty is the progress of the music and the dancing in the streets.

Rio's *carnaval* was strange to me not because of unusual variety in the dancing, the music or the costumes, but because all three were curiously monotonous. Most negro men appeared as African savages and a great many other males dressed as women. I could understand why the negroes chose the cool, cheap grass skirts, but it puzzled me to see so many white and near-white Brazilian men in female costume. Most of them made graceful, pretty girls and obviously had not chosen the disguise for comic effect. Nor could I believe they were all inverts; there were too many of them. I came to think that this Brazilian peculiarity must parallel the ritual celebrations of the primitive hunting tribes in which the male dancers costume themselves as the animals that are their chief quarry. Since the object of the Brazilian males' compulsive quest for women is always a new sex victory, their pursuit, like animal hunting, is a game lost the moment it is won, for a new chase must inevitably follow. Thus the Brazilian men's only real relief from the eroticism which is like a sickness among them would be to change sex and become women, as so many do in fancy at *carnaval* time.

As *carnaval* week progressed I watched the spectacle develop during the daytime and went to the dances at night, from the fancy ones at the Copacabana Hotel to the middle-class cabarets. But the daytime spectacle, the jogging street crowds, the beat of the *favela* drums, ended by capturing me. I would find a balcony and watch hour after hour. I had always loved dancing, but I had never before known how absorbing it can become to look on at mass dance ceremonials.

For the Brazilian *carnaval*, as its volume swelled, ceased to be simple merrymaking and began to take on the nature of a communal ceremonial rite. The small parties of friends who had started out together broke up and merged into the crowd; the whole city at length ran melted through its own streets.

The multiplying drums and the minor, weak singing of the same unisonous, simple music over and over seemed to take dominion over the senses until finally the consciousness became divorced from its everyday self. There were as many people watching the dancers in the crowd as there were dancing and the watchers came to have the same somnambulistic look as the dancers. No one was himself, all of us seemed to move in mystic suspension, the stranger because the world around us was shot through with sunshine and gay colors.

Toward the end of *carnaval*, the sporadic unison singing grew ever weaker; gradually the drums established their sole dominion, Africa prevailing. Their patient, unhurried beat pacing the kaleidoscopic milling of the costumed dancers was like the pulse beat of a simpler world, of a heart so vast and timeless it was beyond emotion. There was no gaiety, no excitement in these drums, only relief from feeling. I had not been conscious of unhappiness, but it was if I had been very unhappy and now was no longer so, under the final magic of the drums. They were forgetfulness, nirvana.

When the *carnaval* was over, I found it extremely hard to face work. It seemed wasteful to spend time on the innumerable details of my job when I remembered the sense of merging into all eternity induced by the *favela* drums. It was unpleasant to focus my attention and to tighten my mental and spiritual muscles to the necessary grip. Perhaps I was more susceptible than most foreigners to the African mysticism in which rhythm rather than revelation opens avenues of communication with the Universal Spirit; I was nursed by negroes from birth and spent my very early years mostly in their world, where I took refuge from my warring, Victorian-minded parents. But I question whether anybody who is caught by the *carnaval* drums comes back to what he was for some time thereafter. The experience, which may be that of dipping back through eons of time, marks our civilized realities with a faint, persistent question mark.

An immediate sequel to the *carnaval* for me was another

accident. Already the Brazilian chapter of my life had had more wrecks and near-disasters than my whole previous existence. In the new one I was injured.

Only a few days after the *favela* drums ceased their throbbing, while traces of their drug were still in my veins, I broke a rule rigidly followed ever since my first visit to Rio in 1941 and climbed into a *lotação*, one of the ramshackle old jitney station wagons that pound through the city at the rush hour. A few minutes later its brakes failed and we rolled inexorably, as in a bad dream, into a shiny new passenger car that brashly tried to beat the lights in front of us. My ankle was badly wrenched; the accident put me on crutches and the crutches brought back the old shoulder pain.

At this point, providentially, I was sent to the coolor airs of Goiás on business for the IRO. After I completed my assignment, I asked for and received permission to spend part of my accrued leave there arranging for the harvest at Fazenda Chavante.

When next I started north from Anápolis to the forest country, my mood was very different from that of my last visit. Under the constant if not severe harassment of the pain caused by my injury, my spirit seemed to have become more on guard. I knew I could never ignore the strong attraction of the back country, but I was beginning to mistrust it. Reflecting on it as we set out, I sensed a familiarity in the upland's spell. The blue distances beyond the mountains ahead always promised lasting ease and sweetness of the kind I had known for a moment when we plunged unguided into the dark clouds over Rio or the easeful oblivion induced by the *favela* drums; so similar both to the complete release following the part of love that mankind with apt imagery has named the little death.

It always came back, the idea of death in a form not associated with fear or dread. The truck I rode lumbered through the too-quiet steep slopes of the old pastures toward the mountains, and I mulled over the curious circumstance.

It had started with Alfredo, I was almost sure. Alfredo's calm disregard of the danger of death had aroused my admiration and imagination. Then had come the premonition causing me to write my farewell letters when I agreed to fly with him. Alfredo could almost have been an emissary of death, not a dark angel, but one clad in the brilliance of the thin upland sunlight. Alfredo had been an escapist who had achieved more complete freedom from mundane bonds than anybody I had ever known, yet in the end I felt he had invited his disaster. He had once encouraged me to return to the struggle I had dropped when I came to the backlands, it was true. Instead of being influenced by his advice, I was being influenced by his example, it seemed.

Once I was on a Spanish packet tossed by a wicked storm in the Mediterranean's Gulf of Roses, called the graveyard of ships. Wind-danger had always come to me out of the black tornado-breeding clouds that sweep up through the American South from the Gulf of Mexico and I did not perceive the danger in the sea storm because the sun continued to shine and the sky stayed resolutely blue. Something similar had happened when I came to Goiás. Until then, I had associated death with old age and illness, both dark thoughts. But here, at a time when the forward movement of my life was temporarily halted, the idea of death had crept in under another guise and it kept returning without tripping the proper alarm bells. Was it not possible to go on from accepting the thought of death too readily to inviting and then seeking it? I sincerely believed something of the sort had happened to my friend Alfredo.

When I came to the backlands, I had thought it was to build anew, not to escape. But when I could not even begin to make the dream come true, it had affected me profoundly. The complete failure of the dream, down to the minutest details, had proved crucial; and I had begun to turn and turn, always seeking an easier way out of difficulties as they appeared ahead.

In the process, I had apparently picked up something of

Alfredo's aura of fatal recklessness. Irene, who heard about my scrapes and near-accidents as they happened, did not need second sight to warn me I would end as Alfredo had. But lately it had gone further. Shortly after my jitney crash, Bill Mizelle had cabled from Buenos Aires to ask if I was all right without even knowing I had had a mishap. He was the least fanciful of men and it was completely unlike him to express any such anxiety without a known reason for it.

More than anything else this persuaded me my misgivings were justified: those who cared for me sensed my danger too.

Though my thoughts came clearer in the cool uplands, Goiás made me uneasy now. I reminded myself it was only a countryside, magnificent country ancient in geologic time though new to history. By a fairly logical train of events I had come to plant a crop of dreams here when I was disappointed and tired and I had been disconcerted and puzzled and upset when I could not at once start harvesting them. That was it and that was all.

The truck in which I was riding topped the mountain ridge and I began to glimpse the fabulous country beyond, lost world enough for any dreamer. All at once my reasoning dissolved into wonder. This wide sweep of all imaginable beauty seized on me like great music, and once more drew me against my will, like obsessive love.

We rounded outside curves crossing the ridge and I watched eagerly for the blue distances to the northeast where lay my forests of Chavante. As they had never failed to do, they held out to me a promise. But even as I felt their spell once more, uneasiness persisted and I could not be sure they promised happiness. I could see the life of the foreground with clearer vision than on my last return and its harshness scratched across the sheathing of my heart like a rough fingernail. How could there be a place for happiness here in the midst of this cruel, slow-motion battle between man and nature?

And now came the traitor thought, a new temptation. Why not drop all the struggle and vanish away into the quiet places beyond the edge of the brutal conflict of the frontier?

It would solve everything, this complete escape into the backlands.

Scattered all through that vast mysterious region stretched out before my eyes stood old homesteads. They had cool dark floors of packed and hardened earth. They had whitewashed walls, inside and out, and peaked tile roofs of soft, weathering red. Most of them had little streamlets led from far away to run near the kitchen door or through the house itself. You would sit on a long bench and eat off a table of long scrubbed hand-hewn boards in the midst of a big family. Your bed would be a clean ticking bag filled with fresh corn shucks or new rice straw. You would bathe in a clear running branch somewhere near the house. You could appear there and be accepted without question, stay there days or weeks and then move on. You would never have to work or worry but only distribute small presents and be a pleasant guest, ready to talk or listen.

Could a woman do it? I would need a horse and a bedroll and a good gun. I could wander endlessly, right up to the forbidden country of the wild Indians. I could get one of the backlanders' heavy wool capes that made them look like batmen in the dusk, and one of their broad-brimmed hats. The backlanders already considered me slightly touched by God, I supposed; in spite of dire warnings, I had never been molested in the *sertão*. I could be like the *sertão* "walkers," people who pick out a stretch of country and walk up and down it without ceasing all their lives, fed and cared for by families along their route; only I would ride, and range far.

It was not impractical. I could sell out everything, convert all my money into cruzeiros and deposit it in an Anápolis bank, where it would draw ten per cent interest a year. The little income would be all I'd ever need, wandering here.

I was amazed at the reality the idea began to assume in my mind. It was not entirely new; my thoughts had been tending in this direction when Alfredo came along—the little inn near the São Patrício river had started it. And then Alfredo had offered me a much broader version of the wandering life, in a plane.

Memory of Alfredo always set up a train of doubts and questions. He had actually embarked on a kind of aimless meandering after I left; he had no real reason for the flights he was making around the country although he said they were favors to friends and yielded a little expense money. Alfredo had been the first one to point out we were "missing the point" of Goiás in our struggles here. He himself had not struggled much, but rather had drifted, and Alfredo was dead.

I was still convinced Alfredo had drifted so fatally because no human tie held him firmly to life. I myself had had no close tie when I planned to fly with him. But had I not contracted a new obligation since the time of my adventure with Alfredo —my promise to Bill not to yield to the very temptation that now so strongly summoned me?

My thoughts dwelt long on this promise as we covered the dusty miles. (Truck trips in the *sertão* were excellent times for recapitulation and I had never needed to recapitulate so much as now.) The instant my pledge to Bill rose to the surface of my thoughts I knew it would keep me from giving in to the backlands, but I wanted to know the reasons why. Very rarely in my life had I ever made an agreement without an escape clause and I had previously avoided involving Bill and myself in any kind of obligation. Out of my long reverie, I realized why I had contracted this one and why it was absolute.

The person who can learn to love enough to put another's happiness first is supremely fortunate, for the experience crowns life, ran my thoughts. I had discovered this in the development of my own feelings toward Bill over three years. But it is not necessarily a bond to life, I realized now. The other person's true devotion forges the bond.

What evidence convinced me now that I was fortunate enough to be so loved? I had had it spelled out for me in Bill's letters from Argentina, most unforgettably at the time when he thought I was falling in love with Alfredo. Separation had been a revealing test. When Bill asked me not to vanish into the backlands, he asked for a protective lien on my life. His cable out of the blue at the time of my injury in the jitney had been like a hand pulling me back to firm ground; mankind is impressed by mysteries and this evidence that he could reach across space to me moved me deeply. Ultimately it was a matter of faith, rather than reason; I had come to believe and the promise held.

No such tie had existed when I left the big cities and newspaper work to start swinging high and wide into foolish adventures and unwise projects. But the bond was defining itself even as I was being drawn further and further into this curious existence one degree beyond ordinary reality, the world of waifs and wanderers and people who don't care what happens to them. On this present long slow drive through the back country, I had been like a dizzy person who steps to the window for a breath of fresh air and is unexpectedly seized by an impulse to jump out. But that was over now; my promise to Bill would always protect me against this magnificent region's invitation to a final involvement. Even so, I was deeply committed here and I did not know how it would come out.

One thing was certain: from this time on, unlike Alfredo when I knew him, I consciously did not want to die. I set my will against death.

It was midafternoon by the time the truck took me down the forest trail to the Rio das Almas and I crossed in the dancing canoe. Painfully I limped up the dusty track on my crutch. At the top of the trail, where the path led through the forest to my clearing, the French people had started a work camp to clear and plant a large acreage in coffee. The women in the quiet huts stared at me curiously as I limped by and entered the woodland path.

When I came out of the forest into my clearing, I found that most of the rice had already been cut. Only patches of late planting had been left standing to ripen more. The rich red of the loamy soil came up strong between yellowing

clumps of rice stalks jaggedly hacked off some six inches above
the ground. With the tall rice gone, I saw to my dismay how
many enormous tree trunks lay about like lifeless giants
sprawling amid the ashes of the fire that had put them to the
torture. Many were rare and precious hardwoods, wasting
here for lack of means to get them to a mill.

As I approached the first house, Manoel's, I saw he had set
up in a bare place beyond it a ten- or twelve-foot pole structure rather like a miniature Eiffel Tower. Manoel himself was
on a platform atop this tower and he had a bucket in his hand.
At my first view of him, he was pouring out of the bucket a
stream of threshed rice which fell onto a light yellow-gold pile
on the ground below while a cloud of chaff fluttered away on
a gentle breeze.

Manoel spoke to me, letting the bucket down on a rope for
his wife to refill from another larger pile of threshed rice lying
in an open shed nearby. His wife, more polite than he, stopped
her work to shake hands with me and commiserate about the
crutch, which I briefly explained.

"You've got a real skyscraper—this looks like Rio de
Janeiro," I said to Manoel, examining the way he had tied
his tower together with vines.

"Dona Virginia, a man has to do what he can up here in this
mato," he said, his Othellolike face serious. "Next year I can't
have people tramping back and forth through my crop. I've
lost too much rice already."

I had expected unpleasantness from Manoel and I was not
disappointed.

"Come on down and we can talk about it," I said with
determined cheerfulness. "That little path through your field
couldn't have hurt much."

Manoel made no move to come down. He remained still, on
one knee, dangling the rope to the ground. Silhouetted there
in his work-stained, patched clothes, he might have been a
statue on a pedestal, representing his kind the world over, the
man who works the land with crude tools. Whenever he
opened his mouth, he spoke trouble for me, yet Manoel com-

manded my interest. I could not help admiring the way he always tried to find a better means to do his work. Obviously his system of separating the rice from its chaff was much faster than the usual method of tossing it up into the air from trays. Yet in all this countryside I had seen only one other tower such as Manoel's and that was at the farm of Davino, a literate white man from the progressive south.

"I can't stop now, Dona Virginia," said Manoel. "I'll be down later. You can go and see the others."

Always the busy man, Manoel, controlling the scene to prove he was as good as anybody else.

"All right, Manoel," I said. "Until later."

Emílio's settlement had grown. Emílio loved to build himself houses and before it was over he had a separate one for cooking, as well as a sleeping house and several miniature barns, which were perhaps more weatherproof than his houses. The family was busy with the harvest tasks. Emílio's wife and his growing son were winnowing rice by tossing it up into the air again and again on big round bark trays. Near a shed housing a pile of grain, Emílio was beating sheaves of rice over a shoulder-high pole platform to thresh it. No new-fangled mechanization here, as at Manoel's. These processes could not have been more primitive if designed by an ineffi-ciency expert and through centuries they had stayed the same.

All work stopped when they saw me and we had to go through the explanations about the crutch and the offer of a *cafezinho*. The big log by Emílio's cookhouse was still the best bench in sight and I perched on it in the shade with the man and boy while the woman made the coffee. They closed me round with a soft generous courtesy and I was glad to be there.

The direct sun had been hot and I was grateful for the shade; the afternoon breeze drying the sweat under my light white blouse made my skin tingle a bit. I tossed my big straw hat down and leaned back against the hut wall. I had picked up a handful of Emílio's new-threshed rice and poured the prickly fluidity from palm to palm. The grains were enormous, longer and bigger than any rice I had seen last year in the harvest.

"This looks like fine rice," I said. "How much do you think we'll have?"

Emílio ruminated, a yellow rice straw in his mouth.

"Dona Virginia . . ." Long pause. Out of politeness Emílio rarely looked me in the face, as if a frontal stare were somehow too bold. Yet Emílio was not humble, for humility implies consciousness of being on a lower level in some sense. Illiterate Emílio, in his late middle years and with only his fine sons to show for a lifetime of toil, was the most perfect philosopher of us all, if wisdom lies in accepting your fate. He was a classic example of the victim in a system to which passive resistance had for long been the only defense, yet he did not resist, even passively. He detached himself, was compliant and did the best he could within the scheme.

"Dona Virginia, it will not be as much as it would have been if the rains had come right. It won't be the best grade. It won't be the worst."

"How many sacks do you think you can fill?" The owner is expected to provide sacks to the tenant, collecting for them in the final settlement.

"I have the fifty you sent and I need fifty more, at least. I still have some rice to cut and you can't tell till after the threshing. Maybe I'll have a hundred and fifty sacks."

Chico and Ezequiel appeared at this juncture, summoned by Emílio's youngest son.

We all perched in a line on the big log by the pole hut in the wild clearing and communed about our harvest. This council gave me a certain atavistic satisfaction, a sense of taking part in a long-established, needful observance. I am not sure whether it came from the many generations of people close to the land behind me or whether it went back further, to the life of the tribe. There was a family feeling in the air, as if the *roçeiros* and the soil and the crops and I were all kin.

Chico said his rice would be first class and that he would have as much as Emílio. Ezequiel was vague and behind in his work.

'S'hor Ezequiel, how did you get delayed? I had money sent to help with the harvest."

"Dona Virginia . . ." Pause.

"Well?"

"Dona Virginia, the little money was not enough."

A backland problem in discovering truth and determining justice here confronted me. It was a task for a Solomon and I dodged it.

"Chico, I'm here about the harvest," I said. "First of all, about getting out the crop. We can cut a track through to the Frenchman's camp and go out to the river that way."

Chico was grinding a handful of rice between the heels of his palms, the ways backlanders roughly dehusk their rice and test it for hardness and ability to emerge whole from the husking and polishing machines. The less the rice breaks up in this mechanical cleaning the higher its grade and price.

"There's a cart hauling Dona Joana's rice to the river and you could speak for it to haul ours next," he said.

"I'll do that. But our rice ought to be guarded day and night till the truck can come for it. Can you men stand guard by turns?"

Chico alternately ground the rice in his palms and poured it from one hand to the other, gently blowing the freed husks away.

"The truth is, Dona Virginia," he said slowly, "the rice ought to be looked after all the way through to Anápolis because those truckers will swap your good rice for bad and they tear holes in the stacks and steal part of the rice and then say it wasted out. All of us men will have as much as we can do to finish up the threshing. We'll have to trust the *senhora* to arrange for the rest."

Emílio and Ezequiel murmured assent.

They were telling me the rice was my responsibility once it left the clearing. The owner officially "receives" his share on the farm and he has the right to buy the tenants' whole crop there, at prevailing prices. The owner always does this, to insure receiving his proper share. But though the tenant delivers the rice in the clearing, settlements are made on the basis of weighing and classification done at Ceres or Anápolis warehouses. Since the owner obviously has as many chances to cheat as Chico ascribed to the truckers, he had used the exact word, "trust."

The men's willingness to trust me made me feel close enough to them to bring up a question that had existed ever since the last visit, when I had been far from satisfied with what they told me.

"Chico," I said, not looking at any of them for fear of frightening away the moment of confidence, "what really happened up here during the rains?"

Chico did not answer me, and the ensuing silence lengthened. With his right forefinger he separated the whole rice grains in his left palm from the broken ones and showed me the two little piles were about equal—this was *um por um*, one to one, considered a good grade of rice. I ignored this attempt at diversion.

"I appreciated your staying on here after José burned the clearing the way he did," I persisted. "And I'd like to know how you made out."

Old Ezequiel surprised me.

"Have you spoken with Manoel?" he asked in his deep, halting tones.

I should have known it would come around to Manoel.

"I'll speak with him again," I said. Ezequiel's hint, I knew, was as far as they would go, but it was enough.

When I came back to Manoel's house later on, he had descended from his rustic tower and was sacking his threshed and winnowed rice. I walked over to the shed where lay a big pile of threshed rice and sat down on it. I loved to plunge my hand into it and run it through my fingers. People always do this around loose grain, whether highland rice in remote Goiás or ripe, threshed wheat in Tennessee, half a world away.

Manoel was busily rubbing a handful of rice between his palms. He blew the loosened husks away and separated the whole and broken grains, classifying it.

"Just look, Dona Virginia," he said, pointing to the high proportion of whole grains. "That's four whole to one broken, the best rice in this *mato.*"

I suspected he had not borne down very hard with his hands in rubbing the rice; an expert can vary the breakage somewhat by the way he grinds the grain.

"It certainly looks wonderful, Manoel," I said. "How many sacks will you have?"

"Mm, Dona Virginia, that depends. The rains weren't good. I lost some rice up there by the edge of the woods because my wife and I couldn't cut it in time. It dried and fell to the ground. If we'd had enough cash to get the help we needed as you promised, I could have saved that stand of rice. Maybe *you'll* owe *me* something when we settle up."

I had sent the men the amount of harvest cash usual in Goiás grubstaking deals and Manoel was being provocative and insolent. He veiled his insolence with a smile, as if I must of course know he was only joking.

"I can't understand why you ever left Goiânia, Manoel," I told him. "You never like anything here in the *mato.*"

"Certain promises were made when we started out here but they all were changed."

"You know very well we had to change our deal when Davino gave up the store," I said.

"Did we agree to starve up here in the rains?"

"You've talked like that before, Manoel, but it isn't true. Not a person starved up here or was seriously sick." My heart sank to think of the risk I'd run.

Manoel turned grim and bitter. "I didn't see any *dono* up here handing out food or medicine."

"I had food and money and medicine sent. I have the accounts."

He threw down the rice. "Very little knocked on my door."

"While the bridge was out, nothing could come in!"

"Mm," said Manoel.

The whole mystery about what had happened during the rains was now clear. Manoel intended to try to get an advantage in the harvest settlement by claiming I had not lived up to my bargain through the growing season. The others had known this all along but had committed themselves as little as possible to see how the game went. If Manoel ever forced a formal showdown, as in a court of law, I could probably never establish the truth I was convinced of, that my agent had done everything humanly possible, because Chico and the Feitosas would probably change sides if it meant an advantage in the settlement for them too.

"You'd better sack up a load of rice," I said to Manoel. "I'll be back here soon to get the hauling started."

"What about a road out of here?"

"Sack your rice," I said. "At the proper time there'll be a road and a cart to take it out of here and a truck waiting over the river to haul it."

Pondering my brave words to Manoel, I limped away toward the *caboclo's* hut on the Bowens' place to hire the cart for hauling our rice to the river. Whom could I get to see to all the necessary details of the harvest and how could I hold both him and Manoel in line while he was doing it? It had long been a point of honor with me to do things on my own, asking aid from the Bowens as little as possible. Besides, they were very busy and neither was well.

Later I struggled down to the port and engaged our drunken, one-eyed canoeman to ferry our rice over the river in the canoe, promising him a bonus if he'd guard it on both banks. When he rowed me over the river, I heard there was a truck loading rice at Davino's and I limped there and engaged a place on the front seat for the trip to Anápolis.

Full dark had come when we left. Davino climbed into the seat by the driver, leaving me the preferred place by the window. Half a dozen white-garbed, murmuring *roçeiros* climbed up on top of the load of 130-pound rice sacks. The heavily overburdened old truck creaked distressfully as deep ruts and sudden holes in the forest trail made it twist and sway. Under the big trees, the jolting headlights weakly diluted the velvet forest blackness; in the clearings their pale glow thinned out under the misty light of the stars and the young moon.

The clearings were ever more numerous. Gone were giant trees that less than a year before had been welcome landmarks, each in turn promising a nearer relief from the nervous expectation of a stranding injury to the old Plymouth's undersides. The country was filling up. And the forest was going down.

When we finally eased over the last rustic bridge, Davino and I both agreed the day we wrecked the Bowens' old Ford there seemed long ago. Soon we were passing the crude building where we had in all innocence set up our store. The clay tiles were gone from our end of the building, leaving it unroofed, like a ruin.

"What happened to the tiles?" I asked Davino.

"They were mine. I took them to the new house."

The hut was dark under an uncertain new moon, with only a tiny gleam of fire to tell of the family huddled within. The flick of the light out of the desolation impinged on me like a tap against a crystal glass, evoking universal sadness, reminding me how many failures each man has to walk away from, how many shelters made warm by temporary hope later stand abandoned, the salvage carted away. For me now the darkened hut called up not only my own necessary desertions of scenes of loss, but the failures of millions of wanderers. I had first witnessed and felt here the elaborate difficulty of the Brazilian land people's lives, the hard lot that millions of them roam ceaselessly to escape, yet never do. The little store had been an infinitesimal stockade, a miniscule outpost in their wilderness of hope foredoomed, for it was an attempt to ease the way for a few of them, if only a handful. The look of the small ruin, hollow under the muted light of night, evoked a vast limbo of patience and forlorn effort, the land people's world. For a moment, I felt its wastes echo all around me and could comprehend the backland phenomenon of *paixão*, grief and discouragement at a final blow of fate so profound that a backlander will take to his bed, turn his face to the wall and wordlessly die.

"We should have charged three times the prices we did." Feckless little Davino, kindly and sensitive, had almost read my thoughts and he was trying to comfort me.

"I don't think that would have done it," I answered. My moment's emotion trailed away, faded out.

The old truck nosed into the highway and roared away toward Ceres, its new vigor spattering gravel out from under its wheels. The cabin, none too comfortable but warm and faintly illuminated by a tiny light under the dashboard, gave us refuge in a world turned subtly hostile since the departure of the sun; the roaring old truck was a friend, it would take us to the comfort of familiar places.

Outside, the high flats dipped into sharp valleys and then the steep hills began to rise. During the first miles, forest occasionally surged forward to cover us over, but south of Córrego Sêco it finally fell back behind the calm rice fields, where it stood like a wall, a band of deeper darkness between the earth's frosty silver and the sky's silvered black.

What should I do about the harvest? A decision had to be made now, for time was pressing and tomorrow at Anápolis I would have to start making practical arrangements for it.

12

My whole experience in Goiás warned me disaster would result if I hastily chose a deputy and left him to manage the harvest.

The driver we were with had been a truck-owning rice buyer until he endorsed his brother-in-law's notes, lost his truck and had to work for hire again. I decided to consult him.

"S'hor Antônio," I said, "do you know any decent truck-owning rice buyer who would buy my crop in the clearing?"

Antônio considered, then he shook his head. My farm was too far from the big road, they wouldn't pay me anything, he said. I should ship the rice to Anápolis and store it for a rise in price. It was the custom to weigh and grade the rice at the warehouse and unless it was closely watched, he warned, either the tenants or the truckers would steal heavily from me before it ever got there.

"You ought to get yourself a *jagunço* to watch them all," advised Davino. The hired killer is the backland's easy solution to many problems.

"Then I suppose *he'd* steal the crop," I said.

The men laughed at the wry reflection, soft backland laughter. In the *sertão*, laughter does not stem from humor, its place is reversed with that of tears. When people weep, literally or figuratively, it means they still have hope this appeal to sympathy will win help for them. But when things are beyond help, they laugh.

"*Êste Brasil!*" said Davino. "This Brazil," a familiar Brazilian expression of despairing pride.

"*Brasil é grande*, Davino." "Brazil is great," I quoted, another favorite expression among Brazil's people. I repeated to the men one of Captain Bowen's favorite anecdotes, about a big black truck driver who backed up to a foreign woman's house in Anápolis to make a delivery and knocked the whole front porch down.

"*Brasil é grande, senhora*," he told the excited, indignant woman, and calmly went about his unloading. In so large a country, what does one front porch matter?

Brasil é grande, ran my thoughts, and millions of her people were like my tenants. If I failed them in the harvest they'd salvage what they could and, as millions do yearly, shift to a new farm, make a new clearing or drift back to a town, as penniless as when they left. Brazil was great, there was a lot of room for imperfection, and it was big, they could always "go somewhere else," their old solution. But where could I go? I had come to Brazil from "somewhere else."

Chico still had some faith in me, since he obviously thought I would stay and see to the harvest myself. Emílio probably did also, if his life-instilled acceptance of whatever came permitted him to speculate about it. Old Ezequiel was no doubt waiting to see, without thinking at all. It was much better for him not to think, at his age, with his strength failing. And how Manoel would love it if I let the situation slide into a tangle of disorganization and failure. He was no doubt hoping I would.

I broke the silence.

"Is Manoel a communist, Davino?"

"I don't know, Dona Virginia," he replied. "They say so. He talks like one, about dividing up the land."

"The communists would chop off Manoel's head the first time he let go his nasty temper," I said. "I'm going to move him to a lot in the *Colônia* and get him off my hands."

"Do you think he'll go?" asked Davino.

This came as a complete surprise.

"Why not? He wants land, doesn't he? I told him last year I'd help him get land in the *Colônia*. That's our understanding."

"Dona Virginia, I don't like to *fuchicar*," Davino said hesitantly, "but I heard Manoel say he intends to stay four years on your place."

"Four years! I never heard of such a thing. Manoel's a troublemaker. I want him off my place after this harvest!"

The old truck roared up a grade. Antônio shifted gears, intent, eyes straight ahead. Davino did not answer me. With Manoel storing up surprises for me, the harvest was growing ever more complicated. It was an appalling prospect.

Everything I had ever had to help cushion the hardships of the frontier was gone. Even my protective ignorance was wearing away, the ignorance that had kept me moving ahead through many past situations I could never have gotten through if I had known in advance how bad they would be.

Worst of all, I should have to go into the clearing at Chavante myself and work out my problem. I had always avoided going to the clearing or had fled from it after the briefest possible visit there. I would linger nearby, at Davino's or Getúlio's. I had always liked going to our first work camp on the riverbank after they cleared the underbrush under the big trees. But I did not like the clearing.

Chavante had started as the focus of a dream, but I had realized none of the dream. Instead I had dodged conclusions until I went off at a tangent to a temporary job with the IRO. Gradually, there had developed the temptations into pure escape, temptations hinted in the dark cloud above Rio and in the *carnaval* drums, which finally took form in the thought of complete immersion of my life in the wild country beyond the edge of the frontier.

My promise to Bill would keep me from going to this last extreme. But what if I turned my back and walked away from Chavante, back to the coast and the cities? Would I have more and graver accidents or take refuge in some imaginary illness, on the order of my imagined "cancer"? I began to check over the things I had uncharacteristically dropped when they appeared too hard. It began when I made the big break and left newspaper work. I had turned my back on Susana, a friend whom I loved. Next, I had turned away from the farm, focus of my dreams, to the inn. Without even visiting it a second time, I dropped the inn for flying with Alfredo. Alfredo in turn was dropped when I became afraid of his flying as well as of his little blue plane. At Bob Rossborough's hint of new perplexities about Bill, I was ready to drop out again there too. If I now walked away from Chavante, where would it end? Already I had been amply warned about becoming like Alfredo, and yet I had in fact become like him: when I ignored the most elementary caution and climbed into the old jitney in Rio I'm sure I felt as he did when he got into his blue plane for the foolish, fatal last flight. I had been luckier than Alfredo; my accident had only been a timely reminder of my mortality.

It is always difficult to know exactly when and how decisions are made. I am sure a conscious about-face began within me when I felt my promise to Bill holding me against the spell of the blue distances. The trend of decision may have been in preparation ever since I first suspected I was thinking too much about death. I believe it was strengthened when I studied old Emílio's face in the clearing and unexpectedly saw in him some quality of wisdom close to primitive sainthood; this quality of his that kept him from bleeding when life's swords passed back and forth through him made it surprisingly hard for me to abandon him in the harvest. And Manoel challenged my conscience, taunting me to turn.

I had never fully accepted Manoel's accusation of neglecting my tenants, since I knew it was part of his tactic of harrying the owner class and trying to jockey me into a disadvantageous position for the harvest settlement. Yet my conscience was not entirely at ease. I had now done a great deal of work and study on Brazil's land and population problems as part of my duties with the IRO and my information went far beyond the surface. I knew that greater shares of the harvest were far from being the key to the landworkers' problem. Not even increased production alone could solve the people's hunger.

The one statement most often made about Brazil by prosperous city Brazilians explaining their country to foreigners is that "all the poor people have to do is reach out and get food from bountiful nature." But this did not represent the truth for the vast majority of the many millions who live by working the soil, I had learned. Though the Brazilian poor in many places do live where they can reach out and pick food from trees or gather wild vegetables, their preference for rice and beans or in some regions, manioc and fish, is so firmly fixed that they consistently leave the fresh growths for the birds. There is even a fixed belief among them that certain of the most healthful fresh fruits "give fever." They call the *mamão*, which is almost a specific remedy for some stomach disorders, "cold to the stomach" and they dislike it. The Brazilian sociologist, Gilberto Freyre, whose patriotism cannot be questioned, reports fully in *The Masters and the Slaves* how the Brazilians' bad food habits were forced upon them in early times by the Portuguese colonists, who used their slave labor exclusively to produce commercial crops—sugar first of all—and neglected all other produce. The almost universal practice of the one-crop system, whether the growing of sugar, coffee or other products, has crystallized these bad habits.

(The same Portuguese colonials who fixed bad food patterns also set precedent for the Brazilian males' feverish sex quest, says Freyre. He notes that while their "feet slipped" in sadistic frenzies among negro and Indian slave women, a distinction between sensual and marital sex relations led them to have intercourse with their wives through a hole in a counterpane.)

From my own observation, I knew of other customs besides monoculture that discouraged changes in Brazilian food habits. According to one which I assumed is based on law, anything a tenant plants by way of permanent improvement, whether stands of the starchy manioc or fruit trees, has to be paid for by the owner when the tenant leaves. As a matter of policy, the owners discourage such plantings and resist paying for them. Since the sharecroppers move so often, they have no real incentive to plant fruit trees that will bear only after they are gone.

How convenient for the comfortable top-dog minority to salve their consciences with the national myth that life can be very effortless amid Brazil's natural riches, ran my thoughts. Their credo is even written into the national anthem, which says, "*Deitado eternamente em berço espléndido, refulgas, ó Brasil . . .*" "Reclining ever in thy splendid cradle, thou shinest, O Brazil . . ." Yet I knew this easy philosophy to be a trap for the unwary.

Through the chill night, these thoughts came in fragments. But this was a part of my brain at work that I had always dodged applying fully to Goiás, my land of escape. This was the seeker of understanding and of causes that I had left behind me when I laid aside my character of adjuster of the times.

My fallacy had been to dream even for an instant there was any frontier far enough away to be outside the problems which we call the problems of the day, but which are old problems, those of man on earth. In Goiás was the very fountainhead of the political troubles I had run away from when I came here. If Argentina was the end result of a series of American stupidities in dealing with an ambitious military leader installing a dictatorship, Goiás typified the causes that lead to dictatorship the world over, whether fascistic or communistic. And Brazil is far bigger than Argentina—take Brazil out of South America and you have only a rim of land, mostly mountain.

The significance of Brazil went further: it was our best and most powerful friend in the Southern Hemisphere, yet it was raddled with similar evils and agitated by the same ground swell of unrest that we had seen rise to mighty waves in China, in Indo-China, in India, in the Moslem world. Did I not have on my very own farm, a tiny property by Brazilian standards, one rebel out of four, with the other three waiting to see which way it would be more advantageous to jump?

If I assumed my full responsibility at Fazenda Chavante, it would have to go far beyond saving my own financial neck in the harvest. In the early 1940's, long before Point Four had even been mentioned, in my *Washington Post* column I had urged the political wisdom of aiding the development of "backward" countries; I had editorially urged Congress to grant more funds for the work of the Inter-Departmental Committee on Co-operation with the American Republics which since 1938 had been lending New World neighbors scientific assistance on a very limited scale. My second book had expounded at some length the reasons why such assistance comprised enlightened self-interest. I was hoist by my own petard: once I should take up the continuity of my life before I came to the *sertão*, I should be impelled by my own dicta to try to carry out these principles in developing Fazenda Chavante.

I would have to try to teach the people how to eat vegetables, have them build better houses and clean the stream. The country was filling up and the Chavante stream would soon become polluted from above as the people in the Frenchman's camp were even now polluting it for Getúlio and others living below their camp. I would want discipline on the place about the crops—someone to see that the rice was planted and cut early enough. I would want to "mechanize" with simple hand planters and elementary work aids such as Manoel knew and used. Real mechanization would have to come later, when we could get the stumps out. There would have to be a central authority at the *fazenda*, a man to whom I could send money. I would have to provide him with a cart and horse with instructions to take to the hospital at Ceres anyone on the place who might be injured or become ill during the rains.

Even as I considered the ramifications of the task, I knew I had decided to do it. Rightly or wrongly, it seemed to me now that if I did not turn and fight, I was very likely to keep running and to go very much further in the other direction than I ever intended to. Perhaps I had been overimpressed by the fate of my friend Alfredo, but the aimless drifting into a disorganization of life and purpose which I now saw as the alternative to assuming responsibility appeared to me as a yielding to the currents drawing away from life and toward death.

Somewhere along the road between my farm and Ceres on my return from this second harvest visit, I completed an about-face on my long journey toward escape, which proved impossible for me so long as I valued my life. Everyone, sooner or later, dreams of a complete and radical escape. I had the chance to try it and I found out that it meant, for me, a destination as cheerless as the Goiás night.

My land was rich, excellent for coffee. If I could find a Brazilian overseer who knew coffee culture, I could offer him a contract making it worth his while to carry out my wishes about the part of the farm kept in other crops. Also, I could make it advantageous for the men who stayed with me as sharecroppers—Chico, Emílio and Ezequiel—to improve their houses, their sanitation and their farming. I would make Manoel a landed proprietor in the federal farm colony, satisfying his belly communism with the possession of land. (The *Colônia Agrícola* had been founded to start solving the problem of the wandering farm worker, the "hidden" problem so dangerous to Brazil and to the continent.) I was very happy to think my particular "communist" had his cure waiting so close at hand.

The trip seemed long; the backlands were playing their old tricks with time. It was around midnight when the old truck creaked across the rickety, flood-battered pontoon bridge and set me down at Donato's for a bite to eat. Dona Anita happened to spy me and exclaimed in mild horror when I told her I intended to finish out the rest of the night asleep on top of the loaded truck. She had only one bed I could possibly occupy, in her servants' room, but insisted I take it. I was tired, dirty; the offer came like manna. It was a great relief to drop all problems and merge briefly into the humble household, accepting generosity and shelter.

Dona Anita came to sit with me while I munched canned Vienna sausages and hard rolls. She bent over hand sewing in the dim light and I warned her she'd ruin her eyes. She said she had to steal what moments she could to make clothes for her baby.

It was her first baby, she volunteered suddenly, though she'd been married twelve years. She had treatments from a doctor in Anápolis in order to be able to conceive. I said I was glad it had turned out so well.

"I'd have gone to the doctor before if my husband had let me," she said. "I finally got him to let me take the treatments. In these last few years I've started standing up for myself, Dona Virginia. I often look at you and think how free you are. You don't know what it is to be a woman up here."

Donato, a mild-mannered man, courteous and obliging in his ways, had not impressed me as an ogre. At the moment, I could almost have envied Dona Anita for having any man at all to do the rough work of the backlands.

"But he gives you a good home and the business is making money," I said.

Her story, once started, had to come out.

"I work in this business, too. I work so hard sometimes I think I will die," her voice continued, low and flat. "You don't know how it is here, Dona Virginia. I married when I was fifteen. My father was dead and I thought . . ." She hesitated, eyes on her tiny stitches. "I suppose I thought he'd be more like a father. . . . But he shut me up in the house and I didn't go out for years and years."

"You mean you literally didn't get out?"

"I could go to church sometimes and to the store sometimes, but not often. The *roça* women are better off than we are in the towns, *dona*. I had no family in Goiás and there was nobody else in the house. He used to stay out late and I cried every night for years, every night. If I'd had children, they would have been company for me. But he's different since I started standing up to him. He even stays home more."

She glanced at her husband, quite close to us, within easy hearing. There was no dislike or resentment in her glance, but she did not lower her voice out of caution or tact. I have never forgotten the way she looked at the man, as if he had no meaning for her. He had chosen to signify authority only to her and now he was a shell even of that.

"You should have several children," I said, the safest remark I could make.

"Oh, I intend to," she said. "I want sons."

It was a revealing glimpse into the life the town women led behind the closed shutters of their quiet houses, these women who love their sons so passionately and whose husbands breed them regularly but are prevented by stern tradition from being their true lovers. The freedom to move at will beyond the limits of their homes is yet to be won by these women, though rebellion is stirring among them. A Goiás ranch princess whom I knew, a strapping, beautiful girl brought up in the somewhat freer life of her father's vast cattle domain, was threatened with a gun by her town-bred husband because she went to market in Goiânia without his sister's chaperonage; she settled the matter by beating up her husband in a fist fight that lasted most of the night behind locked doors. The servants had to send for her uncle to stop the battle.

My snack finished, Dona Anita led me into the clean if airless brick-floored rooms where her two servants slept. One of the maids brought me a big tin basin of warm water which, as usual turned brick-red with road dust as I bathed in it. The two servants climbed into one of the narrow cots together and I unrolled my sleeping bag on top of the other. I was sorry to crowd the girls, but I obeyed the backland law of *maior necessidade*, the pressure of the greater need.

I had been lucky this night, but I could not count on such good fortune to continue. My shoulder ached miserably; I realized the task ahead would test my physical endurance and my capacity for understanding to the utmost.

It was a time to ask the help of Heaven, but I did not pray. A wise minister once told me a Christian's life is a series of new beginnings: a few short years before I had made such a new beginning and since then had felt I was supposed to get along for a while without troubling Heaven to pull me out of any new difficulties. It was not that I believed a human being can turn over one leaf in his relationship with God, however important the turning, and then continue on a crowned saint the rest of his life. The testimony even of the great saints is against it. Yet the familiar text, "By their works ye shall know them," had sunk too deep for me to feel that I, personally, should become a pensioner on Heaven. I had to believe that if I did right I would automatically receive the help of Heaven. But I felt the Recorders there were eying me with tolerant skepticism about my staying powers.

The next morning as we drove south in the cool early mists, I planned my campaign.

The first thing I did at Anápolis was to wire the IRO I would need my full leave for the harvest. (There was confusion about this wire and quite a bit of heated inquiry as to my whereabouts before it was all over.) I wrote a letter to Bill saying I might not communicate regularly for a while, but that I had *not* vanished away into the *sertão* for good.

I inquired around town for an overseer. Francisco Lage, one of the more important rice buyers, offered to help me find a man to grow coffee for me, but he warned me it would take time. I was very anxious to get a man who had some kind of recommendation, ever mindful of the prickly pear I had plucked in taking Manoel on faith. The Frenchman, Jazz Antoinette (who was living in Liberty Hall) was pleased with his contractor, Tito, and we asked the latter to suggest someone.

As we might have expected, Tito nominated his brother-in-law, Sebastião Carlos de Nascimento, called Batão, who was acting as Tito's straw boss. I did not like to take a man off my neighbor's place, even though he was working for a contractor and not the neighbor. But Jazz was in Tito's hands and he added his recommendation to Tito's. Time pressed and there was no other prospect in sight.

When I rode north again one day to see Batão (pronounced Ba-*tonh*) and start fulfilling my rendezvous with conscience, chance put me in the International truck I had once owned. After long months, it had finally emerged from the repair shop and been sold to an old man named Aquiles.

The harvest was on full blast now and the big road alive with traffic. Heavy clouds of dust hung almost continuously over it all the way to the *Colônia*. When we came in sight of my favorite vista from the top of the mountain ridge, it was visible only for the moments when the dust had thinned between passing trucks. (We must have met over a hundred trucks, more than one every mile.) I was ready for the impact of the panorama this time; the country beyond the mountain ridge was beautiful as ever, but I was set against it. I could easily imagine it was waiting to see what I would do, to be ready with a countermove, and I meant to stay on guard.

There were always wrecks along the big road, as well as many trucks with their axles broken from overloading. As we came down the mountain ridge this day we saw a big truck lying upside down in a deep gully to our left, with its four wheels in the air and rice sacks scattered all around. A man riding on top of the load had been injured when it went over and a dozen others jarred and bruised in falling clear.

Aquiles was indignant as we left the scene.

"It's only good luck those people riding on top weren't killed!" he exclaimed. "They ought to shoot that crazy driver!" Yet only a short while after, when we came to a level and newly graded and graveled stretch of road, Aquiles screwed up his weather-beaten face till he looked like a gleeful baboon and began to bear down on the accelerator.

I remembered how the main beam of the truck had been twisted in my wreck. Also, a new canoe we were taking to the river port for the Bowens was whamming away like fury in the back and I wondered what was happening to our passengers. But I expected the backlands to present me with these tests for the nerves and I dealt with the crisis calmly.

"This isn't exactly the place to speed, is it?" I asked in a mild tone.

"I want to see how much it will make, Dona Virginia," he answered. Down went the accelerator a little more, the steering wheel jerking madly in his hands as the whirring front wheels bit into the loose gravel.

"This truck had a bad smash-up when I owned it," I reminded him. I happened to know Aquiles still owed the bank money for it.

We were racing insanely now, every bolt, nut and beam in stress.

"I never thought she'd get up this high!" Aquiles exclaimed in triumph.

I had only one card to play, the emotional appeal.

"S'hor Aquiles, please, I'm very nervous. We can't see in this fog of dust—can't we go slower? I was in a wreck in Rio only recently and I'm afraid I'll get sick at my stomach if you don't slow down."

"But I've never had a wreck, dona," protested Aquiles plaintively.

I kept quiet, dramatically bending forward, my hand on my brow, eyes closed, a picture of human suffering. Aquiles, amenable through his good heart if not through reason, reluctantly slowed down. He made me feel like a wicked stepmother who has denied a child a toy.

(A truck owner in Anápolis once told me he caught hired drivers with two of his loaded trucks lined up on a shaky bridge and a third about to drive onto it. The drivers just wanted to see how much weight the bridge would bear!)

In the early afternoon we arrived at the river and unloaded the canoe, which provided a further test for my new resolution. Goiás canoes are usually long, shallow and narrow, for maneuvering in the swift waters of the floodtime, they tell me. The new one, however, had been built short and deep and broad, to accommodate a maximum number of rice sacks. She wobbled crazily when we climbed aboard her and danced like a half-broken filly as one-eyed Josué paddled her upstream along the bank before cutting across the current.

We slowly pushed out into the swift current, which was not raging now as in the midst of the rains, but was still yellow and strong and sullen. I felt the canoe would tip over if one of the precariously balanced passengers so much as drew an extra-deep breath. I looked around me. Each bank of the river was covered by a wild confusion of vigorous, heavy growth of vine, bush and trees; the only gaps in its heavy barriers were raw scars in the earth where we had scratched out our steep-banked little landings and the edge of the new clearing just downstream. Upriver were the low islands, unpenetrated, virtually impenetrable. Below, the wide yellow river surged powerfully on through the tremendous continent toward the river world of the Amazon Valley, and the sea.

Out in the main current of Ghost River, where I invariably was reminded of my poor swimming ability, I had often wondered for an instant what in the world I was doing there, and wonderment had never come so strong as now. I could not appeal to canoe or river as I had to Aquiles—I could only sit tight. I had always been a firm believer in free will, yet at this moment it would have comforted me if I could have justified the folly of my situation by belief in ineluctable destiny.

Batão had heard of my coming by the grapevine and received me, with his brown little Portuguese wife, in their hut. Batão was one of the skinny, long-headed, long-nosed and sharp-chinned white Brazilians so often encountered in the level of society just above the manual laborers and the landworkers. His appearance and manner were not unpleasant; he missed being ferretlike, though a suggestion of the ferret was there. I guessed he was around forty. He was a Protestant, as many people are in the backlands. They have a reputation for exceptional reliability, not too well deserved in my experience.

I told Batão I wanted to clear and plant about a hundred and twenty acres of coffee on land between the present clearing and the river. I said I'd pay two cruzeiros per *cova* or clump of trees and the contractor could plant certain crops between the trees for four years. At the end of that time, he would deliver me the coffee, then beginning to bear. This was roughly the usual contract for planting coffee in Goiás.

Also, I told him I wanted my coffee contractor to act as overseer for the clearing where my present tenants were, making sure they carried out their own contracts with me. I offered ten per cent of the first clearing's profits for this service.

Batão and Tito set out to convince me Batão was the very man for all this. In recommending himself, Batão repeatedly went back to the time when he administered a big plantation in São Paulo. According to Batão, the *dono* there thought so much of him that when a big crop of cotton failed to come up one year, he just said, "That's all right, Batão. We'll replant it."

This was scarcely an ideal recommendation and it made me uneasy when Batão emphasized it so strongly. Batão was trying to tell me that even though the weather or something else might cause us trouble, he would remain a good fellow throughout. I would have much preferred a sterner character whose plantings would not fail to come up, but I was in the middle of an uncertain situation as I had been in the middle of the Rio das Almas in a wobbly canoe not long before. I had to sit tight and go forward. I agreed to deal with Batão, further details to be worked out.

Batão and Tito invited me to remain in their camp, once again making it possible for me to dodge an overnight stay in the Chavante clearing. I sent Batão's son to fetch my tenants and soon after dark they began to appear silently out of the shadows to join the workmen sitting on boxes around burning wood fires. It was damp in this hollow after the dark came down.

Manoel was characteristically unavailable when I went to speak to my men after supper, so I drew the other three to sit with me on a long log a little distance away from the fires. (It was almost impossible to obtain privacy in the backlands, but I still tried.)

I wanted the men on my place to have better conditions and do things a better way, but in the true tradition of American free enterprise, I also wanted them to earn the improvements and to produce more for me. I told them I would rent the land to them again for twenty-five per cent of the produce if they would agree to follow certain farming practices, early planting, early cutting of the rice, etc. I offered to supply them tools and hardware and door and window fittings if they would build better houses and keep the stream clean. I also told them I would advance cash, not supplies this year. The Frenchman intended to put up a store and they could trade with him.

I explained how I wanted us all to prosper together; I didn't expect to take any money out of the farm for years, I said. They appeared to understand what I was driving at.

Now for Manoel. I sent Chico to find him and bade the others good night. When Manoel appeared, we sparred verbally for a while. As usual, I started out with the determination not to let him make me lose my temper.

"Everything is going fine, Manoel," I said, grimly cheerful. "I spoke for the cart and you can start hauling out your rice as soon as we cut the road. I'm planning to take yours out first."

"Mm," said Manoel.

He was an expert at making this sound that meant neither yes nor no. It registered the fact that I had said something, nothing more. I sometimes wondered if the communist underground had a special course teaching their rank and file how best to employ irritating personality tricks in destroying the capitalistic system. If so, they could have used Manoel as a model. One had to practice great patience with Manoel, or lose a point to him. But at the end of a hard day, it was almost too much.

"Won't you sit down?" I motioned for him to sit on the log,

conscious ever of the tremendous significance small gestures of this kind had for his inflamed, angry spirit.

He sat.

"Can you have a load ready day after tomorrow?" I asked.

"I don't see how you can haul out anything until the road is opened," he said.

"How much will you charge to open it? You're in better shape on the harvest than any of the other men."

"Are you going to pay for the road? Ezequiel said we were all four going to have to cut the road, for nothing."

I sighed.

"Manoel, do me a favor, please. Don't believe *anything* you hear people say I say. Just believe what *you* hear me say, won't you?"

"Mm."

I thought of the bottle of rum in my baggage. Later I would sneak a quick drink, after I'd gone to bed.

"How much will the Frenchman pay for our rice?" Manoel asked.

"Who said he was buying it?" Such a deal had been discussed, but Jazz couldn't raise the cash.

"Rice is selling for eighty up here in the *mato*, but it's a hundred in Anápolis," Manoel told me.

"It's seventy on the big road and ninety in Anápolis if it's one-for-one grade, Manoel. Will yours be that good?"

"I just want to know if we're going to go by Anápolis prices," said Manoel.

I suspected a trick in this.

"I haven't sold the rice yet, Manoel. I may sell it in Ceres." I would puzzle it all out later. "What about opening the road?"

"I'll do it for a hundred cruzeiros."

This was about three dollars. I'd expected to pay fifteen.

"Then start tomorrow," I said. "You ought to be able to finish by midafternoon. All you really need to do is widen the path somewhat."

"Next year you'll have to make the others go around my piece of land, Dona Virginia," said Manoel. "They can't go through again."

I was ready for him.

"Manoel, you remember, I'm helping you get a lot in the *Colônia*, as we agreed. You're going to have land of your own next year."

He suddenly turned, his whole face alight.

"Dona Virginia," he said, "there's a lot half cleared on the road to the port you can buy for three *contos*. I was talking to the man."

"Buy a lot! I'm not buying you anything, Manoel. I'll help you *get* a lot free. They're giving them away."

"I can stay on your land for four years, Dona Virginia, did you know that? The law says that when a man clears forest, he can stay there four years."

This was it; Davino had warned me.

"I never heard of it and I don't believe it. We agreed for you to move over to the *Colônia* and I have witnesses that you did agree."

"Mm."

In a following silence, I watched the groups about the campfires, shadow-figures. The picture suddenly recalled the parable of the speculative old Greek who compared the men of his day to captives in a cave, believing true reality to be what was only a shadow-show moving on a wall.

One of the workmen had a guitar, and he was strumming it and singing softly. It was a minor melody, sad in tone, but I am sure it gave comfort to the singer and pleased others who heard it as much as it pleased me. The flames of the campfires flickered, and throughout the camp, other tiny gleams of flickering light came from wick lamps in the hands of the women putting the children to bed. I could hear little ripples of laughter, brief laughter, the *roçeiros'* punctuation for their gossip about life's tangles and disasters—their *fuchica*. I could smell the camp, a faintly sour smell, for there were nearly a hundred people crowded here, and the strong sun-dried sweat

of the man on the log not far from me. These were not shadows on a wall, but a scene so many times repeated since mankind began to walk erect that it was an absolute of reality.

"I cut two *alqueires* of big trees all by myself last year and
my pregnant wife helped me hack out the branches after
José burned the clearing the way he did," said Manoel suddenly. Two *alqueires* is about twenty-five acres. "I can't do
that much work again this coming year."

I had to resist a quick impulse to sympathize.

"If you don't go into the *Colônia* this year, it means never,"
I said. "The *Colônia* is filling up." If Manoel could get me to
buy a cleared and improved lot for him, for riddance, this
would penalize my good tenants. I could not afford any such
course; they might all start making trouble to try to get
cleared lots for themselves out of me.

"It was hard work, putting down those big trees."

"All work is hard, Manoel," I cut him off. "Many men
spend their whole lives cutting trees. Many work even harder,
digging coal under the ground. How do you suppose I got
the money to buy my land? Nobody gave it to me. I did work
harder than chopping trees, and plenty of it."

"Mm . . ."

There was a point beyond which I could not afford to
temporize with Manoel and keep respect in the balance. I got
up to leave.

"Open the track in the morning, and I'll have Joãozinho
start hauling your rice. Good night, Manoel."

"Good night, Dona Virginia," said Manoel, immobile on
the log.

They found a place for me to sleep in a corner partitioned
off from the big barracks. Tito's wife had a rickety bed there
and I piled my sleeping bag on top of it, wondering how these
houses with straw walls and roofs survived as well as they did
the constant risks of fire from cigarettes and the chimneyless
wick lamps. On the other side of the partition I could hear the
workmen murmuring and laughing very softly as they settled
into their rude beds for the night.

The camp stirred early, while the mists were still heavy all around us. Manoel also went out early, and by midafternoon he had cleared a track through the four hundred yards of forest. Joãozinho showed up to start our hauling, in a big cart with two enormous wheels, pulled by a small, starved-looking horse and a mule whose sides were galled raw by a wicked trace chain. Though his cart and team were all Joãozinho owned in the world and all that held him above the status of common laborer, he ended by beating the galled mule to death in the harvest hauling. (Nonmaterialism in action?)

In the late afternoon I happened to notice the sacks Joãozinho had on his cart were marked with an E. This was Emílio's sign, not Manoel's, and Joãozinho told me he was indeed hauling Emílio's first truckload. I had been all over the farm earlier and I was too tired to go back and take the matter up with Manoel, whom I had clearly instructed to send out his rice. I had to get to the river to be sure the canoeman, Josué, followed my instructions to build a pole platform for the rice sacks on the *Colônia* side of the river, since loose pigs roamed there and had already torn open some of Nilo's rice. Earlier I had borrowed one of Batão's crew to help Josué ferry my rice and to guard it night and day, watching Josué, my first guard. I was taking Batão with me to Anápolis to start working out our coffee contract.

While I was walking along down the dusty track toward the river in the quiet, late afternoon, I heard a soft padding of footfalls behind me. Glancing around, I saw to my surprise it was one of the Feitosa women, Ezequiel's wife. She was smiling nervously and I knew she meant to ask me for something.

Ezequiel was a sore problem, for I knew he was losing money for me and was hopeless, yet I could not see him apart from his obvious history. I knew I'd have to keep him another year and lose more money, which I could not afford to do, especially if I meant to improve the farm. I did not know what favor or advance his wife meant to ask for; I dreaded hearing it, for I dreaded having to consider whether or not I could afford it, when I knew perfectly well I could not.

We padded along and gradually she came up to walk almost beside me. Her very following after me and the way she did it was an eloquent supplication. My heart rebelled at the cruelty reason was forcing me to practice, and I stopped. Against my own sense of practicality, even of justice to my other tenants, I asked her if I could bring her something from Anápolis. She swallowed hard, for her courage was not great and she dreaded making any request as much, I suppose, as I had dreaded hearing one.

"*Dona*," she said timidly, "the rats are eating the rice and even the clothes in the houses. . . . If you could bring us some cats . . ."

Cats! The humility of her need made me ashamed. Cats were something we had for pets in my world or sent to be drowned when they multiplied too fast. But here in the forest, everything was precious, one seed, one egg, one cock, one hen, one pig. Women, who are held to no great account in many places, were an absolute necessity here and even cats were an integral part of the scheme of survival.

"I'll try, *dona*," I said.

(It was not so easy to get them; the wild little half-grown cats we tried to capture at the Chacra scratched the Bowens' Indian cook Vitalina and the Captain himself on the hands and arms. Then they fled to the roof where they sat and gaped fiendishly at us, helpless and furious on the ground below. After two days of this, the usually mild Captain had some difficulty restraining himself from shooting them.)

Batão and I rode all night to get to Anápolis and this time I was wiser than to stay awake in the cramped cabin all through the long hours. I took my sleeping bag up on top of the loaded truck and stretched out among the dark people on the hard rice sacks.

With my body fitted to the unyielding contours of the rice sacks, I lay and watched the night landscape for a while. In the daytime, the magnificence of Goiás's colors and the variety of the countryside itself gave a sense of drama as you passed through, making this vast, thinly peopled world seem full of incident. But at night, with the colors dead and nothing moving, not even puny man, the clearings were pitiful and the occasional huts with their stray scintillas of warm light were poignantly forlorn. I turned on my back and watched the cheerful, friendly stars until at last I dozed.

Early next morning, Batão and I went to the home of a lawyer, Alfredo Melorosa, and slowly started dictating our contract. I sent a truck to the river landing for Emílio's rice and it came back the day after, with news that Manoel's rice was now being put across the river.

While waiting for a ride to the Chacra that afternoon, I overheard a man named Euclides, caretaker for Mr. Cecil Cross's land, saying he had heard one of my sharecroppers trying to sell a load of rice in Ceres. I called him over and asked him what had happened.

"It was a real black one," said sooty Euclides. "He was saying something about selling the rice to a trucker. That's all I know."

Manoel had the ebony skin. I knew I had to get back to the forest at once. If I had a chance to make any profit at all on my three productive tenants, losing a load of rice would sink the chance.

I sent a messenger running to Batão's *pensão* to tell him to join me at once, prepared to ride north in haste.

13

BATÃO and I could not find a truck free to fetch the Chavante rice. Early next morning we caught a ride to the *Colônia* to see if we could find one there.

The whole region was alive with harvest activity, the big road roaring with traffic. Though it had been a poor crop season, the many new clearings of the region of the Goiás Great Forest poured out an aggregate flood of the pale straw-yellow grain greater than last year's. And the migrants were pouring in, on foot and by truck. Day and night, you could hear the deep-throated, intermittent roar of the big machines as they beat their way north carrying five or six families at a time.

The big International in which we were riding swung into the main stream of the trek, its whine swelling the cacophony of straining motors and clashing gears on the long rise leading out of Anápolis. I did not lose myself in the changing beauty of the Goiás countryside on this trip. Instead I peered anxiously at the dark-faced, white-clothed human freight swaying atop southbound loads of rice. I knew no truck ever left our landing without carrying somebody from the neighborhood and I hoped to spot any load from there by recognizing a familiar face on it.

Trucking on the big road had turned into a deadly, exciting game. The wiry, gun-toting backland drivers fought time and each other and the orange-red dust. They overloaded their trucks with sacked rice and then piled passengers on top. They neglected their machines until something gave way, then performed miracles of improvised repairing and ran them till they broke again.

For nearly seventy miles, I stood in the back of a wildly bouncing truck—empty except for a few passengers—and tried desperately to detect Manoel's load through the choking, swirling dust. I steadied myself with hands loosely clasped on the strongly vibrating wooden frame—it would jerk your arms out of their sockets if you held too tight—and kept my knees loose to absorb some of the harder shocks to my body. When an occasional passenger car swooshed arrogantly by us, fanning up clouds of new and thicker dust, I could understand at last the explosive hatred the truckers feel against automobiles.

Twice on the trip north, we paused at roadside inns for *cafezinhos,* and I climbed up on parked southbound trucks looking for my rice. I did not find it.

At Barranca, where the truckers congregated, our International left us. It was dark before Batão and I were able to find a truck free to go for my rice. When we entered the forest trail, the driver of this truck began to say the punishment his old Ford was taking made him doubt he could bring a load out. Though we coaxed him nearly to the river, he balked at last and insisted on returning empty. He agreed to wait while I could walk to Davino's and find out about my rice.

Davino informed me a truck had come in about dark and gone out without a load. I sent Batão to reinforce a round-the-clock watch on Manoel's stacked rice at the river landing and returned to Barranca with the Ford.

It was very late when I staggered into Donato's, tired, dirty and discouraged. This time one of the maids spotted me and called Dona Anita. Once more they both insisted I share the servants' room. Once more I accepted gratefully.

The next day I established headquarters at Donato's and looked for a truck for hire while watching for Manoel's rice. I could not relax my vigil one moment. The broad red main street of Barranca, thinly graveled as it slashed slantwise across a long hill above the river, became an inferno of heat, glare, dust, flies, the roar of trucks and the blare of a public address loud-speaker playing Argentine tangos and de Falla's *Ritual Fire Dance* over and over. In this melee I carried my plea from truck to truck, only to meet courteous refusal. Most truckers from Anápolis had promises to fulfill. Those who worked north out of the frontier town bought rice in small quantities from the *Colônia* farmers and transshipped at Barranca to Anápolis warehouses.

About dark Donato engaged for me a ferret-faced white trucker named Aristide, a former employee of his.

By this time I had invested so much effort in the endangered rice I could not bear to contemplate failure. On the road to the farm, I told Aristide my story and he helped me watch the southbound trucks. He knew most of the truckers we met.

"It's not that one, Dona Virginia, he's from Sant' Ana. . . . It's not this one, he's hauling for an old man above São Patrício. It's not this one. . . . Not this one . . ."

The closer we came to our turnoff, the higher my hopes rose. Aristide entered fully into the spirit of the chase. He helped me check the parked trucks at Córrego Sêco and stopped voluntarily for another check at a new way station some miles farther on.

Here we quickly cleared all the parked trucks but one. I thought I recognized a youth from our trail atop it.

"I'm going up on this one," I told Aristide.

"I'll come too. I've got my gun."

"Keep it out of sight," I warned.

The black boy's eyes bugged as we came up over the side of the truck and began turning rice sacks over to see their markings.

"It's not yours, Dona Virginia, it's not yours!" He knew me, confirming my impression he was from our neighborhood. Manoel's mark was not on the sacks.

We pushed on, surer of victory with every mile. When we

reached Davino's, I was told Manoel's rice was still at the landing. Batão, who was awaiting my orders in the forest camp, had wisely stationed our extra guard at Davino's to avoid trouble at the river.

The moon had not yet risen and it was pitch dark under the fringe of trees by the river landing when we arrived. Our headlights briefly gleamed along the stack of rice, then Aristide turned the truck around and backed up to it. I got out of the cab, flashlight in hand, and walked to the rear of the machine.

"Josué, it's Dona Virginia!" I called to the canoeman, my chief guard.

A movement in the shadows farther on drew my light. Josué, his round battered hat falling off the back of his head, tumbled off the stack of sacked rice where he had been lying. He lurched and grinned foolishly and I realized he was quite drunk. (He was killed here not long after, in a rum-fogged brawl.)

I half turned, sweeping the light around, and all at once Manoel seemed to jump at me out of the blackest part of the darkness. As he advanced into the beam of my light, a trick of the shadows made him appear to be charging at me, though he was not. His thin face was stiff with repressed thunder, his mouth thin and cruel, his eyes glaring.

"You didn't expect *me* here, did you?" he demanded hotly. "You won't get this rice till we settle some things!"

His sudden appearance had startled me badly and I blazed into anger.

"Manoel!" I exclaimed. "Let's have no foolishness! I've had too much trouble over this rice already. It's going with me and you can come too if you want to. . . . Josué, help us here with the sacks, won't you?"

Aristide was behind me in the shadows at the rear gate of the truck; Josué was near Manoel, at the edge of my light. Josué now laughed drunkenly and reeled out of the cone of light into the darkness.

Manoel squared himself up between me and the stack of rice.

"You brought a truck at midnight last night for my rice,

thinking I wouldn't be here," he accused me. "I want to know how we're going to settle up."

"I'd like to know who brought the other truck in here, the first one that went out empty," I retorted. "You seem to forget it's my obligation to haul this rice. We'll settle just as we agreed to and signed in the book over there by the river."

"I never signed any book!" he flung at me. "I want Anápolis prices if I take Anápolis weights and I'm going to get them, do you hear?"

Vaguely I remembered Manoel had indeed been missing when we finally signed our rental agreement.

"I have half a dozen witnesses who know you agreed to our deal," I answered, still furious. "I've had about enough of your smart tricks, Manoel. What are you trying to do now, threaten me?"

I was as indignant and exasperated as I had ever been in my life. I took a step forward, holding the light full on his wrath-twisted face, watching for his next move. His hands hung empty.

"Would you dare threaten me?" I challenged him again. My gold automatic was in my slacks pocket, bullet in chamber, but I was too angry to think of it or of needing it.

At this moment, I heard a small sound behind me, a movement of Aristide's, and I felt death near, not from Manoel, but behind my back, reaching out for Manoel. Aristide was one of the breed of wild backlanders who have swapped the horse for the truck but are still as quick with a gun as our cowboys of old. They have a natural feud with the darker newcomers who work the soil and an emotional allegiance to the *dono* class. Besides, I was a woman and he could not imagine I could handle Manoel. I knew all this, without thinking it out thus in detail. I knew Aristide was already enlisted against Manoel and I was sure his finger was tensed to crack down with his old thirty-eight.

We were frozen for a moment. My anger, which had set up the crisis, was suddenly gone; instead fear for Manoel curled inside me as he stood trapped in my light, opposing me with a stubborn silence. I wanted more than anything now to warn Manoel not to make any foolish move and provoke Aristide's bullet, but I was myself afraid to move or speak, lest I should tip the men into violent action. After a second or two, the automatic reasoning that works for everyone in emergencies provided a solution: I stepped forward again, close enough to put my fingertips very lightly and briefly on Manoel's sleeve.

This is a disarming gesture in Brazil, and it was meant to calm Aristide as much as Manoel.

"I'll do what's *direito* (right) about the rice, Manoel," I said in a much quieter voice. "We can settle it in Anápolis. Help the men load the truck."

Manoel may have smelled his death as close as I did. Or his surging rebellion, like that of a rearing, plunging horse, may have been checked by the brief, confident touch. However it was, he kept silent and faded back toward the far end of the stack. He did not join Aristide and his helper in loading the rice, but the violent scene was over.

We started the hundred-mile drive to Anápolis with Manoel riding on top of the load. Aristide said to me in the cab:

"That *preto* (black man) is crazy, *dona!* I was ready for him back there."

"I am very much obliged, S'hor Aristide," I said, still shaking and cold deep down inside me to think how close we had come to dealing out death. If Aristide had shot Manoel for threatening me, he'd have been a hero. "Manoel is mostly big talk," I said. "If he really had a truck in here after the rice last night, he was probably scared I'd come down on him for it. But it could have been Josué trying to steal the rice, after all. These things get so tangled up. . . . I'll never know what happened."

"É mau mesmo," said Aristide. "He's a real bad one."

"I'm moving him over to the *Colônia* at the end of the harvest," I said. "I'm trying to get him off my place without any serious trouble."

We reached Anápolis in the early light of dawn. It had been days since I had had a bath or clean clothes. I washed up as best I could at the gasoline station and ate breakfast as soon as one of the cafés opened. The post office yielded an irate telegram from the Rio office of the IRO demanding to know where I was. Evidently my wires were still not arriving as they should; all I could do was to send another.

I went to see a lawyer recommended by Captain Bowen and he advised me Manoel was legally bound by the agreement under the trees, which he did not, at the time, protest. Manoel was trying to trick me under a law defining squatter's rights. If a squatter moved into privately owned forest land and was permitted to clear and plant a crop, he could not be dispossessed for four years, although he had to pay a rental. But if a man moved onto property as a tenant, with a clear understanding he would stay a limited time, he had to abide by the limit, said the lawyer. The testimony of my other three tenants would throw Manoel out of court, he was certain. But I was none too sure of the three.

After talking with Melorosa, I decided to have my agreements written out and registered legally in the future to protect me from embroilment.

Manoel had ridden the disputed load of rice to the warehouse of Francisco Lage, where I meant to store it, and I heard he had a violent altercation there, insisting that Lage's grader had downgraded our grain. I could easily imagine he was right. But since there was no official standard, the man who sold the rice was at the mercy of a grader in the pay of the warehouse which expected eventually to purchase it.

Later in the morning, I myself spoke with Lage, asking the custom ruling settlements with tenants. He insisted I should pay Manoel five cruzeiros a sack less for his rice than the Anápolis price minus hauling costs.

I asked why this should be. If the tenant paid for the sack and the hauling and accepted weights tallied at Anápolis, why should he take less than the present Anápolis price? My agreement was to settle *preço por preço*, at the going price.

"All rice loses some weight on the road," said Lage. "*Nobody* pays the tenants Anápolis prices. You should pay *mato* prices."

"But nobody weighs in the *mato*. The tenant loses far more than the owner in the shipping. This is one deal that looks like a squeeze on the tenant."

"Squeeze! Dona Virginia, every single one of them holds out rice on the owner and sells it. Five cruzeiros a sack won't cover what they steal."

"It's the principle involved," I told him. "Which comes first, the squeeze or the stealing? I've kept my tenants bottled up without a road to stop the stealing and I'll stop the squeeze too. I think I'll pay Anápolis prices, less transport."

He had a look of horror engraved on his face when I left to meet Manoel at the Bowens'.

"I'll pay Anápolis prices, less transport," I told him. "But it will be according to our contract, which was twenty-five per cent for me plus repayment of what I advanced you."

Without acknowledging my fairness about the prices, Manoel sullenly pressed for further advantage. "Nobody signed a contract for me."

"You're trying to twist the facts," I countered. "You heard the deal on my farm and you stayed. The law says you accepted it." You have to know law as well as many other things to keep up with the "ignorant," "illiterate," "simple" backlanders. Manoel had advisers, I was sure of it.

"I'm going to Goiánia, *dona*. Will you advance me fifty cruzeiros on the rice?" asked Manoel.

I myself had not yet received an advance on the rice and as it happened I had with me only a note for a *conto*, a thousand cruzeiros.

"It's Saturday, the bank's closed," I answered. "All I have is a *conto* and nobody around here will change it." Fifty cruzeiros was like two dollars; a *conto* note like a fifty-dollar bill.

"*Granfa*, eh?" said Manoel. "Big shot, eh?" It was the perfect sneer.

I walked away, struggling against the thought that I should have let Aristide shoot him.

There were at least three more loads of rice to bring down.

The more trouble they cost me, the more determined I became. It seemed as if the backlands were challenging me with every difficulty over this rice. Getting every sack safely into the warehouse became far more important than the money involved. I knew I was risking my job with the IRO, but I could not let go.

Batão was now at the other end of the line, awaiting me, with our contract still to make. I found a trucker to bring down overnight a load of Chico's rice that was ready and waiting, and contracted with another to come for an additional load the next day. I rode north on the first truck with my three tenants, sent Batão back to Anápolis with Chico's rice and spent the night in the Frenchman's camp.

Though the next day was Sunday, I routed everybody out early and made them hump to get another full load of Emílio's and Ezequiel's rice ferried across the river. Manoel arrived on the truck that came for this load late in the day and I asked him to go back to Anápolis with me and the other three to settle up. For once he agreed and I shepherded the whole crew on top of the load of rice.

It was night when we started; the long, weary, hundred-mile night journey on top of the jolting, swaying load of rice was no novelty now. I had lost about ten pounds in the rough, constant travel, and my shoulder was chronically sore. I rested as best I could in my sleeping bag, turning and twisting in the hard embrace of the rice sacks.

One by one we picked up passengers until we had about eight dark-skinned people on the truck, all shivering in the wind that whipped through their light cotton clothes.

I dozed briefly and when I awoke, it was quite cold. One of the farm people was sitting at the edge of the load, full in the cutting breeze, cracking jokes. To my astonishment, I suddenly realized that Manoel, the thundercloud, was the group comedian! I had never before seen him out of the character of angry man harrying the landlord, or good father nursing his baby. I listened more sharply and it became plain his ironical wit about the chill wind and their thin clothes was tending to draw a contrast between me, snug in my sleeping bag, and the shivering roça people. Chico, Ezequiel and Emílio, sensitive to Manoel's growing insolence and not sure I was asleep, soon ceased to laugh.

I knew the roça people preferred to travel at night rather than under the hot sun of day, but this did not ease my certainty the wind must be very cold on them nor banish the thought that old Ezequiel, in particular, might curl up and die of dust pneumonia. There was a big canvas folded on top of the truck, which the men would not dare to touch. I knew I could get away with unfolding it for a shield from the wind; but I had to find some way to deal with Manoel to avoid the appearance of yielding to his pressure. I decided the best way I could return good for evil and spit in his eye at the same time was to wait until he ran out of funny sayings, and then unfold the cloth.

When he fell quiet a little later, I spoke up dryly.

"Terminou, Manoel?" ("Have you finished?") Then I started unfolding the stiff canvas and motioned Chico to spread it over the others. My three friendly tenants snickered at my having caught Manoel, and old Ezequiel muttered something about Manoel's big mouth as they settled down to sleep.

Sleep did not return to me quickly. I had salvaged "face" by getting a last laugh on Manoel and by making it plain I'd deliberately left the protective canvas folded until he finished his talk. But I had no illusions about my three "friendly" tenants. The minute I allowed Manoel to gain an undue advantage, they would go over to him, I was sure. In a sense, I was at their mercy, for they were my only witnesses against Manoel.

During the next two days, I had Chico legally empowered to sign agreements and receipts for the illiterate Feitosas and we made contracts while I sent Batão to the farm to bring down the last load of rice. Chico and Emílio and Manoel all stood to clear tidy sums in the harvest, while Ezequiel, who had obtained the largest advance and produced the least, owed me a small amount.

As I finished discussing plans for the coming year with the three tenants I had kept on my farm, Manoel called me aside. "You've made contracts with the boys," he said. "What about me?"

"Tomorrow we'll get your papers in order so you can apply for a lot in the *Colônia*," I answered.

Manoel looked at the ground. He had kept his wild temper in check since our confrontation by the river. Also, he was always quieter in town; he even looked smaller.

"I want to take you to a friend of mine to add up my accounts," he said. This was reasonable and I agreed.

We walked along the dusty street.

"I wouldn't make a contract like the one the other boys signed," Manoel volunteered.

"You probably never will get a chance to, Manoel," I replied. "Nobody in this whole country gives seventy-five per cent to the tenant after the land is cleared. The custom is half and half, as well you know."

"Yes, but what about cleaning the stream and building the houses?"

"The extra percentage will more than pay for the cleaning and the work on the new houses," I said. "I want the children on my place out of the weather next rainy season. You'd clean the stream for yourself, not for me. You know you can catch leaf-mold fever drinking from a dirty stream."

"Mm."

We came to a house with an official-looking sign on it.

"In here, *dona*." Manoel ushered me into a little office and I immediately knew this was no "friend's" house. Automatically I shook hands with a small, slender, stern-faced man introduced as "S'hor Silvano."

"I thought I was to see a friend of Manoel's," I said. "Is this a law office?"

"I'm the local representative of the federal labor department," said Silvano. "This man came here about his case and said he'd bring you this afternoon."

"What case?" I asked. "I only came to have a friend of

Manoel's check his accounts. If this is a legal hearing, I want to get my lawyer. I don't know what's going on here."

"He says you are trying to dispossess him."

Dispossession is a long, difficult process under Brazilian law. I turned full around and looked into Manoel's face. Our eyes met hard and in understanding. This was his way to trick me into the toils of officialdom and to involve me, perhaps for years.

"Manoel knew he was to leave and my other tenants heard the deal," I said.

"He says you're only giving him seventy-five per cent and and he claims eighty."

"All my tenants get seventy-five per cent. If there's a law saying they get eighty per cent, I want to see it." The only reference to this percentage I'd ever seen was in communist propaganda.

I did not say this to Silvano but began to explain to him how I was trying to improve conditions and production on my farm. All this was obviously quite different from what he had expected; Manoel's advance billing must have pictured me with eight white tentacles and the map of Wall Street in my face.

"Let me see the account book," he said at last, in a more friendly manner.

"Unofficially?"

"Very well, then."

Together we checked Manoel's book. I was fully confident here, for I knew the prices charged were lower than present Anápolis prices. Silvano's attitude changed the more he studied the book; he noted I was not asking Manoel to pay for medicine supplied his family, for one thing.

The official made additions, took the warehouse receipts showing weights and qualities of Manoel's rice, and spent a few minutes busily figuring. His final calculation had me owing Manoel more than I had estimated. When I asked if he had counted Manoel's share at eighty per cent, he nodded. I picked up my papers and said I'd come back with my lawyer.

Silvano made a gesture, as if wanting to throw up his hands, but it was one of friendly surrender. He made a new calculation that gave Manoel seventy-five per cent, confirming my idea that he and Manoel had tried to run a bluff. He wrote a receipt for Manoel to sign with a thumbprint and I made out a check for the amount due my tenant.

"I told Batão to meet me in Ceres tomorrow and we'll push through the application for your lot in the *Colônia*," I said to Manoel as I paid him.

Check in hand, Manoel spoke to the official very rapidly.

"I've made the calculations, I won't have enough money to get through on a *Colônia* lot by myself," he said. The way he said it, without bluster, made it sound like the truth.

I was suddenly brought up short against the thought that Manoel might have preferred to fight me rather than reveal his need to stay on the farm. It would have fitted in with his independent, forward-driving character.

"Let him stay," said Silvano, as we shook hands.

"He won't sign my contract," I replied. "I can't give him one different from the others."

"Why should I clean that stream and improve your farm for nothing?" demanded Manoel, who obviously had never heard of incentive, only of ways and means to destroy the landlord.

"You'll get a bigger percentage by far than any other *dono* gives," I repeated wearily. "You know they give only fifty per cent after the land is cleared."

"They ought to give eighty!" Manoel rejoined hotly.

I looked at Silvano, shaking my head. Here we were back at the starting place. Manoel clung to the only education of any kind that had been brought to him. He had been taught to fight blindly for a particular impossible figure as his goal, and to nurture his hate.

"Meet me at the bank in the morning and I'll get your check cashed," I said as I left. "You'll be much better off in the *Colônia* on your own land."

The very fact he was unable to cash his own check at

the bank reminded me he was illiterate and this always weakened me a little. I had never known anybody, not even a negro in the backward South at home, who could not at least sign his name.

I had to think very hard what to do about Manoel. He came very near to outmaneuvering me at every turn and his new plea of lack of money to get through till the next harvest may have been another dodge. Yet I had agreed to make new advances to my other three tenants; suppose Manoel's story was true and still I forced him off the place? Would I not risk subjecting him to real hardship, which would not only be wrong but also impolitic, since it would justify Manoel's every villainy, put him in the right? What if I made him leave the place and one of his family died of the hardship caused by lack of resources while he was struggling through the first year on his *Colônia* lot? Would I not incur moral guilt for the death?

Was I my brother's keeper, or my tenant's baby's keeper—? The issue was as old as Cain, who first dodged it. A woman's curiosity, men have recorded, led to the Fall of Man and his expulsion from the Eden of innocence into the hard responsibility of knowing good and evil and having to choose between them. But the first choice of evil made under this uncomfortable state of affairs was Cain's, who refused to be, indeed, his brother's keeper.

It seemed probable that Manoel's new mildness and his dodge to get me into the labor official's presence was part of advice given him in Goiânia, where we were now sure he knew native communists. Obviously they would welcome any chance to make trouble between a Brazilian tenant and an American landlord.

How strange, I thought, that an illiterate woodsman-farmer in the depths of one of the world's last frontiers, thousands of miles away from Russia, on the other side of the world, could go directly to a source of advice that came by stages straight from the Kremlin. Why could I not invoke some counselor who had a set of tactics all ready to help me prevail as a representative of enlightened free enterprise in the best American tradition? Manoel and I reflected in miniature a titanic struggle: he had help and advice and I had none.

I could well imagine the counsel of the local landowners, representatives of capitalism: boot him off the place, no matter if such action did speed the probability of the ultimate destruction of all of us.

I remembered the look of real shock on Lage's face when I proposed my rice-pricing policy with my tenants. If he knew how I was now pondering the Manoel problem, he would think me a simpleton.

It occurred to me then, with something of a jolt, that the local landlords and Lage were as ignorant as Manoel of what I was trying to do. With business practices handed directly down from feudal times, they had not the faintest notion of promoting better treatment for workers and producers in order to have a more productive, more active business life.

The *donos* and businessmen knew as little as Manoel about the unique form of society developed in very recent times in the United States of America, the Industrial Revolution in reformation. Nobody had ever brought the ideas to either class. Instead of that, they had both had a generation of heavy propaganda picturing us as avid oppressors squeezing wealth from all the "weaker" peoples of the earth.

What a mess! I thought, scuffing along in the deep dust of Anápolis.

But my immediate dilemma had to be solved, and I worked out my next move as I trudged along. I would talk again to the lawyer . . . make Manoel move to the *Colônia*. I would offer a small loan against Manoel's next crop, as much as he would have had as advance from me if he stayed on my place. I'd have to push his application through at the *Colônia*. Next year I could take part of the loan, or renew it if he had bad luck. Thus I could ease Manoel's situation without appearing to yield to his force-play.

Time was pressing: it had to be done quickly. I caught a ride north with old Aquiles and we traveled through the night.

This was the tenth or eleventh trip I had made to the Great Forest in less than three weeks and each round trip was over two hundred miles. I was a hardened truck traveler now. We arrived in Barranca before dawn and parked in front of Donato's. While Aquiles curled up in the cab, I finished out the night in my sleeping bag in the empty bed of the truck. Contrary to Dona Anita's dire predictions of throat-cutting, I was not molested. If anybody saw me, I suppose they thought I was a bundle of empty rice sacks.

Batão did not show up the next day to meet me as I expected him to, so I went alone to talk to the *Colônia* authorities about a lot for Manoel. I was promised seventy-two acres for him, an average sized lot, and I prepared a letter for him to present as identification. Then I left to look for Batão.

Plodding along the baking, dusty streets of the wide-scattered nascent little city of Ceres, I busily figured the next step in winding up my affairs. I felt the situation was well in hand, at last. To save my rice, I had fought the country and its disorganization and sharp practices till victory was in my grasp. I had not flinched before any hardship; rather I had taken all the risks, and had prevailed. I had managed to stay out of Manoel's traps, fighting a duel in which advantage was heavily on his side, since he knew the game and had no scruples. I had even fought death, instinctively making the one move certain to stay Aristide's itching trigger finger.

My new formula for moving Manoel to the *Colônia* would cheat him out of overt victory over me, and cheat hunger out of a chance at his family. I wanted very much to see Manoel an owner of land; then indeed he would become, I was sure, an ardent capitalist. This would be my victory.

One more trip to the farm to tie up loose ends, then I'd take Batão to Anápolis, sign our contract and be free.

My arrangements were nearly completed. Batão would receive money from me each month through the bank and pass it on to the three tenants, taking receipts. I would send money for him to buy a cart and horse, the latter to be boarded on the *Colônia* side of the river. This would provide transport, especially for the sick or injured, during the rains. I was extremely thankful there had been no deaths on my place and it was increasingly important to me to keep the record bright.

Batão would have the men work their land properly and plant early, so that we could get a maximum yield. He would buy tools with money I sent and have them build better houses and clean the stream. I would pay for a fairly good adobe house for his family and work crew, and for a well and privy for their use. I planned to plant about a hundred and twenty acres of new-cleared land in coffee and about forty more in rice, for a one-year money crop. In all, I'd have about two hundred and fifty under cultivation. Batão would plant a garden, and I'd provide seeds for the others.

I spied a jeep parked in front of a store and went inside to find its owner, Jean Panz (called Jean-Jean), partner of the Antoinettes and my neighbor in the forest. Here was a ride to the farm.

"Have you heard about the murder?" Jean-Jean greeted me, tense and excited.

"Who got killed?"

"A workman of ours. His body is at the hospital. I'm going there now. I'm sorry, Virginia, but it looks like Batão is in this."

My heart plummeted. I was never prepared for these things, never! The special cruelty of the backlands was to strike from a new direction every time I had won the least advantage.

"How, Jean-Jean?"

"There was bad blood between them in the *mato*. I found the boy in convulsions yesterday and the doctor says it could be poison. Batão had trouble with the father. I'm sorry, Virginia, but it was Benedito's only son and he'll go after Batão."

It was as bad as it could possibly be. If Benedito killed Batão, Tito's sons would take it up. We'd have open war in our forest camp.

"If Batão's a murderer, I want to see him punished by the

law," I said. "Will the autopsy prove whether it was poison?"

"They're going to send the liver to São Paulo for analysis. I'm going up there now; come along."

I followed him, feeling literally as if I had received a dull blow on the head. No matter how well I managed to cope with the backlands, there was always some undreamed-of new and higher hurdle awaiting me.

At the small frontier hospital we found two white-coated men, one a doctor, working on the dead youth in a small out-house, a simple shed with three walls. The young man, about twenty, lay on a narrow metal table, naked except for his stained and torn work trousers loose about his lower limbs. His feet, at which I stood, were crossed one over the other and tied in place with a strip of rag, their pink soles washed clean at last of the red backland dust. Another band of gray cloth bound his forehead, holding back a mass of kinky black hair. I was surprised to see how black the boy was; I knew his father, Benedito, and he could have been a white man deeply burned by the sun.

Jean-Jean asked if there was any new information and the doctor said no, it would depend on the tests.

In the presence of the dead youth, while we waited in silence for the doctor to do his work, anxiety gradually ceased roiling in my mind.

It was the first time I had ever seen a dead person informally, as it were, in everyday clothes. In my experience death and burial, even of people I loved, had taken place virtually off stage, with doctors, nurses and undertakers sharing the last intimate moments, not myself.

I looked down at the boy. With quick breath gone and ardent blood stilled, this human body now belonged to the slow-moving part of the world, to the hills which change only through decades, to the rocks which weather slowly under centuries of rain and wind. His spirit, quicker and more ardent than breath or blood, had emerged into an even greater mystery, the limitless quietude of eternity.

The doctor worked expertly, making a small incision, and as I watched, I seemed to see through all the man-made structures around us. I saw and felt a whole panorama of peaceful hillsides and sun-warmed rocks surrounding the youth, welcoming him to become part of them once more; yet his dead body, not yet gone back to earth, was a bridge still to the spirit newly entered into the calm encompassing all time. For an instant only, it was as if I could see what he would go back to and what he would go forward to; I saw nothing dark, no shadows.

The sharp little knife had made a short cut in the cool, purplish side and the doctor's gloved finger probed inside, briefly showing the strongly pink inside lips of the wound. It surprised me how small the cut was and how small a piece of flesh the doctor brought out. Was this all they meant to do to settle whether or not murder had been committed? The doctor placed the fragment of blackish liver in a wide-necked little bottle and sealed and labeled it.

We exchanged only a few words. I asked the doctor if a quick-striking disease could have caused death. He said it could have, but did not venture to name a likely disease. Jean-Jean took the sealed bottle and we went with it to the Ceres police, who promised to send it at once to São Paulo.

Jean-Jean told me he had arranged in Ceres for burial of the young man, for Benedito would not go near his dead son.

In downtown Ceres, we met the father, a lanky, six-foot *roçeiro*. As we all climbed into the jeep, the old man bent over to pick up a coin glittering in the dust. He looked at the coin blankly for a moment; then he raised his arm to throw it away again with a gesture of despair. Jean-Jean caught his arm, preventing him. Finding a coin promises luck almost everywhere in the world and the two unstudied movements were an eloquent dialogue. "How can there be any good thing with my son dead!" the *roçeiro's* gesture said. "Brother, do not rebel, fate can be kind as well as cruel," meant the restraining motion of the white man from far away.

Benedito was silent until Jean-Jean stopped the jeep to perform an errand in the town and left us alone.

"Dona Virginia, *que do meu filho?*" he asked sorrowfully. "What about my son?"

I was in a most difficult situation. The man's grief and rebellion affected me most strongly. Yet a blood feud was forming and I meant to defend Batão until we had some clear evidence against him. Then I intended to insist on delivering him to the police, cheating private vengeance.

"S'hor Benedito, I cannot say how distressed I am. I hope the autopsy will tell us something. When did your son fall sick?"

"He came home from Anápolis yesterday about noon. He told his mother he had a headache and later he had a fit. He was out of himself when S'hor Jean-Jean took him to Ceres in the jeep that night."

"Where did he eat that day?"

"His mother killed a chicken for him, but he ate little. By the time it was cooked, he sat suffering greatly, bent over, his hands on the back of his neck. He was my only son, *dona*. The doctor says it could be poison. I will have to do something about this."

"But when could he have been poisoned?" I asked. "He only ate in his mother's home at the camp."

"It could have been at the *pensão* where they stayed in Anápolis and I know who could have done it."

This sounded more and more like a typical backland tangle of conjecture, ignorance and gossip. The grieving father, seeking some way to strike back for his pain, was impelled to blame a personal enemy upon whom he could revenge himself, rather than impersonal fate, against which he was powerless. The people around him would not try to check him, but would spur him on. When tragedy loomed, they leaped quickly into supporting roles that gave play to their emotions, making them important in the immensity of the *sertão*.

"S'hor Benedito, you know there are diseases which strike

very suddenly. You should consider that." It was as far as I
dared go yet.

When Jean-Jean rejoined us, I discussed the matter with
him in English, which he spoke very well. Jean-Jean was new
to Goiás. I wanted to warn him that when men went against
each other here in the wilds, the untamed earth itself seemed
to set up active forces urging them to mutual destruction. But
I thought better of it; such reasoning would weaken my arguments. No one can tell you about the backland powers. You
have to learn about them yourself.

I did warn him that feud killings would give his plantation
a bad name, creating labor difficulties for him. Already one
man had been crushed by a falling tree and the workmen did
not want to go to that part of the *roça*. Also, I stressed my substitute theory of sudden disease.

We reached camp, which was quiet under the hot afternoon
sun. The men were away at work, the few women inside their
dark huts. Jean-Jean left us. I walked behind Benedito, whose
will to do murder I somehow had to reason away. I could not
solve this new situation with a quick action prompted by instinctive reasoning, always my salvation in acute emergencies,
as when Manoel's life hung by a thread under the trees by
Ghost River. This one I would have to do another way, using
great tact and patience.

Benedito's wife was waiting for him at the door of their
home. When he spoke a word to her, she threw her arms up
over her face and fled silently to the back of the hut where a
partition divided off their sleeping bunks. No sound was heard
from her during the long afternoon.

The young man who had been with Benedito's son on the
last trip appeared. He heard the news in silence also.

It was cool and pleasant in the hut, though the stinging
gnats continually pestered us. We sat on long, hand-hewn
wooden benches on opposite sides of the room. The sunlight
made occasional faint streaks on the dirt floor through the
close-set vertical poles of the walls. A pet chicken wandered

around our feet, occasionally making a soft cluck. I asked the younger man to go over the story. It was as Benedito had told me. I asked if they had seen Batão in Anápolis. The young man said no, but they had stayed at the *pensão* where Batão usually stopped. Carefully calm, voice low, I reasoned about the poison. The men agreed Batão would have had to bribe someone at the Anápolis *pensão* to administer it. Absurd as it may seem, Jean-Jean had already suggested this to me and I had an answer thought out. I asked where Batão could have obtained the money. There had been no recent payday in camp and I had not advanced funds to him. The most hardened criminal would not commit a paid poison-murder on credit, I argued. The doctor himself said it could have been a swift disease, I told them, slurring the fact he had also said it could have been poison.

Benedito at last came out of his silence. His whole life was gone, he said, in a long monologue like a primitive funeral speech. His son had been his right hand. He told the story of his family's wanderings. This had been the first time they had had a chance to plant a large acreage of rice, with a good *dono*. It was all impossible now, he said; he had no heart for anything.

The man's grief, simple and universal, was deeply moving; it was a world crashing down. With conscious intent I used my very real sympathy to draw the rank poison out of him, asking him about his other children and his grandchildren. When at length he said he would send for one of his daughter's young sons to bring up at his side, I felt the festering wound was open and would drain.

I would not risk my advantage by leaving the hut. As the men came in at dusk and gathered to hear the news, I repeated over and over my own account of the autopsy, enlarging on the possibility of disease. Gradually the story evolved until it appeared that Benedito himself believed this theory. Whether from politeness or because he had felt my sympathy, Benedito did not contradict me and the version caught on. At length, I obtained a promise that nothing would be done in the matter until we heard from the autopsy. I hoped that the whole thing would peter out while they were waiting for the report, and this in fact happened. Actually, the jar containing the fragment of the boy's liver got lost somewhere between Ceres and São Paulo and no report ever came.

Batão showed up late that night and offered proof he had not for weeks been near the *pensão* where the dead boy had eaten. I made him promise to keep quiet and avoid trouble.

Bound for Anápolis and my departure for Rio the next day, I felt deep satisfaction at having met so many challenges with such a measure of success. The trouble over Benedito's son, unexpected and disturbing, had brought an unexpected reward. Like most people, I had only with difficulty learned to curb my natural and primitive impulses into civilized behavior and I felt that when I first came to the backlands, I lost much of the ground I had won. But in my long harvest campaign, I had prevailed through self-discipline and self-control and in Benedito's hut, I had used the highest of the civilized faculties —patience, reason and sympathy—to impose restraint on the universal primitive instinct to see death as the work of a hostile will. It was as if I had won a victory not only over the backland powers, but over savagery deep-buried within myself.

It was only a beginning; I knew there would be other contests, but I felt confident I could meet them.

14

The new and sterner tests for which my harvest travail in the *sertão* had been a rehearsal came very soon. Called there urgently in the fall by Batão, who had exceeded his budget and said the *fazenda* work was at a standstill, I found a far more serious trouble threatening our world in Goiás: my good friends, the Bowens, were in grave distress. Joan was ill with some malady the local doctors could not diagnose and in spite of constant sedatives suffered at intervals the most frightful convulsions from intestinal pain. At these times she clung blindly to her husband, who was nursing her night and day with the doubtful help of frightened, lugubrious servants. The Captain had had yellow fever and other illnesses in the wilds— he almost died when Alfredo was in Anápolis—and I wondered if he might not collapse before Joan's strong vitality was exhausted.

While trying to decide what to do, I dealt with Batão. His sins went far beyond overspending, and imperiled my entire farm venture. He had cleared land on the back of the place instead of near the river as I had ordered, thus upsetting my whole long-term plan for Fazenda Chavante. Topping this outrage, he had kept Manoel on the farm. I had sent elaborate instructions and money to him and the lawyer, Melorosa, directing them to help Manoel get his *Colônia* lot and to lend him in my name the sum needed to help him through his first year as an independent landowner. Instead, they had permitted Manoel to sign the same contract as my other tenants and to remain.

The first person I saw when I returned to Chavante was Manoel. Smooth and silky in triumph, he told me he had not started work on the new house because Batão hadn't given him the tools for it; it was obvious he intended to ignore every improvement clause in my contract. When I asked Batão about the tools, he said he hadn't wanted the men to take time out to build the houses during the planting season. After the rains started, it would of course be next to impossible.

Deeply angry at both men, I looked over Batão's contract to see if I could find grounds for breaking it. Yet it was inadvisable to start a court action, because I could not get an exit permit from the country while involved in court and therefore could not continue my IRO work. I decided to use a Brazilian approach and try to weep my way out of my four-year obligation with Batão.

Concealing my rage behind a friendly face in Brazilian fashion, I took Batão to Anápolis with me and we talked it over. I began by mournfully revealing I did not have any more money to advance than the sums stipulated in the contract. I "wept" in true Brazilian style. I was an orphan, I told Batão, painting a pathetic picture of how hard it was to be a woman all alone in the world. This self-dramatization, half confession, half pharisaical boasting, could grow on me, I discovered. I began to be somewhat affected by the touching picture and to enjoy myself in a dank sort of way.

Then I hinted at getting tough. Suppose he planted sketchily because he had overspent. I'd count every coffee plant that came up and break his contract if there was one plant less than our agreement stipulated, I said.

Batão had his say. He wept copious metaphorical tears, dwelling on his twelve or thirteen children (mostly living). I did not see the direct connection between coffee planting and unrestrained child getting, a luxury I had never been able to afford, but it served as the script for Batão's turn on stage.

Next, he enlarged on the rigors of life in the *sertão,* on which we were agreed. Then he told over, as if fingering a string of prayer beads, the virtues of his character, his kindliness, his desire to please me, his willingness to prove his eminent worth. He dwelt lovingly on the great profits I should reap through him, in the future. He figured them for me on the back of a grubby envelope.

I took Batão to lunch and for a time we rested. In the afternoon the deadly duel began again. Taking my turn once more, I drew a tear-jerking picture of my labors for the refugees and the future greatness of Brazil. Could I permit money so earned to be wasted on a poorly-done, skimped coffee planting? Never! But representatives of two great friendly nations should always keep things friendly. We skirmished back and forth with self-laudatory protests of good will and mutual international admiration till at length I suggested we might plant only rice this year and so have plenty of money for coffee planting the second year. Brightened considerably by the suggestion of plenty of money, Batão agreed to postpone the four-year undertaking of coffee planting.

We now spent long hours alternately weeping and orating over terms of the new contract. Batão naturally wanted a year for the rice planting added to his existing four-year coffee contract, which would have tied me to him for five years. I wanted a one-year deal only, since I meant to get rid of him. I stuck to the point that I had no money to back up anything but a one-year contract, and he finally weakened and agreed. The next day we abrogated our four-year agreement, which was worth the whole value of my farm, and signed another for a year only.

I had out-Brazilianed a Brazilian! This took away not only much of my deep anger at Batão for his blithe reversal of all my dearest wishes, but also some of my resentment over many other frustrations suffered in Goiás.

My concern about the Bowens had been growing hourly and I became convinced that unless Joan was taken to a hospital in São Paulo, they would both die. When I went to see their doctor, he refused to order the trip, but said he would prescribe the sedatives necessary if we wanted to risk it. I would take the responsibility, I told him, mindful that my failure to face the responsibilities of friendship had led me to abandon Alfredo in my first months in Goiás. With me along to help, the Captain agreed to go.

And now as I pushed our preparations, there arose around us a powerful, voluble, almost engulfing wave of sympathy from our Anápolis friends. These people who live with death at their elbows and who deal so softly with each other in their daily lives were overready to commiserate and suffer with us emotionally, but you could see in their eyes that they thought Joan would die from the trip and considered me rash and heartless for promoting it. Nine-tenths of them would never have money for such a bold solution; moreover, the Brazilian middle class as well as the poor use suffering acceptance as a defense against the unimaginable thicket of difficulty surrounding their poverty-ridden lives. I had glimpsed another truth at the feet of the dead son of Benedito: amid all this natural splendor, the very process of dissolution was not dark or chilling. But lack of dread of death did not make it any more acceptable to me and I wished for a few worriers around to help me fight it.

To carry through, I had to transmute all my doubts and pity at the sight of Joan's frightening agonies into unshakable determination. She had a panic fear of being put off the plane if she had an attack, for there was a regulation compelling airlines to offload the sick. I promised her if we were thus stranded at some backland airstrip, we'd hire a private plane and continue to São Paulo. The airline clerks were unsure about us and demurred when I first asked for tickets; finally I sat one full day in their lobby and won out by silent pressure. Just as our flight came in at the airport, Joan went into a convulsion that raised a tidal wave of hesitations and doubts in the little circle seeing us off. While our friends stared bug-eyed, as if we were creatures from Mars, the Captain and I calmly gave her the maximum dose of easing drug and walked her onto the plane by force of will.

We completed the uneasy trip without incident, our patient resting quietly all the way. She went into a hospital at São Paulo, where a skillful surgeon found and relieved her trouble, severe abdominal adhesions and an encysted appendix.

Capping a series of crises in which I faced the challenges of the *sertão* rather than dodging them, this experience completed a profound change in my life that began when I first resolved to turn and fight. I had come to charge myself with a long record of weaknesses, vacillations and mistakes in Goiás, and the worst of them, I had come to believe, was the decision to leave Alfredo. Though I had argued to myself my desertion was meant to be only temporary and had finally tried to put the whole question out of my mind, I did feel guilt over it. Looking back, I saw that in seeking an escape from my growing fears about flying with Alfredo, I had seized the excuse of financial need, and fled. After I discovered the strong attraction to death that enters into the search for escape, I believed my influence with Alfredo, the escapist par excellence, would have protected him from death.

"I didn't run away this time!" I said to myself and to Alfredo when I learned Joan would live. All my efforts to resist and overcome the complexities of the backlands could have been a preparation for this most important emergency, in which I had to marshal judgment, determination and courage to know what to do and to insist on doing it. At the final showdown, the big crisis, I did not abandon my friends to the mercy of the beautiful and cruel *sertão*, and this set me free of a burden of remorse for abandoning Alfredo.

I was all the way back now from my journey toward escape. I had gone to the backlands to rebuild my life in a beautiful setting, found more difficulty than I could absorb, began to dodge and became entangled in evasions. In untangling myself, I lost the common illusion that other times, other places and other peoples are simpler and kinder. Gone forever from my mind was the idea common among people on pavements and children in schoolrooms that refuge lies in some leafy woods, some distant forest. No longer did escape seem either possible or desirable to me. The desire to escape vanished when I realized its ultimate, deadly destination.

The idea of escape in the American civilization is very often associated with neurosis or maladjustment. Self-judgments about emotional stability are always suspect, but by chance I have qualified opinions on my own. In the last stages of my dissolved first marriage, I insisted on taking my problems and uncertainties to one of New York's most competent psychiatrists to see if I needed his help. After a most thorough probing, he sent me away with the consoling opinion that I was "very well-balanced." Since returning to New York I have taken an equally thorough and complicated series of psychological and psychiatric tests to oblige a doctor friend engaged in a research program of much interest to me; this time the verdict came out "exceptionally well-adjusted." Both of these professional judgments of personality are significant in summing up my experiment in escape, I believe. They indicate that even an exceptionally well-balanced person may fall into involvement with escape after delving too deeply into the complex hopes, fears and disappointments of the times.

I have often thought that when I do wrong, punishment comes very quickly, while other people get by for years with their misdeeds. But it is also true that my rewards come quickly when I try to do right. My great reward followed very swiftly after I worked through my final expiation in the backlands, though the *sertão* still had one lesson for me to learn. This reward was the happiness of marriage based on steadfast love, a whole dimension in itself.

During my travail in the harvest I kept writing to Bill and at last I had to go to Chile and Argentina for the IRO once more. Our welcome reunions continued. Bill had always been extremely sensitive to the workings of my spirit and had an uncanny ability to read my mind. Though we did not try to analyze what was happening to me, he knew there was a change. When he first met me, there had been a grinding of the gears within me over my work and this became more apparent just before our break. There was little inner grinding now, and when it started, we both hastened to get away from the disturbing subject. Our unique achievement, which had spoiled both of us for anybody else, was that from the first we practiced happiness together. Bill set the tone, but my own appreciation for his unselfishness and his ability to resist dark emotions set me trying to be unselfish and even-tempered too. Freed at last of the grinding of gears over the imperfections of mankind, I could contribute more when I was with Bill and uphold my side of our good tradition.

In the fall I told Bill I did not intend to subject my whole life to the farm; I meant to make it an investment and an experiment in developing my own "backward area." We both agreed it would be good for us to return to our own country—Bill had been away four years and I five. With a job offered him in New York, Bill asked if we could be married when we returned, and I said yes. This decision came easily, though my former self would have surrounded it with doubts, hesitations and a desire for impossible guarantees. I guarded no escape clause deep in my mind, for I was free of the illusion of escape. Our separation had proved what most couples can only guess at, that we would never be so well suited as together. We had cultivated tenderness and affection, channeling the exciting rapids of a strong mutual attraction into the deeper and quieter waters of permanent union, and it seemed eminently desirable to consecrate this with marriage.

Bill's new job was as a magazine editor with McGraw-Hill in New York and I left the IRO to marry him there in December, 1949. Setting up our new home was a lovely new occupation for me, but among other good things, Bill and I shared a rediscovery of our own country. My experience in the backlands gave me new eyes for my country, this fabulous place I had been away from for five full years. It was like coming into the world of tomorrow, in being today. I was at last through with my emotional entanglement with the backlands, though the *sertão* was not yet through with me.

Though it was a wrench to leave Bill, I flew back the following April for the harvest weeks at Chavante, where the news was encouraging. When I had last seen it, the rice had sprouted well. There had been minor troubles then: Manoel and Batão had been feuding and I'd told Batão to make a path around Manoel's lot and isolate him there "like a wild animal." The tenants' new houses had not been built; Batão claimed he had bought them cottonseed with the tool money as insurance against a fall in the rice market. The garden, after one failure, had come up, but the privy had been built too close to Batão's well and I had ordered him to fill up the privy. Batão could not be trusted to transmit my monthly advances to the tenants. But I had learned that people in the backlands suffer compulsion to keep the cash and let the credit go; I had arranged to have the tenants get their money through a new branch bank at Ceres.

On my return in April, the Bowens, now well and strong, met me and drove me north to the farm. They said someone had estimated my crop at ten thousand sacks of rice. Ten thousand sacks! That would yield enough money to develop Chavante in fine style. I had just sold an optimistic article to *The Saturday Evening Post* about my clearing, and that was a good omen: I was writing again. The big road was busy with early harvest traffic; it was an artery of hope as northward-moving hundreds surged steadily forward in roaring trucks toward a new life on the land and the pale rice flowed south to turn into money and goods, the recompense of gigantic effort in hewing down a forbidding forest.

When I passed through them, the old slopes approaching the mountains were as still as ever, guarding their secrets. And the magnificent new country beyond that I feasted my eyes on had its final lesson locked deep in its heart. But I was caught up in my own happiness and the general optimism, and I sensed nothing.

Barranca and Ceres were booming. The small freeholders of the *Colônia*, with big crops, were building new houses. All along the road, I noticed new ones going up, new piles of clay tiles and latticed framework soon to be covered with mud plaster.

As usual, the details of the picture at the farm were less pleasing. If the rest of the region had improved, Manoel at least had not; he began a harangue about Batão taking the workmen through his rice field and hinted he might sue for the damage done. I had no intention of penalizing Manoel for ignoring his obligations, but I did not intend to let him penalize me further. I had contracted to advance my tenants a substantial sum of money to hire extra help in the harvest and I instructed the bank to have the tenants sign a receipt for the money stating their full satisfaction with my performance of contract. This was to forestall any legal shenanigans by Mr. Manoel.

He had not withdrawn his harvest money and I knew why he had not, and he knew I knew why.

"When are you going to draw your harvest money, Manoel?" I asked him. We were calm, old adversaries circling for advantage.

"I haven't needed it yet," he said.

"That rice is part mine, see that it doesn't get too ripe," I said.

"Mm," said Manoel.

Emílio, even without the promised tools, had built a new, fairly weatherproof pole hut which he showed me with pride. His crop and Chico's were good, he said. I asked about Ezequiel's. Amid many long pauses and much deep soul-searching, Emílio revealed to me that old Ezequiel had taken to getting falling-down drunk every time he got his monthly cash advance. His family had fared worse than when I advanced supplies only.

When I went to see Ezequiel, he cringed like an old dog expecting a whipping. He confessed his crop would be small. "How did you happen to fall behind, S'hor Ezequiel?" I asked mildly. "Plenty of money was sent this year to help you. I think you could do a little better and get out from under your debt."

"Dona Virginia, I guess I'm just *frouxo*," said Ezequiel. *Frouxo* means indolent, lax, "no 'count."

There was no room for argument here, so I left. A chronic sufferer from empathy, the habit of putting myself in the other person's place, I could understand Ezequiel only too well. I remembered how much comfort the curious Menelik's rum had given me; in Ezequiel's place, I should probably have spent the crop money on rum too. I could do nothing about Ezequiel. I fervently hoped he'd leave my farm, but if he did not choose to, I could see us going down the years together.

Batão, when we met at his house, gave me a severe jolt by saying to begin with that it would take three times his original estimate to finish financing the harvest. He was overspent and refused to let me see the books. Though I had heard of his sprees in Anápolis whorehouses, he claimed the money had gone for treatment for his son and a workman, who caught fever drinking at the well. It was his own fault, I told him; he had been warned about letting the women wash dishes at the well and pour out the waste water there, a habit formed by washing beside running streams. (I should have had him fill up the well as he did the privy, I thought; how complicated it was to change patterns of culture!) We dickered and wept back and forth until at last he offered to sell out to me. This was what I wanted and I agreed to buy his share, at a price to be set when he had finished cutting the grain.

I already had a new overseer in view, Pedro Torres, recommended by the Bowens.

I returned to Anápolis at once and brought Pedro Torres to see the farm. Pedro was a man of some education and had picked up notions of scientific farming while working around one of Brazil's best agricultural colleges. I was happy to find someone with even a smattering of such knowledge and as we drove through the closed-in hills around Ceres, I called his attention to the erosion already beginning on these slopes so newly cleared.

"It's the way they hoe," said Pedro. The *roçeiros* laid their hoes flat on the ground and scraped, always from uphill downward, and they themselves made tiny gullies for the heavy rains to deepen. At Chavante, I asked him about the cultivated soil that always looked so abnormal to me. The *roçeiros*, he explained further, in scraping the earth rather than chopping it as they hoed, left a slick surface which the sun's heat cracked open in the dry time. The cracks allowed the deeper moisture to evaporate. As the first thin film of humus was exhausted or washed away, the land would become less and less productive. The men should chop the earth fine with the blade of the hoe, making a layer of insulation against the sun's rays, he said. The soil around us, he said, could be ruined in a few years by this kind of cultivation and letting it lie fallow would do no good. There was a big ant that ate leaf and twig in the deserted clearings, preventing the formation of new humus.

I knew this was so, because the DP farm colony we had started in Goiás had lost its first crop by planting in old clearings instead of in virgin forest land. The secret of the quiet old clearings of Goiás was at last made clear to me— they were comatose land, the graveyard of the soil and man's effort.

Pedro was tempted by my offer to turn the harvest over to him and have him plant coffee with its proceeds. But he gave me my first suggestion of the undreamed-of catastrophe that was coming.

"My brother at the bank says the rice crop in other parts of Brazil is very big," he said. "The crop begins to come in here first, but prices may break later on. Maybe we'd better wait and see what happens."

"S'hor Pedro, a price break? I've checked the statistics, the price of rice has been going up for several years!"

"I'm more than fifty years old, Dona Virginia," he said. "It always happens. I've been through it with sugar and cotton and coffee. Half the ranches in this country are still mortgaged to the Bank of Brazil because of a big boom in Zebu cattle that went flat a few years ago."

"But, S'hor Pedro, Brazil needs food, the world needs food!" I protested. "They can't let a thing like that happen. It's an election year. The government will have to do something."

"That may be, *dona*," said Pedro. "If you can make a contract to sell the rice, I'll make a deal with you."

Still sure the government would act, I tried to sell my rice at Ceres. I found the buyers there uneasy. One of them, a second-generation Pole, went with me to see my crop and offered me fifty cruzeiros a sack for it, delivered in Ceres.

I took him to Manoel, who had sacked some of his rice. When the Pole repeated his offer, Manoel burst into a torrent of outraged protests.

The buyer laughed at him.

"You men on this place are lucky," he said. "You should see what's going on in the *Colônia*. They haven't got *donos* over there to see them through this harvest and the next, and they're selling by the roadside at forty cruzeiros just as fast as they can sack their rice."

Fifty cruzeiros a sack would not pay half my costs for producing the rice, and we did not make a deal. Instead, I borrowed a thousand dollars from the bank and advanced Batão small sums for food for the workmen.

Like low thunder growing gradually louder, calamity crept upon us. Brazil, nation of chronically underfed people, nation distressed by decaying agriculture, importer of food, was about to have a bumper harvest.

Shuttling between Anápolis and Chavante, trying to sell my rice and dickering with Batão, I watched the drama unfold. In Ceres, people seemed dazed. In Anápolis, near the railhead, they pinned their faith on government action, as did I. The truckers pounded their machines to death on the big road, trying to get rice delivered before contracts began cracking. The small buyers who roamed the *Colônia* making roadside purchases were timid, offering ever lower prices.

A curious phenomenon developed among the homesteaders of the *Colônia*, for whose benefit the federal government had in the early 1940's started opening up this wilderness. They broke into a spree of gambling that pinpointed the velvet night of the Great Forest with many flickering lights. Driving along the big road after dark, you could see in front of many huts small groups huddled over guttering candles and wavering wick lamps, gambling feverishly with each other for the rice they had sweated all day to thresh and sack, wagering the sacked rice which still had a chance to sell. I had never before seen any signs of life around the huts after dark and the change was weird, as if an unsuspected race had suddenly crept out from underground to perform mysterious evil under the vaulting, sullen night sky.

Pedro and I haunted the office of a local paper to read their telegraphed news from Rio and at last it came: the Bank of Brazil would buy rice, the good grade, at from one hundred to one hundred and twenty-five cruzeiros per sack. I had sold at one hundred and thirty the year before, when all costs had been much lower, and had barely broken even; this bank price would not even repay the cost of producing my crop. All I could hope for would be to get back enough money to plant some coffee and eventually cover my losses. The bank's decision automatically cut off from help those producers who could not find funds with which to finish harvesting their rice or to pay for hauling it to storage. Local banks and buyers would not advance credit except to farmers reasonably near Anápolis, but I found a man willing to pay me a hundred a sack for my rice, delivered at my expense.

Even after the bank announced its support price, I had not believed I would have to sell at that figure. At a hundred cruzeiros a sack, I would lose a good part of the money I had

put in. I thought surely the rice market would recover from
its present staggering, and that rice would move and prices
firm up. But the people around me thought I was lucky even
to have a chance at a firm offer for rice.

I met the rice buyer from Ceres, the Pole, on the street one
day and discussed the offer with him.

"Make the deal, *dona*, make the deal," he urged. "Nobody
knows what will happen. Price support may not work for
months. All we need is for one big buyer to crash and there'd
be panic. There's panic now in the *Colônia* and back in the
hills. The small farmers are begging to sell their rice for the
price of the sacks and nobody will buy at any price. Make
the contract if you can."

I made the contract, accepting an advance of fifteen *contos*
and several hundred empty sacks for my rice, for which I
gave a note of hand for twenty-one *contos*. I bought off
Batão for about five hundred dollars, one-sixth of his original
demand, and Pedro signed an agreement to finish the harvest
and plant coffee the next year. In paying off Batão, I bought
only my freedom to put the farm in Pedro's hands and leave,
for no one could guess what his share of our rice would
finally be worth.

On my way to install Pedro on the Fazenda Chavante, I
learned in Ceres that the wily Manoel had at last slipped
through my fingers. Driven by necessity to withdraw his harvest money, he had signed my quitclaim receipt, picked up his
money and the receipt in one motion and slipped out the door
before the befuddled little girl clerk who served him even
noticed what he had done. I was sure I would have serious
trouble with Manoel now.

Driving north toward Chavante, I saw that all life on the
small farms of the *Colônia* seemed to have come to a standstill after the announcement of the inadequate support price.
The stacks of tiles grew no higher; they remained stacked.
Here and there they were beginning to fall off and break.
The house frames did not take on sheathing, but remained
skeletal, ruins before they had ever been dwellings. Some of

these buildings could have been finished with materials at hand and their paralyzed state bespoke profound discouragement, the endemic malady of this farming people, along with hookworm, syphilis, malnutrition, malaria, goiter and other life-sapping ills.

On the road from the river to Chavante, we met old Benedito, staggering drunk in the daytime. The Frenchman had mortgaged his land to the Bank of Brazil to harvest his rice. Nilo and the Bowens were the lucky ones. Nilo, after taking a loss, had sold his land to a wealthy doctor in São Paulo, Dr. Job Lane, and the Bowens' operations were being handled by one tenant, Getúlio, and a small crew.

We met Manoel on the path entering Chavante. I did not mention his trickery at the bank, for there was nothing to be gained by bringing it up. I knew he'd make all the trouble he could now. Manoel and I had through it all waged a battle in which principles and morals and *direito*, what is right, were involved. Manoel's counselors told him any foul means was justified by the desirable end, which was to destroy the landlords, beginning with me. But Manoel had other knowledge in him and he knew he had lost self-respect by stealing the receipt from the soft little girl clerk. It was an unworthy act. He would be truly dangerous now, for some of his own self-respect was gone.

At our approach, he stepped back off the path, far out of the way, this strong personality who had always seized the center of the stage. His Othellolike face as he stood among the tall cotton was drawn hollow, his mouth thin under his chiseled, proud, narrow nose. I had the distinct feeling that he had thus drawn apart to prevent me from offering him my hand. It would have wounded him to shake my hand, for he had lessened himself in our sharp battle and he was now determined to hate me fully and to destroy without any mercy.

I told him Pedro was taking over and that we had a contract to sell the rice on the basis of one hundred cruzeiros a sack for the one-to-one grade. He made no comment.

"Will you be at your house later, Manoel?" I asked. "I'd like to speak with you."

"I'm going to Goiânia," he said. "I'm on my way now."

He was lying and he knew I was not deceived. But he was running from me because he had stolen the receipt and I would not see him again. Manoel's advisers in Goiânia would tell him how to take me into court on trumped-up charges that Batão's workmen had damaged his rice, I was sure. But before he had time to, I would be out of the country and Pedro would have to handle it. Manoel would take his time over the squeeze, to see how much he could get and for the sheer pleasure of it. Manoel, the belly communist, wanted far more than food for his family, land of his own, or books for his son. He wanted the pleasure of winning and he wanted to savor the broad revenge he had been promised.

"Good-by then, Manoel," I said.

"Good-by, *dona*."

What could I have said to Manoel if I had seen him again? I understood him completely now. Manoel, the belly communist, had refused to go into the *Colônia* not only because he would have no protection as an independent small producer, but because he wanted to exercise the prerogative of moving where and when he willed. He had never experienced any form of capitalism except an outworn European kind any American would want to improve, and he had never had any teaching except communist tactics to destroy. Manoel had not been born a communist, he had been born a fighter and the communists had reached out for him, as no one else had. What Manoel did not know and had never been told was that he in fact could never get what he wanted most of all, his free prerogative to seek fortune and happiness in his own way, in any system not based on the individual's freedom.

In the evening, I called together my other tenants and told them I had made the best arrangements I could. Pedro would keep on advancing small sums of money for food until we could finish the rice harvest and get in the cotton. All of us knew the price crash meant the prolongation of a grim struggle. Chico had contracted to buy a lot in the *Colônia*, but now could not make the down payment. Emílio had told me he intended to move back to Goiânia with his little stake, so that his son could go to school; now he would have no stake. Old Ezequiel asked me if he could have a small cash advance but I was forced to deny him. I meant for Pedro to supply him with food only, for his family's sake. His throat must have been very dry, for it worked pitiably.

That night I slept for the first time in my clearing at Fazenda Chavante, in a lean-to beside Emílio's kitchen. From the dust I had breathed on the road and the evening chill, I caught a deep cold in the night. The next day, showing Pedro our boundaries, I climbed to the highest spot on my farm, a new-cleared hillside that I had never visited but had picked from afar as a site for a future home.

The homesite was perfect, just under the brow of the wooded crest, overlooking a broad expanse of cleared land that gave a vista all the way across the river, across the more distant forests and to the blue mountains far beyond. It was incomparable, as I had dreamed it would be. I withdrew my eyes from the distant view and looked at the clearings spread out below me, at my farm, the Frenchman's *roça* and that of Galeano, my neighbor upstream. The scene was hideous with the wreckage of the forest, with the bleaching trunks of great trees thrown about like matchsticks scattered by the hand of a heedless child.

I saw it all with final clarity, without the illusion cast over it by my desires and my hopes.

For countless ages the rain and the sun and the forest had built rich soil here and we would destroy it in one generation, if not in a decade. This land would be destroyed perpetuating a set of evils already condemned, evils which my own country was spending its substance to correct the world over and which the informed Brazilians themselves knew were wrong. My husband and I, if we worked very hard and put our entire lives into the place for fifteen or twenty years of struggling forward one step and slipping back two, might finally realize my dream here and have a decent farm. But what would there be all around us? The plundering and the laying waste of the Valley of the Rio das Almas, the valley of Ghost River, once my vale of dreams.

From my own hilltop I could see it stretching to the northeast in a splendor of forest and hill and river and far mountains. There it lay, a glory of natural richness, a tremendous treasure garden. I had felt this country in many moods, but never understood it before. This beautiful savage country that fought man with a force the primitive within me could feel as a transcendental enmity, was waging a just fight, for man's penetration here was nothing more than a wanton, murderous attack, wasteful and wrong. This was the final thing I had had to learn.

In all the time behind them, the so-called "civilized" men who were flooding in here had not learned so much as to hoe the earth and not destroy it. The men who worked the land here had not made one single improvement over the crudest scratching in the earth, and their lords over them had not seen or cared. Now even the fruits of their folly would be snatched away from them by the paradox of their success.

I should have seen all this the first time I came here, but I was blinded by my own illusion. I should have known on sight that all this "progress" was nothing more than the spilling over of an evil system, the corrosive spread of a plague that has eaten for ages into the vast continents and the backward peoples of the world. Emotionally, I had perceived a conflict here, but I was self-blinded to the nature of it.

Wanton, cruel, painfully-wrought destruction. Who would profit by it? In spite of the government's fumbling gesture at price support, everyone who produced rice would lose and all those merchants who lived by supplying these producers would suffer. I had seen communist leaflets saying the middlemen, the big rice buyers, would get rich in the price break, but that was not true. Most of them had bought rice and advanced to the producers money which they themselves had borrowed from the banks at high interest rates. Though property would change hands—gravitating into the hands of the people financially strongest—and would rise in value as more land was destroyed, everybody actually would lose and the princes of privilege most surely of all, since this would breed their eventual destruction. This debacle enriched no one, for it was sheer waste, of sweat, of food, of hope, of land and of the political stability of the nation.

I remembered how I had once thought Barranca looked like a scene from a Western movie and how easy it was to assume this frontier repeated a stage our own people had passed through a hundred years ago. Nothing could be more mistaken. In the American frontier march, sturdy men and women took along with them a free system, schoolbooks and the best farming knowledge, the best guns and wagons of their day. This frontier in Goiás was being cleared and its soil despoiled with tools forsworn by European man in prehistory, for five thousand years ago the plow was used in Europe. Two systems only were coming in here. One was an outmoded, stumbling, fumbling, suicidal capitalism. The other was communism, bent on nothing but the destruction of the former.

Like the awesome September clearing-fires, it was on far too vast a scale for me to contend with alone. It would only overwhelm me; I felt there would never be a place for me here.

We returned to Emílio's house for supper and my cold worsened. By nightfall I knew I was seriously ill or might soon be. I had had penumonia and pleurisy in adolescence and could remember very well the fevered pain with which the lung involvement came on. We sent Emílio's sons to ask for aspirin and S'hor Pedro, who was himself ill with a deep cold, had only two left. There was no other medicine in any hut anywhere around us, on my farm or the neighbors'.

I sent to the landing to see if a truck might be there, but none came.

Through the night I alternately burned, sweated and chilled. I had bought for Bill a shirt hand-spun from Chavante cotton and woven and sewn by Emílio's wife. In my fever I became convinced the rats would eat the shirt and when the woman arose to make me a drink from some herb, I asked her to bring the shirt from the bushes where it was drying and hang it from the pole rafters of the kitchen hut. I found a crack in the partition through which I could watch it hanging there high above the fire she kept going in the mud stove.

It was a night that would never end, filled with fever. I had imagined myself fighting death hand-to-hand in the *sertão*, in the argument with Manoel, in Benedito's hut, at the Bowens' when Joan was ill. Would my contestant catch me now, just when my happiness was beginning? My husband's shirt took on talismanic importance and became the only real thing in a world of shadows. I watched it through the crack in the wall: so long as it was safe, no real harm could come to me.

The night would never end. I could not stay inside the sleeping bag, for I sweated there and my heart pounded with the heat. When I climbed out of it the chill breeze cut through me. Mist dimmed the stars to which I had so often turned for comfort in Goiás.

There was no help, the world was empty around me. It was not empathy that put me in the place of the forlorn *roçeiro* now, I was *in* his place.

I should never have spent a night in the Chavante clearing, I thought in my fever. I should never have given the righteously angry earth spirits a chance at me. I could imagine them stalking me across the gigantic whitening matchstick tree trunks, skeletons of the forest we had destroyed to despoil the land. It was easy to understand now why the *roçeiros* never let a tree stand near their huts for fear a hostile spirit might hide there, lying in wait for them. Their consciences were probably as uneasy as mine over the destruction they had wrought, for deep down all men know the earth to be their mother, their sustainer, a supreme handiwork of the Divine.

Dawn came at last, mist-wreathed, cool, impersonal, and then the sun burned the milk-white mists away. In midmorning I learned a truck had arrived at the river and marshaled my strength to walk there under the blazing sun. We reached

Ceres about noon and I went immediately to bed in the new hotel. I did not call a doctor, for I was determined to get to São Paulo as quickly as possible and I did not want to be warned against traveling.

I learned of a fast passenger-car jitney going to Anápolis late that day and I fled in it, feverish and coughing in the dusty dusk. There was a feeling of finality about this journey and I was indeed leaving my farm at Chavante for the last time. At Anápolis, I spent an uneasy night with the family of Pedro's brother, and the next day, without even waiting to say good-by to the Bowens, who were briefly absent on a trip, I boarded a plane for São Paulo. Only after we took off and were actually in the air did I begin to feel safe.

Conclusion

A FEW days' rest and treatment in São Paulo put me on my feet again and after a brief stopover in Rio, I left by air for New York, which now meant home.

The denouement at my Fazenda Chavante unfolded by inevitable stages. Even with official support, the rice market stagnated and the Anápolis buyer broke his contract to take our rice on the excuse its quality was inferior. We had no appeal. Pedro managed to get a small loan on our stored rice and Bill and I sent him some cash. But with the rice market still paralyzed through the planting season, we could not plant coffee. Pedro did succeed in planting cotton.

Not long after I came home, just when the rice buyers were breaking contracts with producers, war in Korea created a demand for rice. I found prospective buyers in New York who would have bought by the shipload all the rice stored in Goiás. But it was so mortgaged and controlled all down the line, we could not get at it. The Bank of Brazil monitored rice exports through a licensing system; coast Brazilians who had never before dealt in rice but who had money for speculation and could pull wires formed pools to buy rice from the producing areas at the distress prices. Then they held out for the highest possible export price or sold abroad against imports that brought fabulous prices in Brazil. The price of rice to the producer stayed low for two years, but the surplus never brought lower prices to the poor consumer on the coast, since the part not siphoned off abroad by the opportunists was held over in storage a second year. The holdover kept the prices to the producers depressed through 1951 and they did not plant heavily that fall. As a result, there was a short crop in 1952 just as the surplus ran out. Rice prices to the consumer shot up. The old dictator Vargas had been swept back into office the year of the bumper crop and crash, and when no miracle came down from his new government, food riots began to break out over Brazil. The communists had a heyday, as who can wonder.

In Goiás, many of the small farmers, unable to haul and store their rice in warehouses, stored it inadequately on their farms, where much of it spoiled. My own story illustrates the fate of those producers who pledged their land to weather the crisis: by the time Pedro finally managed to sell our stored rice to the Bank of Brazil in the spring of 1951, interest on the various loans, new sacks for resacking, interest and repayment of money advanced for hauling, storage charges and "expenses" in general had mounted tremendously. I'd have been smarter to let most of my rice spoil on the farm, as many of the small farmers had to do.

Old Ezequiel proved my best tenant after all. Since he produced the least, I lost less in hauling, financing and storing the grain he raised. Fortunately our yield was less than a thousand sacks, instead of the ten thousand originally estimated. Otherwise I should indeed have gone bankrupt.

According to a now familiar pattern, Pedro's cotton looked good when it sprouted out of the rich soil. But the seed had been infested with insects and the chemical sprays Pedro bought proved worthless. With the world price of cotton very high, we took another loss and Pedro jumped his contract.

This was the final blow. After the cotton harvest, my third at Chavante, I agreed to sell the farm to Dr. Job Lane, who had bought Davino's brother's land. He is a cruzeiro millionaire and can afford to develop the land properly. People all around me who had cleared forest and taken losses sold out to big commercial coffee companies which began moving in from São Paulo and buying up properties large and small. My French neighbors lost their land to the Bank of Brazil. Dr. Sayão sold his land and left Goiás after his work at the *Colônia* was sabotaged.

Goiás, they tell me, is now being filled up with coffee planting, which means another wait of three or four years till the big return comes in. Even the *Colônia* farmers are planting coffee, they say. Brazilians believe the high cost of coffee culture, which has to be done entirely by hand, and the small extent of the remaining good coffee land, will keep prices high. But coffee only recently recovered from half a generation of depressed prices caused by overplanting in a previous boom. Coffee prices could crash again from several causes and Brazilians say that if they do, the American government will have to subsidize it to keep Brazil afloat. This would not be a genuine solution for the Brazilians and would make them and thirteen other Latin American coffee-producing countries an economic millstone around our necks. Even if we should subsidize coffee in a crash, I shudder to think what would happen to the small growers, the few that there are, and to the millions of workers on the big plantations who are low men on the totem pole even in prosperous times.

The people who were part of my Chavante story have scattered. Poor little Davino, I hear, developed some form of tuberculosis in the *mato* and went back south with his family. Chico, Emílio and Ezequiel, as well as Batão, were last heard of working on the big commercial coffee plantations. Pedro has faded away into the remote gold fields of the fever-ridden north, and there he seeks his fortune.

And Manoel? Not long after I came home Pedro wrote me he was having trouble with "the communist Manoel." In the fall of the year, a letter came saying Manoel was dead.

Pedro was in Anápolis when it happened and at once went to Chavante with a policeman from Ceres. Manoel was by that time buried. All they learned was that he had sent his pregnant wife to Goiânia and was staying with his baby son to harvest his cotton when a "sudden disease" killed him overnight.

Someone has suggested ulcers, the capitalist affliction; another meningitis, which probably carried off Benedito's son. But I have my own theory.

Manoel, they wrote me, died not long after the rice buyer in Anápolis broke his agreement to buy our rice on the excuse it was a poor quality. Since there was no official referee or legal standard set up to judge between us, we had to accept his grading, which was at once taken up by other buyers. Manoel in all his life never produced low-grade rice, I am sure. Although he was far my most troublesome tenant, he was my best farmer, always trying not only to keep a larger part of the grain for himself but also to improve its quantity and quality. I am sure that when Manoel realized how the bursting rice boom had blocked all his forward drive, dooming him to years more of profitless struggle, he himself burst in frustration and rage.

Manoel's end disturbed me. I had always been proud that there had been no deaths on my place and it was a final bitter reversal of my wishes. The thought that Manoel was buried there, dissolving back into the denuded soil like the fallen, fire-scarred trees, made it easier for me to sever my last tie with Fazenda Chavante.

The irony and the deep tragedy of Manoel was that he, of all the land people I dealt with, was the best fitted by temperament to work for and within a free society. He had the strong will, the drive and the determination of the ideal individualist, so dreadfully needed among the depressed peoples who have taken passivity as their defense against entrenched injustice. Manoel alone tried to improve his farming technique, building the crude winnowing tower, asking for simple equipment for more efficient work. Communism, the only political system sending its teachers into this backward area, had by sheer default captured for its foot soldier the very man best fitted to function in a system based on individual freedoms; his very drive, which was offered no other goal, took him to it. Communism had even stolen our watchword with which to mislead him, the beautiful and much-battered word, democracy.

Manoel could not have fitted into communism, even if it had fed him well, because Manoel's belly was not the center of his motives any more than the bellies are the sole concern of the millions like him. His every irritating action showed he wanted the right to the full exercise of his whole personality; as the wise founders of our nation wrote it in simpler words, to life, liberty and the pursuit of happiness.

The death of Manoel points up another bitter truth. The life-span of his world, like that in most of the backward areas, is little more than half the number of years I may expect to live just by residing in the United States. What a dreadful inequality this is! The drive of men like Manoel is the instinct of survival itself, turning from their age-old passive resistance into an active drive; this is what the -isms are by default capturing to turn against us, the life-force of the species.

In Goiás, I learned things that a lifetime of studying and theorizing about the backward peoples could not have revealed. Only when your life and fortunes are caught into and ground through their system can its full meaning be perceived. It is above all a tragedy of ignorant rule and of waste.

The landworkers of Brazil are wasted men and the land is wasting. Nobody really profits under the system that abandons them over and over to such disasters as I lived through with them in Goiás. In the rice crash, the rapacious opportunists on the coast got only a shrunken pea in comparison with the tremendous melon of our yield that was simply wiped off the books or spoiled in the crude backland storage bins. Goiás, like all Brazil's farm areas, needed tools, seeds, machines, skills and teachers, all of which had to be brought in. How could we ever obtain them unless the people's sweat and the soil's fertility could be converted into the counters of exchange that we call money? It is often said that countries like Brazil are "backward" because they are undercapitalized. The truth is that with their shortsighted disregard for the man who works the soil, they are sink-holes for their own capital. They stay undercapitalized because they are backward politically, because they abort the creation of their own wealth at the source.

What could have saved us all in Goiás, the backland that is the hope of Brazil, a nation without which South America is only a rim of land? The drama is important to the survival of the free world, because there are hundreds of millions of Manoels in the world, and these are the restless backward peoples who today come very near to holding the balance of power between communism and the West. We believe we can combat communism overseas by sending our technicians to increase production. In Goiás, we increased production by clearing new land, and built up to a disaster. As a result came a switch to coffee, a commodity that can make fourteen Latin American republics pensioners on the American pocketbook, and one which shackles a country's manpower to the depressed hand labor that makes for communism.

What could have been done to prevent or mitigate the collapse of the rice boom, which spread much wider than Goiás, into rice-growing parts of Minas Gerais, parts of São Paulo and the state of Rio Grande do Sul in the Brazilian south? The Brazilian government in Rio actually recognized the rice producers' need for aid and sought to give help through the Bank of Brazil. But they missed fire by setting the support price too low to save the small farmers and the economically weaker vessels; for this, all suffered. The men at Rio used their device of price support blindly and there was nobody to warn them that in not saving Brazil's forgotten men, they doomed themselves politically and condemned the nation to a new cycle of familiar economic grief.

The truth is that no small centralized group of rulers can ever provide proper and timely solutions for such problems without corresponding pressure from below to spur and guide them. This is one of the many reasons why rule from the top alone, even well-intentioned rule, invariably fails and induces the rulers to start pushing people around.

What the rice-producing areas of Brazil needed to prevent

the miserable tragedy of errors was a sprinkling of democratic leadership to rally the influence of the big and little producers, the buyers, the merchants, even of the truckers, and bring it to bear on the problem. Native democratic leaders were needed to arouse local action to spur and guide national policy in this truly national crisis; Vargas's supporters would have been forced to follow suit, giving the nation two parties competing to get a genuine solution. A very few leaders could have done it, for the tension was considerable in Ceres, in Anápolis, in Minas, in many places.

Why were there no such democratic leaders when the followers of dictatorship were everywhere, even pinning their posters on the mud walls of Batão's house on Fazenda Chavante? It is a story quickly told. In 1945, the American ambassador to Rio, A. A. Berle, Jr., said in a speech that American public opinion would like to see democracy in Brazil; the stand was not taken because of altruistic attachment to democracy alone, but because it was feared American troops on Brazilian bases would become involved in fighting between Vargas's followers and the rising opposition. At once patriotic Brazilian Army leaders turned Vargas out and in the following elections, a young and enthusiastic democratic party gained a handhold on power. They did not have full control, but the wind stood fair.

Even as this was happening in late 1945, the United States was reversing its policy. As it had been like the sun rising when the United States shone as champion of the democracies, so now the dusk came on. To make it worse, as time went on, American official policy actually began to court Perón's new nationalistic tyranny. The forces of democracy, thus orphaned, floundered. The enemies of democracy surged forward, as is attested by the resurgence of dictatorships throughout Latin America. Communism and Peronism had active missionaries backing them; "democratism" had nobody and nothing but uncertainty and a feeling of betrayal.

In Brazil the top men in the government and the budding democratic parties who could have put force and life into perfecting the democratic processes became bitter and querulous in their orphanhood and insecurity. The secondary democratic leadership became confused, disillusioned, even frightened, for vindictive revenge against the democrats was stalking other countries of Latin America. The nascent democratic movement had won the Goiás governorship, but its force weakened by stages there as elsewhere in Brazil. By 1950 the rice debacle was no more than part of a general dissolution of the democratic movement, which resulted in the election of the men who represented the idea of dictatorship.

If I have learned anything from the tragedy of the wasted men and wasted soil in Brazil, it is this: the American people are deceived if they think we can buy our way out of openly leading the democratic forces of the world, or that we can stem communism's advance by giving material support that strengthens the neo-fascistic nationalisms.

The restless peoples want fuller bellies among other things, but men can be sure of enjoying the fruits of their progress only under our kind of system, in which enlightened local leaders can carry the pressure of the people's need to a receptive national administration. Wherever enlightened national leadership does not exist to bring depressed peoples more and more into active political responsibility as well as into economic productivity, the skills we teach will form mere patchworks on hostile political systems. In many countries today, our overseas assistance is helping consolidate power for groups that have as little intention as the communists of allowing the depressed peoples their full suffrage, and which are out of deep principle hostile to us. Entrenched governmental cliques, whether communistic, neo-fascistic or archaic-capitalistic, believe they have nothing to gain and everything to lose by enfranchising their people. Such regimes will accept our material aid, naturally, but will inevitably use the goods and skills we send them to encompass our own destruction. This makes our effort to overcome rising political antagonisms through assistance programs alone like trying to beat an adversary to death by hitting him on the fist with our chin.

I was one of the first, if not the first American journalist to advocate foreign technical and other assistance as an instrument of policy. I began to support the idea in the early 1940's in my *Washington Post* column on Latin America, the region where we first experimented with this kind of international co-operation, and I still favor it. But I learned a new truth the day I scuffed along in the deep dust of Anápolis and worried about Manoel, the misled captive of the red -ism, and the rice buyer Lage, unenlightened raw material for the black ones. I learned this: we must transmit an understanding of the principles of a free and responsible society to backward peoples through an inspired leadership of their own, which will teach them that civic co-operation pays off better than class exploitation or class warfare. If we do not, *we actually condemn them to a choice between the -isms, red and black.*

Some men who have dabbled in the lives of other nations say that many backward peoples "have no capacity for democracy." I could compile from my personal experience scores of specific incidents disproving this statement. While I was in central Brazil the truckers of the big road in Goiás staged a nonviolent strike which brought the region's commercial life to a stop and reversed a ruling of the state legislature on the methods of collecting a production tax on rice. That was community action in the democratic tradition. In Argentina, while the Argentines thought the United States wanted to see democracies everywhere, civic action openly and stubbornly opposed the guns and every other power of the military regime. The same happened even in Paraguay. When you hear a man say other peoples cannot learn democracy, beware. He either (1) is speaking from a vast ignorance or cynicism, or (2) has a vested personal interest in maintaining a *status quo* overseas, and would like to see the clock turned back in the United States, or (3) in his heart is sympathetic to neo-fascistic state socialism or communism. Continue your exploration of his thinking, and he will reveal himself.

There has been no "capacity" lacking overseas; our own democracy began with a small group of inspired leaders who had the moral and financial backing of a powerful foreign nation, France. What has been lacking is a powerful leadership for democracy in a day when the other systems are recruiting everywhere. Instead of exerting that leadership we have been trying to buy pro-Americanism, but we have failed. We can only succeed in our objective of self-preservation by ourselves standing firm on the principle that all people have a right to their lives, their liberties and their own pursuit of happiness.

I am sure this will sound as strange to many Americans as did the suggestions of technical and other aid in the early 1940's. But I am equally sure that the inspiring of democratic leadership will someday be an instrument of our national policy along with Point Four. We are actually attempting to form democratic forces overseas with our vast aid programs, but we are missing fire. We have not yet fully realized that we must project abroad another indispensable element of our economic prosperity, which is our political liberty.

The effort to foment democracy must be made on two levels. First, our government will have to start influencing foreign administrations to live up to existing international pledges to respect democratic principles; it should aim at creating a "climate" unfavorable to all regimes that do not respect individual liberties. Secondly, the people of the United States themselves will have to exert a tremendous effort to reach potential leaders overseas and give them the inspiration and the information they need to win the masses away from the -isms. We need a Point Five program to this effect as a complement to Point Four.

How great, how vast, how dense is the forest of noncomprehension separating us from other peoples! This is the new frontier for Americans, not some far backland like Goiás. Here Americans can spend energy, initiative, ingenuity and drive for a generation.

There is much to do and the times are against us. We cannot break through the forest without two-way avenues of information, and today our avenues to all overseas peoples are being closed. A report published by Russell F. Anderson, foreign editorial director of the McGraw-Hill Publishing Company, reveals that in 1952 there were less than three hundred American correspondents, not all of them well qualified, bringing the American people news from overseas, while at the end of the last war there were nearly ten times that many. The services taking news of us to other peoples are entirely inadequate. We are the blind leading the blind.

We have brought this on ourselves. At the end of World War II, we had a whole vast network of treaties in which other countries agreed to respect democratic principles. We did not create a "climate" of respect for these treaties, which were the incontestable answer to the inevitable cry of "intervention." In Argentina, our correspondents were harassed, our wire services squeezed, their representatives jailed on trumped-up charges, our publications and films banned. But far from taking any countermeasure to these insults and injuries, we came to the rescue of the offending government with a dollar loan that saved it in an internal crisis. Incidents make precedents: next, William Oatis was jailed in Czechoslovakia on trumped-up charges, and the world knew that American newsmen were fair game. In 1952, groups in Mexico and Cuba, our "friendly" neighbors, proposed that our publications in Spanish be barred from all Latin America, and Brazil banned our newsreels. Where will it end?

We have not defended the good principles; the powers of darkness have encroached.

As China was lost to us before our uninformed public even recognized its importance to us, so Latin America started slipping away when we deserted our leadership of democracy there. How much it would mean to us today to have a strong, democratic, friendly Latin America at our side to show the world as a counter to the communist display of success in China. Instead of that we have uneasy political bedfellows, dictatorships that are veiled enemies bent on blackmail, to be watched and copied by power cliques in the Middle East and elsewhere.

The picture overseas is dark, but here at home, a good ground swell is running. My confidence in my own people, which wavered at the time of the Argentine debacle, has been restored. The extremisms are not flourishing here, nor are the thieves safe. Even our conservative party has developed an important wing dominated by progressives who preach the advantage of mass distribution of privilege as well as the mass production of goods. Thinking Americans are beginning to realize that we have the new thing: that we have proved in this generation how individual freedoms and private wealth can coexist with high mass living standards in an industrial society, exploding the outdated theories of the long-dead Marx. Many of our mistakes have been made because we have not yet come to our own full self-realization. We are beginning to see what it is we must project abroad, and once we see it, it will be done.

I go about my life now in the midst of the biggest city in the world, but the air is just as crisp and exciting in Manhattan's canyons in the fall as it ever was in the dry time in upland Goiás, and the sunshine here is just as gay; it is the same sun shining. Here I enjoy as never before the winter's sparkling snow, which I did not see for five years. The well-kempt trees of Gramercy Park, where I live, have no feud with me and the animal life of the area, the big friendly cats and the small enthusiastic dogs which Bill and I meet as they walk people around, are no menace. (Even my stubborn shoulder pain—diagnosed as "chronic muscle spasm due to repeated injury"—is cured.) We do not find the people of this city the snappish, gouging Americans of the legend familiar abroad. We find them just as polite and a great deal more direct than many of our good friends overseas. The New York subway rush is no more hectic than Buenos Aires's snarling traffic jams, or Rio de Janeiro's mad daily automobile stampedes to the suburbs.

Sometimes people ask me what I think about the danger of the atomic bomb, which I announced half-facetiously I was going to Goiás to escape. I can reply in all seriousness that some violent Manoel or some mysterious killer germ in Goiás would have been as immediate a threat to my survival. In fact, since I am free of the illusion that anybody can escape, whether from himself or from the larger perils of the times, I have a calmer attitude toward those perils. Our danger lies in not opposing them, or in being ruled by fear of them; their threat is slavery and if opposing them brings risks, I offer the credo of an early American who with Washington and Jefferson helped set this republic on its way. He was Patrick Henry, who prefaced his immortal cry for liberty or death with these words, never more topical than now: "Is life so dear and peace so sweet as to be purchased at the price of chains and slavery?" The imperative answer is still no.

Part of my reason for going to the wilds was to seek relief from my disappointment over Argentina and all that it stood for. I thought I would find solace in park-like forests and lush pastures on my farm. But easement came another way, through hardship and action: somehow I worked off my deep anger and resentment over the betrayal of our freedom-loving Latin American neighbors as I battled the *sertão's* hazards, confusions and violences, its distances, mystery and enchantment. I shall never be reconciled to the great betrayal, but it does not eat into me corrosively as it once did.

In the final harvests, I confronted and faced down every challenge of the frontier, only to learn at last that I could not hope to save my farm and my tenants from the eroding way of life backwashing up from the Brazilian coast. Though my struggles in the forest gave me understanding and enlightenment, the final debacle convinced me my place was not in Goiás, wasting with the good land and the forlorn *roçeiros,* but here among my own people. If I can effectively tell what I experienced, it will do more for my backland than a lifetime spent trying to develop a model farm. I am not discouraged by the realization that one person can scarcely expect to work wonders on so vast a problem as our lack of information about the backward peoples; any gain is profit in so urgent a cause.

I went to Goiás above all to find a new way forward and I found I had to go beyond the forest. I mistakenly thought I could build a pleasant haven in which to rest, like Buddha under his Bo tree, until revelation came. Instead, I was forced to find my way through action, which was fortunate, for it not only took me back to my whole self, but also to Bill. I discovered that only a heart can provide safe haven, a place never can. And I see clearly now that to use the great gift of life with true appreciation of its value, it is not enough to rise above selfishness, as I did in plunging into battle on the side of the angels in Argentina and again, at the last, in Goiás. It is also needful to keep the faith when you learn the angels themselves can lose.

THE END

CPSIA information can be obtained at www.ICGtesting.com
Printed in the USA
BVOW02s0012230615

405592BV00019B/253/P